MW01193561

Birding Corpus Christi and the Coastal Bend

More than 75 Prime Birding Sites

Jamie Ritter

GUILFORD, CONNECTICUT
HELENA, MONTANA

AN IMPRINT OF THE GLOBE PEQUOT PRESS

*A*FALCONGUIDE®

Maps by M. A. Dubé © Morris Book Publishing, LLC
Photos by Jamie Ritter unless noted otherwise

Library of Congress Cataloging-in-Publication Data

Ritter, Jamie.
 Birding Corpus Christi and the Coastal Bend / Jamie Ritter. — 1st ed.
       p. cm.
 Includes bibliographical references and index.
 ISBN-13: 978-0-7627-3915-8
 ISBN-10: 0-7627-3915-0
 1. Bird watching—Texas—Corpus Christi Region—Guidebooks. 2. Birding sites—Texas—Corpus Christi Region—Guidebooks. 3. Trails—Texas—Corpus Christi Region—Guidebooks. 4. Corpus Christi Region (Tex.)—Guidebooks.
 I. Title.
 QL684.T4R58 2006
 598.07'234764113—dc22
                          2006011728

Manufactured in the United States of America
First Edition/First Printing

Contents

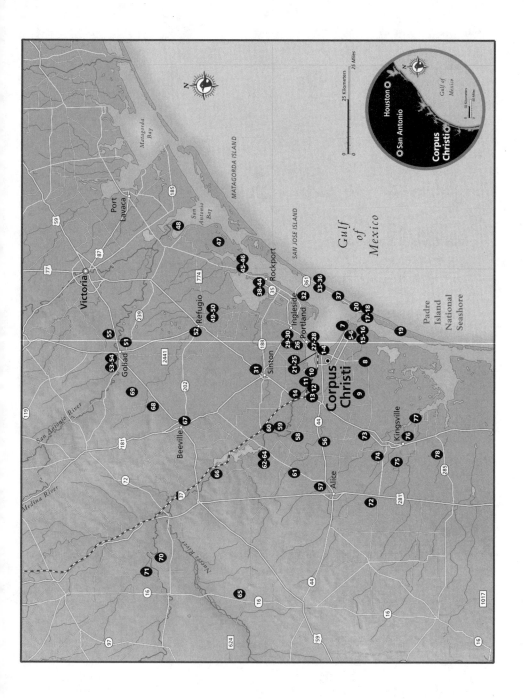

Acknowledgments

Writing a book has always been a dream of mine, and it turned out to be a very exciting event. But even better was the response I got from fellow birders, experts, and friends. Every single person seemed excited and wanted to help. Many, many thanks to Ray Allen, Stephanie Barnes, Claire Barnhart, Tony Baylis, Robert Benson, Sally Bickley, William "Buzz" Botts, Jan Cartwright, Anita Cates, Annie and David Clayton, Suzanne Contreras, Bob Creglow, Sally Crofutt, Murrell Foster, Linda Fuiman, Richard Gibbons, Dennis Gissell, Selma Glasscock, Carolyn Goodloe, Darlene Gooris, Kathy Griffith, Diana Harrington, Joe Herrera, Jake Herring, Francis Hicks, Michael Hill, Jayne Hogg, Lee Hutchins, Jimmy Jackson, Kay Jenkins, Linda Jimenez, Diane Johnson, Larry Jordon, Lowell Kepp, Eric Knecht, Jackie Knox, Leatrice Koch, Wilfred Korth, Tom Langschied, RoseAleta Laurell, Marilyn Lawson, Ray Little, Mary Livingston, Jon McIntyre, Todd Merendino, Derek Muschlek, Gary Mysorski, Juan A. Navejar Jr., Kristine Ondinas, Miles Philips, Richard and Patricia Phillips, Leah Pummill, Brent Ortego, Cullen "Stormy" Reeves, Bill Reilly, Juan Rodriguez, Juan Sanchez, Bill Schmidt, Cliff Shackelford, Callie Shreckengost, Heather Shyties, Terry Simpson, Tom Stehn, Glenn Swartz, Patricia and Jimmy Swartz, Paul Thornton, Chris Torres, Bill Townsend, Leo Trevino, David A. Vela, Mike Wallace, Donna Williams, Jesse Womack, and Bill Wright.

I had five very special angels. The first angels were Joel and Vicki Simon. They just could not do enough to help me. They suggested sites, gave expert advice about birds, introduced me to people, proofread some sections of the book, and suggested other experts whom I could contact.

Another was Jo Creglow. She was so thrilled that the book was going to be written that she read every word that I wrote and gently made suggestions and changes. She also introduced me to other experts.

A bird-watching friend and super photographer, Tony Baylis, offered photographs that he had taken of many of the specialty birds in the Corpus Christi area. He met with me several times to select and organize his wonderful prints for the book.

Glenn and Phylis Lanmon have been friends of mine for over twenty years. We go to the same church. Never did I believe that their aerial photography business, Lanmon Aerial Photography, Inc., would one day help me. Glenn took existing aerial photographs that he had of specific sites and labeled them so that they could be converted into many of the maps in this book. There will never be enough thank-yous for Joel, Vicki, Jo, Tony, and Glenn.

The book is dedicated to Gene Blacklock, my teacher and mentor. I would never have even consented to write the book without his backing. Gene knows everything about South Texas birds, and I do mean everything. He read much of the book and made suggestions about birds at certain locations. He inspired anything that is right in this book; all mistakes are mine.

My family was ever supportive. My cousin, Kim Moore, gave me my first pair of birdwatching binoculars. Kim has gone bird watching with me and gave me the sketchbook in which I took all of the notes for this book. My brother Bill Bryant is a computer expert. He set up the format for the book and helped me with e-mail and other computer problems. Let's just say that he was long-suffering. My brother Paul Bryant and his wife, Shelley, are nature lovers, with their main interest in native plants. They went with me to several birding locations, have discussed unique "bird situations," and have given invaluable advice.

My daughter's mother-in-law, or as we say in South Texas, my *comadre*, Wanda Knecht, is a bird-watching buddy and traveling companion of mine. She was raised in North Carolina and knows about those "eastern birds." Her only problem is that she sometimes tries to turn our bird-watching trips into butterfly trips. She and I are living proof that single women can and should enjoy outdoor hobbies.

I have two lovely daughters, whom I love dearly. Annette Schmidt, my elder daughter, likes birds and will even "watch" them on occasion. She loves the beach and went to every beach or near-beach location with me. She enjoyed taking notes and gave me tons of advice and encouragement.

My younger daughter, Carrie Knecht, required surgery while a freshman in high school. I had offered to do something special with her beforehand and was very surprised when all that she wanted was to see Bald Eagles and Whooping Cranes. I hadn't even known she was interested in birds. Carrie gave the bird-watching "bug" to me. She lives in the Northwest now and calls to brag about Calliope Hummingbirds and Evening Grosbeaks. She has a degree in journalism and read and corrected everything that I wrote.

Again, let me say thank you to everyone who had any part in the production of this book. I hope you are proud of what we accomplished.

Introduction

Corpus Christi earned the title "Birdiest City in the United States" in 2003, 2004, 2005, and 2006, as awarded by the American Bird Conservancy. Along with its surrounding areas, it is one of the greatest birding locales in the country. While Texas is large and provides many opportunities for birding, Corpus Christi is one of the more outstanding spots to bird-watch. Over 650 species are known to breed in the United States and Canada; more than 510 of those species have been found in Corpus Christi and other parts of the Coastal Bend.

The Coastal Bend is home to many native Texas birds. Geography and a temperate climate play a special part in creating a natural haven for birds. Corpus Christi is at the apex of the Coastal Bend. This bend acts as a funnel for migrating species in both the fall and spring. Birds from the Eastern Flyway, the Mississippi Flyway, and the Central Flyway pass through Corpus Christi. Even birds from the Rocky Mountain Flyway often stray through the area. Tropical surprises from the Lower Rio Grande Valley also find their way north to the Coastal Bend. Couple that with prime spots to view seabirds, wading birds, and shorebirds, and the possibilities are endless.

Local birders debate as to whether the spring or fall migration is better for passerines. On a successful spring weekend, one could easily spot and record over one hundred songbird species. Fall is a favorite for hummingbirds and hawks. The Ruby-throated Hummingbird migration peaks in September, and over one million hawks were counted during the 2004 Hawk Watch. Winter can also prove exciting, as waterfowl take time to enjoy the mild weather. Wintering Whooping Cranes, whose population has grown to over 200, make the area a must-stop for even the greenest birder.

Large and small towns alike have taken notice of the economic impact that birders can have. Appropriately, more and more possibilities are opening up for Coastal Bend birders. Conservation groups are at work to protect remaining habitats. The National Audubon Society has recognized the importance of the coastal area. A national wildlife refuge, a national seashore, several state parks, and many small city and county parks are available to the birder.

The 2005 Christmas Bird Count for Corpus Christi totaled 227 species, down from an all-time high of 239 in 2004. In 2003, Corpus Christi ranked first in the Christmas Count with 231 species and has traditionally ranked in the top 5 year after year. Additionally, Corpus Christi Flour Bluff, Kingsville, Port Aransas, Rockport, Choke Canyon, Matagorda Island, and Aransas National Wildlife Refuge can usually be found in the top 30 sites of the United States. This is a winter count.

REPORTING RARE BIRDS

Rare Bird Alerts Texas, (713) 369-9673

Corpus Christi is certainly known as a birding hot spot for Texas and for the United States. If you have purchased this book, I probably don't need to sell you on the many wonders this area has to offer. But just in case, I've included a list of birds recorded during 2006's "Birdiest City Day in Corpus Christi." This list includes 247 species. The second list names those species recorded on the 2003, 2004, or 2005 Birdiest City Day but not seen in 2006. Keep in mind, however, that this list includes only birds found inside the city limits. This is a spring count.

The scope of this book offers even wider opportunities for finding just that bird you are looking for. But don't take my word for it—come to Corpus Christi and the Coastal Bend and see for yourself.

2006 BIRDIEST CITY COUNT FOR CORPUS CHRISTI

Black-bellied Whistling-Duck
Fulvous Whistling-Duck
Gadwall
American Wigeon
Mottled Duck
Blue-winged Teal
Cinnamon Teal
Northern Shoveler
Northern Pintail
Green-winged Teal
Redhead
Lesser Scaup
Greater Scaup
Bufflehead
Red-breasted Merganser
Ruddy Duck
Northern Bobwhite
Common Loon
Least Grebe
Pied-billed Grebe
Eared Grebe
Am White Pelican
Brown Pelican
Neotropic Cormorant
Double-crested Cormorant
Anhinga
Great Blue Heron
Great Egret
Snowy Egret

Little Blue Heron
Tricolored Heron
Reddish Egret
Cattle Egret
Green Heron
Black-crowned Night Heron
Yellow-crowned Night Heron
White Ibis
White-faced Ibis
Roseate Spoonbill
Black Vulture
Turkey Vulture
Osprey
Mississippi Kite
Sharp-shinned Hawk
Cooper's Hawk
Harris' Hawk
Red-shouldered Hawk
Broad-winged Hawk
Swainson's Hawk
White-tailed Hawk
Zone-tailed Hawk
Red-tailed Hawk
Crested Caracara
Peregrine Falcon
Sora
Purple Gallinule
Common Moorhen
American Coot

Black-bellied Plover
American Golden Plover
Snowy Plover
Wilson's Plover
Semipalmated Plover
Killdeer
American Oystercatcher
Black-necked Stilt
American Avocet
Greater Yellowlegs
Lesser Yellowlegs
Willet
Spotted Sandpiper
Upland Sandpiper
Whimbrel
Long-billed Curlew
Marbled Godwit
Ruddy Turnstone
Red Knot
Sanderling
Semipalmated Sandpiper
Western Sandpiper
Least Sandpiper
White-rumped Sandpiper
Pectoral Sandpiper
Dunlin
Stilt Sandpiper
Short-billed Dowitcher
Long-billed Dowitcher
Wilson's Phalarope
Laughing Gull

Franklin's Gull
Ring-billed Gull
Herring Gull
Gull-billed Tern
Caspian Tern
Royal Tern
Sandwich Tern
Common Tern
Forster's Tern
Least Tern
Black Tern
Black Skimmer
Rock Dove
Eurasian Collared-Dove
White-winged Dove
Mourning Dove
Inca Dove
Common Ground-Dove
White-tipped Dove
Monk Parakeet
Yellow-billed Cuckoo
Greater Roadrunner
Groove-billed Ani
Barred Owl
Lesser Nighthawk
Common Nighthawk
Common Pauraque
Chuck-will's-widow
Whip-poor-will
Chimney Swift
Buff-bellied Hummingbird
Ruby-throated Humming-
  bird
Black-chinned Humming-
  bird
Belted Kingfisher
Green Kingfisher
Golden-fronted Wood-
  pecker
Ladder-backed Wood-
  pecker
Olive-sided Flycatcher
Eastern Wood Pewee
Yellow-bellied Flycatcher
Acadian Flycatcher
Willow Flycatcher

Least Flycatcher
Eastern Phoebe
Ash-throated Flycatcher
Great-crested Flycatcher
Brown-crested Flycatcher
Great Kiskadee
Couch's Kingbird
Western Kingbird
Eastern Kingbird
Scissor-tailed Flycatcher
Loggerhead Shrike
White-eyed Vireo
Bell's Vireo
Yellow-throated Vireo
Blue-headed Vireo
Warbling Vireo
Philadelphia Vireo
Red-eyed Vireo
Blue Jay
Green Jay
Horned Lark
Purple Martin
Tree Swallow
Northern Rough-winged
  Swallow
Bank Swallow
Cliff Swallow
Cave Swallow
Barn Swallow
Black-crested Titmouse
Verdin
Carolina Wren
Bewick's Wren
House Wren
Sedge Wren
Marsh Wren
Ruby-crowned Kinglet
Blue-gray Gnatcatcher
Eastern Bluebird
Veery
Gray-cheeked Thrush
Swainson's Thrush
Hermit Thrush
Wood Thrush
Gray Catbird
Northern Mockingbird

Brown Thrasher
Long-billed Thrasher
Curve-billed Thrasher
European Starling
American Pipit
Sprague's Pipit
Blue-winged Warbler
Golden-winged Warbler
Tennessee Warbler
Orange-crowned Warbler
Nashville Warbler
Northern Parula
Yellow Warbler
Chestnut-sided Warbler
Magnolia Warbler
Yellow-rumped Warbler
Black-throated Green
  Warbler
Blackburnian Warbler
Prairie Warbler
Palm Warbler
Bay-breasted Warbler
Blackpoll Warbler
Cerulean Warbler
Black-and-white Warbler
American Redstart
Worm-eating Warbler
Ovenbird
Northern Waterthrush
Louisiana Waterthrush
Kentucky Warbler
Mourning Warbler
Common Yellowthroat
Hooded Warbler
Wilson's Warbler
Canada Warbler
Yellow-breasted Chat
Summer Tanager
Scarlet Tanager
Olive Sparrow
Green-tailed Towhee
Chipping Sparrow
Clay-colored Sparrow
Field Sparrow
Vesper Sparrow
Lark Sparrow

Savannah Sparrow
Grasshopper Sparrow
Lincoln's Sparrow
Swamp Sparrow
White-throated Sparrow
Northern Cardinal
Pyrrhuloxia
Rose-breasted Grosbeak
Blue Grosbeak

Lazuli Bunting
Indigo Bunting
Painted Bunting
Dickcissel
Red-winged Blackbird
Eastern Meadowlark
Yellow-headed Blackbird
Great-tailed Grackle
Bronzed Cowbird

Brown-headed Cowbird
Orchard Oriole
Hooded Oriole
Baltimore Oriole
Audubon's Oriole
Bullock's Oriole
Lesser Goldfinch
House Sparrow

BIRDS FROM OTHER BIRDIEST CITY COUNTS FOR CORPUS CHRISTI

The following birds were listed in the 2003, 2004, or 2005 counts but not in the 2006 counts. All four lists include an amazing 287 birds.

Snow Goose
Mallard
Wild Turkey
Northern Gannet
American Bittern
Least Bittern
Glossy Ibis
Swallow-tailed Kite
Bald Eagle
Northern Harrier
Merlin
Black Rail
Clapper Rail
Virginia Rail

Piping Plover
Solitary Sandpiper
Hudsonian Godwit
Baird's Sandpiper
Purple Sandpiper
Wilson's Snipe
California Gull
Thayer's Gull
Lesser Black-backed Gull
Black-billed Cuckoo
Eastern Screech Owl
Great Horned Owl
Broad-tailed Hummingbird
American Robin

Cedar Waxwing
Cape May Warbler
Townsend's Warbler
Prothonotary Warbler
Western Tanager
Eastern Towhee
Le Conte's Sparrow
Nelson's Sharp-tailed
  Sparrow
Seaside Sparrow
White-crowned Sparrow
House Finch
American Goldfinch

How to Use This Book

Ask a Texas native what the Coastal Bend includes, and you're bound to get a dozen different answers. For the purposes of this book, consider the southern boundary of the Coastal Bend to be Rivera and the northern boundary to be Tivoli.

The heart of the Coastal Bend is Corpus Christi, where Texas does "bend" to encompass the Gulf of Mexico. It is a city of approximately 280,000 people and covers about 150 square land miles. Historically, the city leaders have been aggressive in annexing outlying communities. Consequently, there are many rural areas within the city limits. This, of course, results in more opportunities to see more birds.

There are seventy-eight birding sites described here. They are divided into nine different regions, and a map is provided for each region, showing the site locations.

Each site description includes a detailed map; it is not intended as a navigational tool, but rather for trip planning. Instead, use a reputable road map or the *Delorme: Texas Atlas & Gazetteer.*

Following the number and name of each site, the following headings appear.

Habitats lists the various habitats to be found at the site. Characteristics of these are discussed in the Climates and Habitats section.

Specialty birds includes Coastal Bend specialties that are likely to be found on the site, and those that are classified as endangered or threatened by the U.S. Fish and Wildlife Service.

I consider Coastal Bend specialties as those that occur in the area but are seldom seen anywhere else in the United States. This list includes the following birds: Least Grebe, Black-bellied Whistling-Duck, White-tailed Kite, Harris' Hawk, Whooping Crane, Buff-breasted Sandpiper, Hudsonian Godwit, White-tipped Dove, Groove-billed Ani, Common Pauraque, Buff-bellied Hummingbird, Ringed Kingfisher, Green Kingfisher, Golden-fronted Woodpecker, Great Kiskadee, Couch's Kingbird, Vermilion Flycatcher, Brown-crested Flycatcher, Scissor-tailed Flycatcher, Cave Swallow, Green Jay, Long-billed Thrasher, Sprague's Pipit, Olive Sparrow, Cassin's Sparrow, Botteri's Sparrow, Hooded Oriole, and Audubon's Oriole.

Endangered or threatened birds include Brown Pelican, Reddish Egret, White-faced Ibis, Wood Stork, Swallow-tailed Kite, Zone-tailed Hawk, White-tailed Hawk, Peregrine Falcon, Whooping Crane, and Piping Plover.

Other key birds includes some interesting nonspecialty species. These are birds that are somewhat more common to bird-watchers, but once again would most likely be seen in Texas or the South as opposed to other parts of North America. These are birds that the normal birder would be excited to list. Examples of other key birds are Roseate Spoonbill, Fulvous Whistling-Duck, Crested Caracara, Inca Dove, and Pyrrhuloxia.

Under this section some Neotropic Migrant Traps will be noted also. These sites "trap" migrating passerines both in quantity of species and quantity of birds. These are sites where many species of vireos, warblers, orioles, and other passerines come through in the spring or fall. There is no way to clearly predict which species or numbers stop at each site, but it can be predicted as substantial. Traps fill quickly when fallout conditions occur. These sites often rival more famous traps, such as High Island on the Upper Coast of Texas.

Species are grouped into Resident, Spring/Summer, Fall/Winter, and Migrant. These seasonal categories necessarily are very loose and give only a general impression of the season in which significant numbers of that particular species are likely to be present. For many species, there will always be some individual birds that don't "obey" the seasonal designations and will confound any attempts to categorize them. The birds are placed in the seasonal category in which they are most likely to appear.

Whooping Crane family. PHOTO: TONY BAYLIS.

These lists of specialty birds and other key birds should by no means be taken as complete listings of all the species, even the common ones, to be found at the site, but only those that I think might be of special interest. Thus, the paragraphs can be thought of as highlights, and in the detailed site description many additional species will generally be mentioned.

Best time to bird is self-explanatory. It helps you plan your trip to each site during the right season. Of course, the "best time" will depend on which birds you would like to see.

Directions provide written details on how to reach the site or a logical point to begin birding a large or wide-ranging site. The instructions begin from a city, town, or the junction of two well-traveled roads.

The birding also includes some directions to points of interest and good birding within the boundaries of the larger site. This heading provides tips on how best to observe birds at the site and lists some of the species you're likely to see there.

General information gives additional facts about the site and its history. This is also where you will find information about wheelchair accessibility.

Also, in this section, I have given the Great Texas Coastal Birding Trail-Central Texas Coast number. The Great Texas Coastal Birding Trail was developed to promote ecotourism, especially bird watching, along the Texas coast. The area was divided into the Upper, Central, and Lower Texas Coast. The Texas Parks and Wildlife Department (TPWD) and the Texas Department of Transportation (TDOT) worked with public and private groups and individuals to develop the trails. A map of these trails may be purchased from either the TPWD or the TDOT. In this guide, trail numbers will be listed as CTC, for the Central Texas Coast. *DeLorme: Texas Atlas & Gazetteer* includes the page number and grid coordinates of the site's location in this very useful atlas. These atlases are available in many bookstores and can be procured from DeLorme Publishing, P.O. Box 298, Yarmouth, ME 04096; (207) 846–7000 or www.delorme.com.

Elevation tells the approximate elevation or range of elevations on the site.

Hazards lists things to be found on the site that require your attention and some caution, ranging from poisonous plants to rattlesnakes to heavy traffic. All the hazards can be avoided with a little care, and none should discourage you from visiting and exploring a site.

Nearest food, gas, lodging names towns near the site that can provide the amenities you might need. In Corpus Christi, I have named locations near a site, if possible. Because Corpus Christi is a large city, there are many possibilities. Where a site is rural, I have selected a nearby town with a reasonable selection of services.

Camping lists the name of any national, state, county, or city campground that is near the birding site. For private campground information, you must refer to Appendix F. South Texas is a busy tourist area. There are also many Winter Texans who spend several months in the area, often in motor homes. Consequently, many camping and RV parks service this area. I have included a list of campsites organized by towns in that appendix.

Many campgrounds require reservations. The numbers to call for the national, state, county, and city parks, as well as the other private campgrounds, are given in the appendix.

For more information provides the name, address, and phone number of a reliable agency, office, or organization that can help answer questions not covered in the site descriptions. Because certain organizations may appear in several listings, the addresses and telephone numbers are also collected in Appendix A. Look in the appendix for Web addresses also.

TERMS USED IN THIS BOOK

cayo—the Spanish word for *bay*. One important secondary bay near Corpus Christi is Cayo del Oso. However, local citizens have taken to calling it simply "the Oso."

cendero—This is a Spanish term for a cleared opening in a brushy area through which wranglers would drive cattle. Cenderos can be, but are not necessarily, ranch roads. Today, cenderos are also often cut and maintained by pipeline companies in order to look after and repair lines.

endangered—an official designation of the U.S. Fish and Wildlife Service, to provide protection for a species at risk of extinction. An endangered species is one that is in danger of extinction throughout all or a significant portion of its range.

fall/winter category—from September through February in the Coastal Bend. Species in this category are a mixed group. Some birds, such as hawks, migrate southward through the area at the beginning of this period. Other birds, such as Whooping Cranes, ducks, and geese, come at this time to stay through the winter.

fallout—a phenomenon in which migrating birds literally fall out of the sky after a long, tiring flight. This event most often occurs in the Coastal Bend in the spring and often is associated with a thunderstorm.

laguna (lagoon)—a shallow body of water separating the mainland from barrier islands.

mottes—a grove of trees, especially live oak, surrounded by grassland.

Neotropic Migrant Trap—Migrating passerines stop at some sites in such great numbers, that birders refer to these sites as traps. Migrants may be common for only a few weeks or even days, and absent the rest of the year.

norther—a cold mass of air coming from the north. **Blue norther:** when skies turn dark black-blue; associated with an approaching cold front, usually accompanied by rain.

oso—a Spanish term meaning *bear*. Corpus Christi citizens use the term when referring to a local secondary bay.

passerine—any of the perching songbirds.

peeps—small sandpipers, such as Semipalmated, Western, and Least.

resident—significant numbers of that species can be found at the given locality throughout the year.

spring/summer category—In the Coastal Bend, spring lasts from February through early May. Species included in this category are those that arrive in early spring to stay through the summer. This group is small. The larger group in this category is those migrating through the Coastal Bend in spring. Warblers, for example, move through the area in large numbers, and many are easily listed at this time. However, their stay is usually brief, as they strive to head north to their breeding territories. There are some shorebirds that nest here during the summer. Mostly, summer, from June through September, is a slow season in the Coastal Bend for bird watching. It is really, really hot here!

threatened—an official designation of the U.S. Fish and Wildlife Service. A threatened species is one that is likely to become endangered in the foreseeable future.

Important Bird Areas (IBAs)

The Important Bird Area Program is a worldwide activity to identify areas that are important to birds. It began in Europe in the 1980s under the International Council of Bird Preservation, since renamed Birdlife International. In 1989 Birdlife International published the results of its work in the book *Important Bird Areas in Europe*. This book listed more than 2,444 Important Bird Areas (IBAs) in thirty-one countries.

In the United States, the American Bird Conservancy, in association with The Nature Conservancy, initiated a similar program in 1995. Sites are listed if they include habitat for species of birds showing alarming combinations of population decline, small population size, small ranges, and high threats. Sites can also be chosen if species are moderately abundant with population declines or high threats. A third list includes those sites with restricted distributions and low population size. The final criteria for sites includes those with significantly large concentrations of breeding, migrating, or wintering birds, including waterfowl, seabirds, wading birds, raptors, and land birds.

The recently published *500 Most Important Bird Areas in the United States* (Random House 2003), includes four sites covered by the scope of this guide. They are the King Ranch, Padre Island National Seashore, Hazel Bazemore County Park, and Aransas National Wildlife Refuge. I have noted these sites as IBA.

Climate and Habitats

Corpus Christi and the Coastal Bend lie in the Gulf Coastal Plains of the southern United States. Elevations covered in this book range from sea level to a mere 300 feet above sea level. At a few sites you may encounter some rolling hills or small ravines cut by rivers working their way to the Gulf. These are generally very gentle and few in number.

Climate

The climate exhibits subtle changes throughout the year. Keep in mind, however, the area is hot and humid, and locals often wear shorts in December.

Spring

Spring for South Texas usually begins in March and continues through early May. Temperatures typically range from the 70s to 80s Fahrenheit, with slightly cooler temperatures at night. Occasional thunderstorms, often accompanied by dangerous lightning, produce much of the annual precipitation for the region. The area usually gets about 30 inches of rain a year. These thunderstorms can create fallout conditions for migrating birds.

Summer

Hot summer days start in June and continue through September. While temperatures climb into the 100s during the summer, they usually hover around the upper 80s or 90s. It is always a few degrees cooler along the Gulf. There is little change from day to day during Coastal Bend summers. The prevailing wind is out of the southeast and can be strong at times. The humidity reaches into the 90th percentile. Water temperature for the Gulf gets as high as 85 degrees. It seldom rains during the summer, and some ponds and marshes may dry out. Of course, summer is also the season for hurricanes. These storms can cause great damage from high winds, high waves, and flooding. Hurricanes in the Gulf often drive pelagic birds closer ashore.

Fall

Temperatures in the 70s and even 80s are common in October and November. This can be a beautiful season for the coastal area. The winds and humidity are milder during this time. Migrating birds begin to arrive in the Coastal Bend. Many winter days fit this same pattern, as well.

Winter

Temperatures stay in the 50s and 60s through the months of December and January, but winter northers can drop temperatures 20 degrees in an hour or so. This is the driest season, but early winter storms often trigger rain. It usually freezes three or four times during an average Coastal Bend winter. February can be cold, but it usually warms by the end of the month. Many migrant birds are happy to spend the winter in the mild South Texas weather. These temperate winters also encourage early breeding for larger wading birds and raptors.

Habitats

These habitat descriptions are adapted with permission from *Birds of the Coastal Bend* by John Rappole and Gene Blacklock (Texas A&M University Press, 1985).

Tall riparian forest—This is the southern boundary for the tall deciduous forest characteristic of the moist, rich soils of the eastern United States. This habitat is found only at the northern end of the Coastal Bend. It includes plants such as American elm, green ash, box elder, and black willow.

Birds typical for this habitat are American Crow, Red-bellied Woodpecker, Pileated Woodpecker, Carolina Chickadee, Tufted Titmouse, Carolina Wren, and Downy Woodpecker.

Transitional riparian forest—Bottomlands along the Mission, Aransas, and Nueces Rivers of the Coastal Bend are transitional between tall deciduous forests and the subtropical forests characteristic of river bottoms in the mesquite grassland of deep South Texas. Plants include hackberry, Mexican ash, anacua, black persimmon, cedar elm, red mulberry, Western soapberry, Turk's cap, and poison ivy.

Woodland communities are the best habitats for viewing large numbers of migrating land birds. From late March to early June and late August through October, these forests are often alive with birds.

Mesquite savanna—Much of this habitat has been lost to agriculture. What is left of the mesquite savanna includes plants such as mesquite and silver bluestem.

Birds here include Groove-billed Ani, Bobwhite, Wild Turkey, Greater Roadrunner, Pyrrhuloxia, White-tailed Kite, and White-tailed Hawk.

Tamaulipan scrubland—This habitat is characterized by extensive stands of shrubby thorn forest. Although much of this area was once probably savanna, change was caused by overgrazing and fewer prairie fires. Mesquite, colima, agarita, huisache, plains bristlegrass, seacoast bluestem, and prickly pear are the dominant plants in this habitat.

Birds here include Harris' Hawk, Long-billed Thrasher, White-eyed Vireo, Olive Sparrow, Painted Bunting, Bewick's Wren, and Common Pauraque.

Tamaulipan thorn scrub—The canopy of this dry chaparral is 4 to 6 feet high, less than half that of mesquite chaparral in the Tamaulipan scrubland. The ground between the low, thick, thorny trees is bare, with some cacti and a few grasses during wet seasons. Thorn scrub can be found on caliche or other poor soil sites. Plant species include cenizo, blackbush, catclaw, guajillo, yucca, and Turk's head cactus.

Birds peculiar to this habitat include Scaled Quail, Cassin's Sparrow, Lesser Goldfinch, Black-throated Sparrow, Curve-billed Thrasher, Ash-throated Flycatcher, Say's Phoebe, Cactus Wren, Olive Sparrow, Lark Bunting, Lesser Nighthawk, and Black-chinned Hummingbird.

Prairie—Very little prairie habitat remains in this region. The rich prairie soils have been taken over for agricultural uses. Plants characteristic of this habitat include seacoast and big bluestem, tanglehead, Texasgrass, cowpen daisy, Texas and woolly croton, and wild buckwheat.

Birds found in this habitat include Crested Caracara, White-tailed Kite, White-tailed Hawk, Wild Turkey, Long-billed Curlew, Dickcissel, Sandhill Crane, and Scissor-tailed Flycatcher.

Oak savanna—The oak in this case is the live oak. Other plants of this habitat are hackberry, chittimwood, chapotillo, tickle-tongue, Turk's cap, pigeonberry, purpletop, brown seed paspalum, Indiangrass, and four-flowered Trichloris.

Birds of the oak savanna include Burrowing Owl, Crested Caracara, Wild Turkey, Red-tailed Hawk, Cattle Egret, Northern Bobwhite, Great Horned Owl, Brown-crested Flycatcher, Golden-fronted Woodpecker, Long-billed Thrasher, Loggerhead Shrike, Scissor-tailed Flycatcher, Bell's Vireo, and Blue Grosbeak.

Oak woodland—Oak woodlands are fairly extensive at the Aransas Wildlife Refuge. They once covered much of the barrier islands, where now only a few remnant oak mottes persist. One such motte can be seen at Packery Channel County Park. Oak woodlands are especially attractive to migrants. Included plants are live oak, blackjack oak, beautyberry, sweetbay, wax myrtle, greenbrier, Spanish moss, poison ivy, trumpet vine, ball moss, yaupon, mustang grape, lantana, and dewberry.

Birds here are the Black-crested Titmouse, Carolina Wren, Carolina Chickadee, Sharp-shinned Hawk, and migrant thrushes, flycatchers, warblers, and vireos.

Estuaries—Many species of birds utilize these important salt marshes, which are extremely rich in nutrients. This estuarine habitat is dominated by a few specialized plant species able to withstand the salinity changes that are common in coastal communities. Included plants are cordgrass, sea ox-eye, saltwort, glasswort, coastal saltgrass, and shoregrass.

Many species of birds use the salt marsh, including some spectacular species found in coastal Texas: American White Pelican, Whooping Crane, Roseate Spoonbill, Black-crowned Night Heron, Snowy Egret, Great Egret, Tricolored Heron, Wood Stork, White-faced Ibis, and White Ibis.

Primary and secondary bays—Bays can undergo significant changes in salinity and temperature coinciding with major climatic cycles. They tend to be shallower and calmer than the open ocean. Natural islands and spoil islands, resulting from dredging operations in coastal bays, are excellent breeding sites for many species of colonial waterbirds.

Included birds are Brown Pelican, Double-crested Cormorant, Magnificent Frigatebird, Common Loon, Northern Pintail, American Wigeon, Northern Shoveler, Redhead, Lesser Scaup, Common Goldeneye, Ruddy Duck, Red-breasted Merganser, Black Skimmer, and Least Tern.

Gulf beaches—Though structurally simple, the Gulf beaches are rich habitats that provide feeding areas and, in some cases, nesting sites for many species of shorebirds and wading birds. Tidal pools associated with the beaches are used by various species.

Look in this habitat for Least Terns, Black Skimmers, Snowy Plovers, Wilson's Plovers, Caspian Terns, Gull-billed Terns, Laughing Gulls, Ring-billed Gulls, various sandpiper species, and Great Blue Herons.

Marine—This habitat is home to the pelagic birds of the Gulf of Mexico. Some species can be seen with a spotting scope, but most require a boat trip.

Pelagic birds are less well known to Texas birders. On a trip into the Gulf, it's possible to see Northern Gannets, Masked and Brown Boobies, Pomarine Jaegers, Cory's Shearwaters, Audubon Shearwaters, Magnificent Frigatebirds, and Sooty Terns.

Freshwater marshes, lakes, and ponds—These freshwater habitats come and go with rainfall levels. Dominant plants of these communities include bulrushes, cattails, sedges, and duckweed. In areas of prolonged flooding, look for spiny aster, giant ragweed, and longtom. Lotus, water hyacinth, and waterlily are characteristic of slightly deeper water.

Birds of these freshwater wetlands include Least Grebe, Anhinga, Black-bellied Whistling-Duck, Fulvous Whistling-Duck, Cinnamon Teal, Gadwall, Least Bittern, and Black-necked Stilt.

Agricultural areas—The main agricultural products of the Coastal Bend are cotton, sorghum, and pasture. These monocultures will support some species of birds, particularly when flooded during wet cycles.

Birds that frequent agricultural areas are Killdeer, Black-bellied Plover, Mountain Plover, Dickcissel, American Pipit, Horned Lark, and Lark Sparrow.

Planning Your Trip

The Corpus Christi International Airport is a modern airport with connecting flights from all over the United States. Rental cars from national companies are available at the airport.

San Antonio, which is about 150 miles from Corpus Christi, could also be used as a convenient starting place. Interstate Highway 37 connects San Antonio and Corpus Christi, so many visitors enter the area from that direction. State highways also enter the area from Houston, Laredo, and the Lower Rio Grande Valley.

The sites in this book have been deliberately chosen to be reached easily. Preference has been given to sites that are open every day of the week, do not need special permission to enter, and can be accessed without a group or guide. Priority has also been given to those sites accessible by good paved roads. There are a few exceptions to all of these preferences, but in every case I have noted the exception.

Few places in Texas are in public ownership (less than 4 percent). Most land, except for national and state parks and wildlife refuges, is privately owned. Even some of the sites listed in this book are privately owned, as noted. Consequently, the out-of-state birder may be surprised to find many NO TRESPASSING signs. Never cross a fence or gate without permission from the landowner.

What to Wear

Because it is impossible to predict for certain the weather in the Coastal Bend on any given day, it is best to layer your clothing. Temperatures vary from early morning to afternoon by as much as 30 degrees. In the spring, summer, and fall, shorts or cropped pants can be worn if you expect to bird in open areas, while long pants offer the off-the-path birder protection from thorns and pests. For most areas, it is nice to have a sturdy pair of hiking shoes or boots. A raincoat or an umbrella is also good to have on hand.

Never stay out in South Texas without adequate protection from the sun. Wear long-sleeved shirts, or use plenty of sunscreen. Invest in a broad-brimmed hat, preferably with a strap or tie. Remember, it can be windy here.

In addition to binoculars, field guides, and this travel guide, be sure to bring plenty of water, insect repellent, and additional sunscreen.

Hazards

Birders, have a wonderful time exploring Corpus Christi and the Coastal Bend. It is highly unlikely that you will encounter any problems along the way, but I mention these hazards so that you can plan wisely.

Climate

Of all of the hazards mentioned here, this is the one that should be taken most seriously. It gets hot in the Coastal Bend. Plan to carry plenty of water with you.

Stay in the shade when possible, and wear sunscreen. It is possible, even likely, to sunburn on cloudy days.

Traffic

Texas has an excellent highway system. Because South Texas is so flat, you will find few driving hazards except in spring or fall, when fog can pose a problem. If you find yourself in foggy conditions, slow down or get off the roadway until the fog clears. Otherwise, traffic is only an issue at a few sites, in which case it has been noted.

Poison Ivy

Remember this: "Leaves of three, let it be." Poison ivy climbs up fences and trees, has attractive shiny trifoliate leaves with white berries, and is poisonous to the touch. In the fall the leaves may turn to a rich reddish or brownish color. Avoid this plant in all instances. However, if you do tangle with poison ivy, wash your hands immediately. Your clothes will also need laundering to avoid spreading plant residue.

Downtown Corpus Christi from the T-Heads.

Brown Pelicans in Corpus Christi Bay. PHOTO: TONY BAYLIS.

Mosquitoes

Many of the sites in this book feature standing water, and South Texas is noted for its hordes of gnats and mosquitoes. West Nile virus is a concern throughout the state, and a few human cases have been reported. Therefore, insect repellent is advised.

Ticks and Chiggers

Insect repellent helps here, too. Spray your feet, ankles, and lower clothing. Tuck your pants into the tops of your boots to thwart tick and chigger access. Over-the-counter medication is available to stop the itch caused by chigger bites. Tick bites can be more serious and may warrant a doctor's visit. Lyme disease, although rare in Texas when compared to eastern states, should be a concern for anyone bitten by a tick.

Fire Ants

The imported fire ant *Solenopis invicta* entered Texas in 1957. Its effect on gardens, homes, young mammals, and birds has been serious. Drought conditions, when these insects seek moisture, increase contacts between humans and fire ants.

The best defense against fire ants is to simply watch where you are planting your feet. They do make mounds, but these are often hidden under thick grass. If you find yourself under attack, call for friends to help you brush them off. Their bite will leave a pimple-like spot that can be painful for a day or so.

Killer Bees

The Africanized honeybee migrated from South America in the 1950s. Killer bees have a quick temper. They are more likely to sense a threat at a greater distance, become more upset with less reason, and sting in much greater numbers. They are similar to domestic bees and impossible to tell apart in the field.

Your best defense against bees, killer or otherwise, is to be alert. If you see bees flying around your vicinity or you hear buzzing sounds, leave the area. Don't turn over logs or rocks where bees may nest. Killer bees will pursue you three times farther than regular honeybees.

If you or someone else is stung, remove the stinger quickly in a sideways motion with a fingernail, credit card, or similar material. Seek medical attention if there are signs of a systemic allergy or if swelling extends beyond two joints. Ice may reduce the swelling, and a sting-kill ointment may reduce the pain.

The Corpus Christi area is also home to wasps and yellow jackets. Follow similar steps if you run into either of these insects.

Thorns

It seems as if just about every other plant or tree here has thorns, and I don't mean just cactus. At most sites you will be on trails where thorns should not pose any threat.

Snakes

Texas is home to around 115 species and subspecies of snakes. Venomous snakes make up less than 15 percent of the total number of Texas snakes. They can be separated into four categories: coral snakes, copperheads, cottonmouths or water moccasins, and rattlesnakes.

Coral snakes have a small mouth and are usually nonaggressive. Their bite is dangerous, but they are extremely rare. Fortunately, these snakes are fairly easy to recognize. Their colors always go in the order of red, yellow, and black. Other snakes have similar colors, but never in that order. In other words, a coral snake's pattern will put red next to yellow, while the "copycat" will have red next to black. The easiest way to keep them straight is to remember the following rhyme: "Red and yellow kill a fellow/red and black, friend to Jack."

Copperhead snakes are gray and/or brown and blend in well with forest floors. They are the least dangerous poisonous snake, and they typically bite humans only when someone accidentally steps on, sits on, or picks them up.

Cottonmouths rarely stray far from the water. They will be found in marshes, swamps, ponds, lakes, ditches, and canals along the Gulf Coast. They can be defensive and aggressive. In the spring, they regularly sun themselves in grasses near the water. Just keep your eyes open.

Nine kinds of rattlesnakes are found in Texas. They usually rattle before striking, but not always. Pay attention to where you are placing your hands and feet.

Alligators

There will be alligators at a few of the sites listed in this guide. Stay on paths or trails, and leave the alligators alone.

Lightning

In the Coastal Bend, lightning often accompanies or precedes rain. Get in your car and avoid touching the body of the car.

Rough Seas

Unless you are on a pelagic trip, this should not be a problem for you. However, when walking out onto a pier or jetty, be aware of the movement of the water. Rocks in these areas are slippery, and big waves appear without warning.

Crime

The most common crime encountered by birders is vehicular theft. Don't leave items of interest to thieves in view in your car. For some sites mentioned in this guide, this is a serious problem. Be warned: If crime is listed as a hazard for a site, vehicular theft is usually the problem.

Birding Ethics

The following is the American Birding Association's Code of Birding Ethics.

Everyone who enjoys birds and birding must always respect wildlife, its environment, and the rights of others. In any conflict of interest between birds and birders, the welfare of the birds and their environment comes first.

1. Promote the welfare of birds and their environment.

   1(a) Support the protection of important bird habitat.

   1(b) To avoid stressing birds or exposing them to danger, exercise restraint and caution during observation, photography, sound recording, or filming. Limit the use of recordings and other methods of attracting birds, and never use such methods in heavily birded areas, or for attracting any species that is Threatened, Endangered, or of Special Concern, or is rare in your local area.

   Keep well back from nests and nesting colonies, roosts, display areas, and important feeding sites. In such sensitive areas, if there is a need for extended observation, photography, filming, or recording, try to use a blind or hide, and take advantage of natural cover. Use artificial light sparingly for filming or photography, especially for close-ups.

   1(c) Before advertising the presence of a rare bird, evaluate the potential for disturbance to the bird, its surroundings, and other people in the area, and proceed only if access can be controlled, disturbance minimized, and permission has been obtained from private landowners. The sites of rare nesting birds should be divulged only to the proper conservation authorities.

   1(d) Stay on roads, trails, and paths where they exist; otherwise keep habitat disturbance to a minimum.

2. Respect the law and the rights of others.

   2(a) Do not enter private property without the owner's explicit permission.

   2(b) Follow all laws, rules, and regulations governing use of roads and public areas, both at home and abroad.

   2(c) Practice common courtesy in contacts with other people. Your exemplary behavior will generate goodwill with birders and nonbirders alike.

3. Ensure that feeders, nest structures, and other artificial bird environments are safe.

   3(a) Keep dispensers, water, and food clean and free of decay or disease. It is important to feed birds continually during harsh weather.

   3(b) Maintain and clean nest structures regularly.

Reprinted by permission of the American Birding Association, http://americanbirding.org.

3(c) If you are attracting birds to an area, ensure the birds are not exposed to predation from cats and other domestic animals or dangers posed by artificial hazards.

4. Group birding, whether organized or impromptu, requires special care.

4(a) Respect the interests, rights, and skills of fellow birders, as well as people participating in other legitimate outdoor activities. Freely share your knowledge and experience, except where code 1(c) applies. Be especially helpful to beginning birders.

4(b) If you witness unethical birding behavior, assess the situation, and intervene if you think it prudent. When interceding, inform the person(s) of the inappropriate action, and attempt, within reason, to have it stopped. If the behavior continues, document it, and notify appropriate individuals or organizations.

Group Leader Responsibilities.

4(c) Be an exemplary ethical role model for the group. Teach through word and example.

4(d) Keep groups to a size that limits impact on the environment and does not interfere with others using the same area.

4(e) Ensure everyone in the group knows of and practices this code.

4(f) Learn and inform the group of any special circumstances applicable to the areas being visited (e.g., no tape recorders allowed).

4(g) Acknowledge that professional tour companies bear a special responsibility to place the welfare of birds and the benefits of public knowledge ahead of the company's commercial interests. Ideally, leaders should keep track of tour sightings, document unusual occurrences, and submit records to appropriate organizations.

Corpus Christi: Downtown

The shoreline and Corpus Christi Bay dominate downtown Corpus Christi. In fact, the city curves around the bay so as not to miss even one opportunity for the beautiful view.

The weather near the bay is cooler in the summer because of the ocean breezes. Five of the sites in this section are along Corpus Christi Bay or the Cayo del Oso that connects with it. Three other sites are urban parks.

Obviously, at the bay sites you will see birds such as gulls and terns that are associated with saltwater. Also, at sites where the shoreline is visible, wading birds and shorebirds will be abundant. If you are trying to add Brown Pelicans, Reddish Egrets, or Roseate Spoonbills to your bird list, then this is the place for you.

The three urban parks in this section really do not represent the typical habitat of South Texas, but because of their strategic location near the coast, all three act as Neotropic Migrant Traps in the spring. Visit these parks if you are interested in warblers, vireos, tanagers, and hummingbirds.

1. Blucher Park
2. Corpus Christi T-Heads
3. Texas State Aquarium
4. Rose Hill Memorial Park
5. Hans and Pat Suter Wildlife Refuge City Park
6. Oso Bay Park
7. Texas A&M University—Corpus Christi Nature Trail
8. Corpus Christi Botanical Gardens and Nature Center
9. J. C. Elliot Landfill

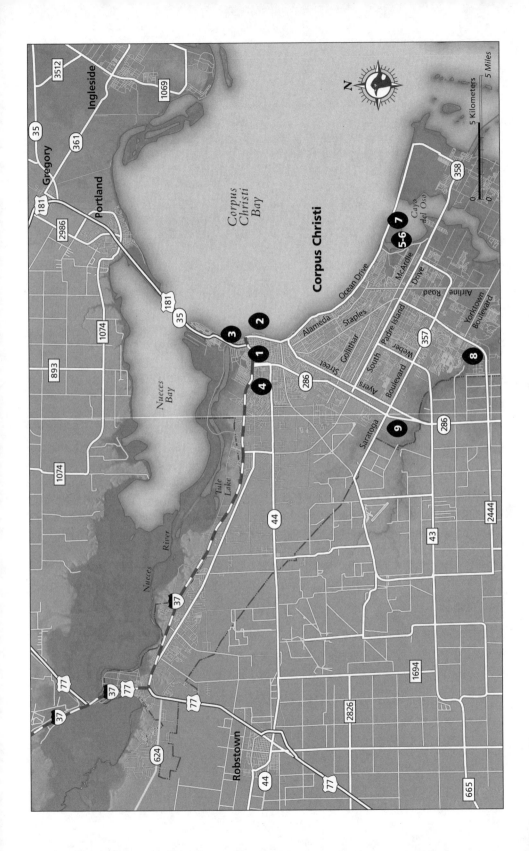

① Blucher Park

Habitats: Urban park, riparian.

Specialty birds: *Resident*—Common Pauraque, Buff-bellied Hummingbird, Golden-fronted Woodpecker, Couch's Kingbird. *Spring/Summer*—Brown-crested Flycatcher, Cave Swallow.

Other key birds: *Resident*—Inca Dove. *Spring/Summer*—Painted Bunting. *Fall/Winter*—Rufous Hummingbird. *Migrating*—Neotropic Migrant Trap.

Best times to bird: March through November.

Directions: When entering Corpus Christi via Interstate 37, take the Buffalo Street exit (Exit 1A). Stay on the access for 3 blocks. It will quickly turn into Buffalo. At the corner of Buffalo and Tancahua, turn right and travel for 0.3 mile. Turn right onto Comanche and travel for 3 blocks. Turn left onto Artesian for one block. Turn left onto Blucher Street for ½ block and right at Carrizo. Blucher Park will be on the left side.

If you are on Shoreline Drive in Corpus Christi, you can take any of the parallel side streets, such as Leopard or Williams/Lipan, to get up onto the bluff and to Tancahua Street, then follow the directions above. Blucher is behind the main Corpus Christi Public Library. This park is open from sunrise until 10:00 P.M.

The birding

Blucher is a small urban park about 1 block square, but it really packs a big punch for its little size. First, it is a densely wooded park, and the Audubon Outdoor Club has added other native plantings. Many of these native plants are labeled. Second, there is a small creek flowing through the park. Third, it is close to the coast. This combination attracts migrating passerines, especially during the spring migration.

There is no real strategy for attacking this park. There are paths that you can follow, but the park is small, and you can just wander around in the open areas. You will be surprised when you start to check every bush and tree carefully. During bird walks in 2004, the AOC listed eighty-eight species in the month of April. At least thirteen additional species have been listed in previous years. Gulls and wading birds can be seen flying over the park. Hawks, such as Sharp-shinned and Broad-winged, have been known to stop over. They're tricky to find, but nightjars such as Chuck-will's-widow and Whip-poor-will have been seen here. Flycatchers can be numerous, from the Brown-crested to the Scissor-tailed. All of the swallows, except the Cave and Violet-green, have been seen at Blucher. Want to see buntings, or tanagers, cuckoos, grosbeaks, or orioles? Try Blucher. During the fall, look in the treetops for Cedar Waxwings. But be sure to keep your eyes open for the migrating warblers. Twenty-five-plus warblers have been listed in the park, including the rare (for South Texas) Prairie Warbler.

General information: This park is owned by the City of Corpus Christi and managed by the Audubon Outdoor Club. The AOC leads free, guided bird walks every Saturday and Sunday during the month of April (except Easter) beginning at 7:30 A.M. This is CTC#71.

DeLorme: Texas Atlas & Gazetteer: Page 98 4C.

Elevation: 35 feet.

Hazards: Steep inclines, fire ants, crime.

Nearest food, gas, lodging: Across the street from Blucher Park is the beautifully restored 1904 George Blucher House Bed and Breakfast Inn.

For more information: City of Corpus Christi, 1202 Leopard, Corpus Christi, TX 78401; (361) 880-3211; Audubon Outdoor Club of Corpus Christi, Inc., P.O. Box 3352, Corpus Christi, TX 78463.

② Corpus Christi T-Heads

Habitats: Primary Bay.

Specialty birds: *Resident*—Neotropic Cormorants, Brown Pelican.

Other key birds: *Resident*—Gull-billed Tern. *Fall/Winter*—Common Loon.

Best times to bird: Year-round.

Directions: Take Interstate 37 to its end, at Shoreline Drive. This drive follows the arch of the bay in downtown Corpus Christi. The T-Heads can be found coming off Shoreline at Peoples Street, Lawrence Street, and Cooper's Alley.

Shrimp boats at the T-Head.

The birding

The T-Heads are not so much a prime birding spot as a site that every out-of-towner should see. Construction of these artificial islands began in 1939. They accompany the seawall, miradores (overlooks), Magee Beach, and city parks that line the bay front. You can drive out on these islands and park for a quick look at Laughing Gulls, Ring-billed Gulls, Franklin Gulls, Herring Gulls, Royal and Sandwich Terns, and Double-crested Cormorants. A lucky find in the winter would be a Lesser Black-backed Gull. The cormorants, and perhaps Great Blue Herons, will most likely be seen on the two breakwaters that curve into the bay. You may walk on the breakwater jutting out from Magee Beach. The other is closed to the public. The most delightful birds visible at the spot will be the Brown Pelicans. They cruise the bay here looking for their next meal. Watch long enough and you will see them plunge headfirst for a tasty morsel. Occasionally, sandpipers and ducks are spotted along Magee Beach.

General information: Actually, there are two T-Heads and one L-Head. The T-Head on People's Street includes a skate park, a restaurant, fishing and sightseeing rentals, and docks for shrimp boats. The Lawrence Street T-Head includes the Municipal Marina. The L-Head on Cooper's Alley is the home of the Corpus Christi Yacht Club.

DeLorme: Texas Atlas & Gazetteer: Page 98 4C.

Elevation: 30 feet.

Hazards: Traffic.

Nearest food, gas, lodging: Shoreline Drive and Ocean Drive.

For more information: City of Corpus Christi, 1202 Leopard, Corpus Christi, TX 78401; (361) 880-3211.

③ Texas State Aquarium

Habitats: Aquarium.

Best times to bird: Open every day except Christmas Day.

Directions: To reach the Texas State Aquarium from Corpus Christi, take Highway 35/U.S. Highway 181 north across Harbor Bridge. Take the first exit (signed for the Aquarium) after the bridge. Turn right onto Burleson for 1 block. Go right again onto Surfside and follow that road to its end under the bridge at the parking lot of the aquarium. Excellent signs mark every turn to the aquarium once you cross the bridge.

The birding

The Texas State Aquarium is devoted to displaying fish and mammals of the Gulf of Mexico. It houses some 300 species of ocean and freshwater creatures in more than forty habitats. Want to see sharks, sea turtles, tropical fish, and even river otters? This is your place.

The aquarium understands the role played by bird life on the marine ecosystem and maintains exhibits of birds. Moreover, it operates a bird rehabilitation center. Injured or orphaned birds, including herons, pelicans, raptors, ducks, and small shorebirds, can sometimes be seen up close. The back of the aquarium faces the bay, and the ship channel is to the south of the aquarium. It is possible to spot gulls, terns, and pelicans in the outdoor area.

General information: At the aquarium, there is an entrance fee and a parking fee. This is CTC#72. It is wheelchair accessible.

As you cross the bridge to get to the aquarium, you should be able to get a good look at the USS *Lexington* on the gulf side of the bridge. The *Lexington* is open to visitors. Also, across the Harbor Bridge from the aquarium is the Corpus Christi Museum of Science and History, South Texas Institute for the Arts, Heritage Park, and the Asian Cultures Museum and Educational Center.

DeLorme: Texas Atlas & Gazetteer: Page 98 4B.

Elevation: 25 feet.

Nearest food, gas, lodging: This area is known as Corpus Christi Beach or North Beach and has many facilities for tourists.

For more information: Texas State Aquarium, 2710 North Shoreline, Corpus Christi, TX 78402; (361) 881–1200, (800) 477–4853.

4 Rose Hill Memorial Park

Habitats: Urban cemetery.

Specialty birds: *Resident*—Groove-billed Ani, Common Pauraque, Buff-bellied Hummingbird, Golden-fronted Woodpecker, Couch's Kingbird. *Spring/Summer*—Brown-crested Flycatcher, Scissor-tailed Flycatcher.

Other key birds: *Resident*—Inca Dove, Ladder-backed Woodpecker. *Fall/Winter*—Rufous Hummingbird. *Migrating*—Neotropic Migrant Trap.

Best times to bird: March through June.

Directions: From Interstate 37, take the Lawrence Drive exit (Exit 1E). Turn south onto Buddy Lawrence and travel 0.5 mile until you reach Leopard. Turn left onto Leopard and go 2 blocks to a stoplight. Turn right on to Palm Drive and travel for 3 blocks to the entrance of Rose Hill Memorial Park. The cemetery is located at the intersection of Palm and Comanche. The gates open at 7:00 A.M. and close at 8:00 P.M.

The birding

A sign at the entrance to this cemetery proclaims THIS IS A BIRD AND ANIMAL SANCTUARY. There is little doubt as to why birds are attracted to this spot. It is lovely. Most of the trees are very old live oaks. The birds you see will be mostly nestled in these beautiful trees. In addition, palms, mesquites, and Chinese tallows have been planted.

If you have never birded in a cemetery, it may take a little getting used to. This is an old and well-established memorial park. There are usually a considerable number of people coming and going. Maintenance men are normally at work, too. However, if you are respectful of any ongoing services or quiet visitors, no one will notice you. I have been stopped by other visitors (they were not bird-watchers) on two occasions. Both times they just wanted to know what birds I had seen. In fact, during spring migration you will most likely see more birders than mourners.

That indeed is the main reason for coming to Rose Hill. In the spring, every tree may literally be alive with migrants, especially vireos and warblers. Pick a parking place and start walking. I like to start on the east side of the park, but I'm not sure why. You can easily spend an entire day at this location. Very early in the morning you may rouse a Common Pauraque or a Chuck-will's-widow. The park is big enough to maintain hawks as well. Great Crested and Brown-crested Flycatchers use this park in the spring. Eastern Phoebes hang out here in the winter. You could see Blue-gray Gnatcatchers, Black-crested Titmice, and Ruby-crowned Kinglets. Look for Couch's Kingbirds, Eastern Wood Pewees, and Summer Tanagers as well. This is a good place for Scarlet Tanagers and Gray-cheeked Thrushes.

The vireos and warblers alone make Rose Hill a fine birding spot. In the spring you can find White-eyed, Bell's, Yellow-throated, Blue-headed, Red-eyed, Philadelphia, Plumbeous, and Warbling Vireos. Migrating warblers include Black-and-White, Worm-eating, Yellow-throated, Pine, Golden-winged, Blue-winged, Tennessee, Nashville, Northern Parula, Black-throated Green, Chestnut-sided, Bay-breasted, Yellow-breasted Chat, Kentucky, Mourning, Hooded, Wilson's, Canada, and American Redstart.

General information: Rose Hill Memorial Park was opened in 1913 and encompasses 55.5 acres. It is wheelchair accessible.

DeLorme: Texas Atlas & Gazetteer: Page 98 3C.

Elevation: 35 feet.

Hazards: Fire ants, traffic.

Nearest food, gas, lodging: Leopard Street.

For more information: Rose Hill Memorial Park, 2731 Comanche, Corpus Christi, TX 78408; (361) 882-5497.

5 Hans and Pat Suter Wildlife Refuge City Park

Habitats: Secondary bay, freshwater marsh.

Specialty birds: *Resident*—Brown Pelican, Black-bellied Whistling-Duck, Reddish Egret, White-faced Ibis, Common Pauraque, Buff-bellied Hummingbird, Golden-fronted Woodpecker, Long-billed Thrasher, Olive Sparrow. *Spring/Summer*—Brown-crested Flycatcher, Scissor-tailed Flycatcher, Hooded Oriole. *Fall/Winter*—Peregrine Falcon, Piping Plover.

Other key birds: *Resident*—Neotropic Cormorant, Mottled Duck, Crested Caracara, Little Blue Heron, Roseate Spoonbill, Clapper Rail, Gull-billed Tern, Inca Dove. *Spring/Summer*—Magnificent Frigatebird, Wilson's Plover, Painted Bunting. *Fall/Winter*—Marbled Godwit, Rufous Hummingbird. *Migrating*—Shorebirds, Neotropic Migrant Trap.

Best times to bird: Year-round.

Directions: Take South Padre Island Drive (SPID) east toward Padre Island. Exit on Ennis Joslin Road and head north toward Corpus Christi. Travel down Ennis Joslin for 2 miles until it intersects Nile. The refuge will be on the right. If you are coming from downtown Corpus Christi, take Shoreline/Ocean Drive and stay on it until you reach Alameda. This is the last road before the Texas A&M University-Corpus Christi campus. Turn right on Alameda and stay to the left as it becomes Ennis Joslin and travel for 1 mile. The refuge will be on the left.

The birding

The twenty-two-acre Hans and Pat Suter Wildlife Refuge City Park is small but popular. If possible, park close to the traffic on Ennis Joslin Road. Auto break-ins are a problem at this park.

As you leave the parking lot, look for hummingbirds and passerines. During the spring and summer, try for Ruby-throated, Black-chinned, or Buff-bellied Hummingbirds; in the winter, you may find a rare Rufous Hummingbird. Many warblers use this park as a stopover throughout spring migration. You may spot a Carolina Wren, an Indigo Bunting, or a Baltimore Oriole. In the fall and winter, the trees can literally be alive with Yellow-rump Warblers. These seasons also bring American Goldfinches (but they will be brown in their fall plumage) and sparrows.

The park is pretty straightforward. The trail to the south leads to Oso Bay Park. The other path leads through the park. This way will direct you past some native and nonnative plants and over a small freshwater stream. The trail is short and ends at a long boardwalk beside a freshwater channel. The channel funnels wastewater from a treatment plant into Oso Bay. The 800-foot-long boardwalk ends at the edge of the bay with a viewing platform. Another platform can be used about halfway down the walk.

Boardwalk at Hans and Pat Suter Wildlife Refuge City Park.

In winter the channel fills with American Coots, Moorhens, and ducks. Look for American Wigeons, Northern Shovelers, Gadwalls, Green-wing Teal, and Cinnamon Teal. You can listen for rails, but good luck on seeing any.

If the tide is out, the Oso beach should be rich with birds. Brown and White Pelicans, Little Blue Herons, and Reddish Egrets may all be there. Check the edge of the water for Black-necked Stilts, American Avocets, gulls, and Piping Plovers. Ducks, such as Northern Pintails, will be farther out. Belted Kingfishers like to hover at the mouth of the channel. In the flats above the channel, you should see Great Blue Heron and a flock of Roseate Spoonbills, who prefer to "spoon" through the marsh there. Watch the sky for Osprey and Peregrine Falcons.

Have fun. Stay a while, as the birdscape changes quickly here.

General information: The park is named for Hans and Pat Suter, prominent citizens and wildlife preservationists in Corpus Christi. Hans died in 1984. Pat continues to be active, especially in protecting habitat. The refuge was dedicated on Earth Day, April 22, 1999. Sadly, this park has a serious problem with guinea grass and Brazilian pepper bushes. At the time of publication, discussions were under way regarding eliminating this invasive plant species. This is CTC#69.

DeLorme: *Texas Atlas & Gazetteer:* Page 85 7F.

Elevation: 30 feet.

Hazards: Crime.

Nearest food, gas, lodging: Corner of Ennis Joslin Road and Ocean Drive.

For more information: City of Corpus Christi, 1202 Leopard, Corpus Christi, TX 78401; (361) 880-3211.

6 Oso Bay Park

Habitats: Secondary bay, Tamaulipan scrubland.

Specialty birds: *Resident*—Brown Pelican, Black-bellied Whistling-Duck, Reddish Egret, White-faced Ibis, Common Pauraque, Buff-bellied Hummingbird, Golden-fronted Woodpecker, Long-billed Thrasher, Olive Sparrow. *Spring/Summer*—Brown-crested Flycatcher. *Fall/Winter*—Peregrine Falcon, Piping Plover.

Other key birds: *Resident*—Neotropic Cormorant, Mottled Duck, Little Blue Heron, Roseate Spoonbill, Gull-billed Tern. *Spring/Summer*—Magnificent Frigatebird, Wilson's Plover, Painted Bunting. *Fall/Winter*—Marbled Godwit, Rufous Hummingbird. *Migrating*—Shorebirds, Neotropic passerines.

Best times to bird: Year-round.

Directions: South Padre Island Drive (SPID) is the major expressway that goes from Corpus Christi to Padre Island. Take SPID east toward the island. Exit on Ennis Joslin Road and head north back toward Corpus Christi. Oso Bay Park is about 1 mile north on Ennis Joslin Road. There is no sign for Oso Bay Park, so look carefully for the first park on the right.

Neotropic Cormorant. PHOTO: TONY BAYLIS.

The birding

Oso Bay Park, as its name suggests, is situated on Oso Bay. In addition to the frontage on the bay, there is an upland brush area and a paved trail leading north to Hans and Pat Suter Wildlife Refuge City Park. Joggers also use this trail.

Take the trail on the right if facing the bay. This way will take you down for a close look at the pelicans, diverse shorebirds, wading birds, and waterfowl. Birding here is usually at its best when the tide is out, revealing mudflats.

Continuing on the trail will lead you into brush, where you can search for passerines, especially migrants in the spring. Keep your eyes peeled for sparrows, wrens, orioles, buntings, and grosbeaks. There is a cutoff on this trail that will return you to the parking lot.

Otherwise, the trail continues about 1 mile to Hans and Pat Suter Park. It leads through the brush, where many plants and trees are labeled, and the birder will be rewarded with an occasional view of the bay.

This park has many nonnative trees, and it has a serious problem with invasive guinea grass.

General information: This is CTC#68.

DeLorme: Texas Atlas & Gazetteer: Page 85 7F.

Elevation: 30 feet.

Hazards: Fog, crime, mosquitoes.

Nearest food, gas, lodging: Ocean Drive.

For more information: City of Corpus Christi, 1202 Leopard, Corpus Christi, TX 78401; (361) 880-3211.

Texas A&M University—Corpus Christi Nature Trail

Habitats: Secondary bay, Tamaulipan scrubland.

Specialty birds: *Resident*—Brown Pelican, Black-bellied Whistling-Duck, Reddish Egret, White-faced Ibis, Golden-fronted Woodpecker. *Spring/Summer*—Wood Stork. *Fall/Winter*—Peregrine Falcon, Piping Plover.

Other key birds: *Resident*—Neotropic Cormorant, Mottled Duck, Crested Caracara, Little Blue Heron, Roseate Spoonbill, Gull-billed Tern, Inca Dove. *Spring/Summer*—Magnificent Frigatebird, Wilson's Plover, Sandwich Tern, Painted Bunting. *Fall/Winter*—Marbled Godwit. *Migrating*—Shorebirds.

Best times to bird: Year-round.

Directions: The Corpus Christi campus of Texas A&M University is situated at the end of Ocean Drive (6300 Ocean Drive). Ocean Drive is a four-lane street that runs along the bay front. Ennis Joslin Road merges into Alameda and ends at Ocean Drive 1 mile from Hans and Pat Suter Wildlife Refuge City Park. At the intersection of Alameda and Ocean Drive, turn right. Take the first entrance into the university grounds. Stop at the visitor's kiosk to get a free parking permit (required) and directions for parking.

The birding

The Nature and Hiking Trail was designed for use by birders, hikers, skaters, and nonmotorized bikers, and is owned and maintained by Texas A&M University–Corpus Christi. It is located on Ward Island, which is connected to the Corpus Christi mainland by a short bridge.

The trail makes a 3.2-mile loop. Part of this loop includes a walk back to your car through the university grounds. Few birds would be found on that part of the trail, especially when school is in session, but there is no way to avoid this section unless you retrace your steps. The university has a map of the site on its Web page.

The trail is an easy one to use. It is wide and paved. Motorized vehicles are not allowed. The trail skirts Ward Island along Oso Bay. White lampposts mark the path. (All other lampposts on campus are black.) It is lighted from dusk to dawn. The map shows that there are three "rest stops" along the way. These stops include a bench, a water fountain, and an emergency call button. There are no restrooms at these stops.

The trail affords a close look at Oso Bay from several locations. You can see something different at each of your stops, depending on the tide and direction and angle of the sun. A spur leads down to the bay. If the tide is out, you can walk on the beach.

Wilson's Plover. PHOTO: TONY BAYLIS.

Spotting a few passerines is possible, as part of the trail goes through modest brush areas. The trail is intersected by a freshwater inflow into the bay, which you can navigate using a footbridge.

Your focus will be on pelicans, shorebirds, wading birds, gull, and terns. This is the "other" side of the bay from Oso Bay Park and Hans and Pat Suter Refuge. Don't be surprised if you see birds not spotted at those sites. On one particular visit, I counted some fifty American Avocets feeding in the shallows at the first bay overlook on the trail. Twenty minutes earlier, I saw Black-necked Stilts at Suter but no Avocets.

Once you have explored the nature trail and leave the campus, plan for a stop ¼ mile farther out on Ocean Drive toward the North Gate of the Corpus Christi Naval Base. Pull over between the university and the bridge leaving Ward Island. Anglers use the stone breakwater on the Corpus Christi Bay side, and some wade fishing also goes on nearby. Birders will want to use this spot on the university side for another look at Oso Bay. Catch a glimpse of a Reddish Egret searching for a seafood supper. Watch White Pelicans bathe. Spot Forster's Terns flashing white and diving. See a Great Blue Heron gulping down a fish while a Snowy Egret wades nearby. At the right time of year and with cooperating tides and weather, expect to see all of this and more.

General information: Ward Island has been inhabited for at least a thousand years, as witnessed by the numerous Karankawa tribal artifacts discovered there. Control of the island changed hands several times between 1889 and 1942. During part of that time, developer John C. Ward owned it. For a while the U.S. Navy operated a radar training facility there. In 1947 it was relinquished by the Navy to the state to be used for higher education. This is CTC#70. The trail is wheelchair accessible.

DeLorme: Texas Atlas & Gazetteer: Page 85 7F.

Elevation: 30 feet.

Hazards: Fog.

Nearest food, gas, lodging: Corner of Ocean Drive and Alameda.

For more information: Texas A&M University-Corpus Christi, 6300 Ocean Drive, Corpus Christi, TX 78412; (361) 825-5700.

8 Corpus Christi Botanical Gardens and Nature Center

Habitats: Tamaulipan scrubland, freshwater marsh, freshwater lake.

Specialty birds: *Resident*—Least Grebe, Black-bellied Whistling-Duck, Reddish Egret, White-faced Ibis, Groove-billed Ani, Buff-bellied Hummingbird, Golden-fronted Woodpecker, Couch's Kingbird, Long-billed Thrasher, Olive Sparrow. *Spring/Summer*—Wood Stork, Brown-crested Flycatcher, Scissor-tailed Flycatcher, Cave Swallow, Hooded Oriole. *Fall/Winter*—Peregrine Falcon, Vermilion Flycatcher. *Migrating*—Buff-breasted Sandpiper, Hudsonian Godwit.

Other key birds: *Resident*—Neotropic Cormorant, Mottled Duck, Roseate Spoonbill, Gull-billed Tern, Inca Dove, Ladder-backed Woodpecker, Bronzed Cowbird. *Spring/Summer*—Painted Bunting. *Fall/Winter*—Rufous Hummingbird. *Migrating*—Shorebirds, Neotropic passerines.

Best times to bird: Year-round.

Directions: South Padre Island Drive (SPID) is the major expressway that goes out toward the island. At the intersection of SPID and Staples Street, turn south onto Staples. Travel on Staples south from Corpus Christi central for 4.5 miles. Staples will narrow from four lanes to two and curve. As the road curves, the entrance to the Corpus Christi Botanical Gardens is on the right (8545 South Staples). There are several signs for the gardens.

The birding

If the term *botanical gardens* conjures images of rare orchids, Hawaiian plumerias, and manicured rose gardens, you may be surprised by Corpus Christi's award-winning gardens. These are only a small part of what this premier birding spot has to offer. Stop by the gift shop first to register and pick up a site map and a bird list. Follow the sidewalk to the side of the gift shop to start your adventure. Take this path around to and through the Exhibit House and on to the Bird and Butterfly Trail.

Before you enter this trail, take a look through the large Hummingbird Garden on the right. Native mesquite trees are used as a backdrop for many luscious plantings used to entice Ruby-throated, Black-chinned, and Buff-bellied Hummingbirds. In the winter, look for Rufous Hummers as well.

The wide bird-watching trail is constructed of crushed stone and is wheelchair accessible except for the stop at the Birding Tower. On the way, you should easily spot Mourning and Inca Doves, Northern Mockingbirds, and Northern Cardinals. Also enjoy all of the signs naming the plants and trees. The tower overlooks Gator Lake, a freshwater pond with no "gator." Wading birds such as the Great Blue and Little Blue Herons and Great, Reddish, and Snowy Egrets are found feeding in the shallow water. In the summer, this is a likely place to see Wood Storks. Other residents of this area include Pied-billed and Least Grebes, Yellow-crowned Night

Herons, and American Coots. An occasional Neotropic Cormorant or Anhinga can be seen sunning on the banks. Red-winged Blackbirds can be heard and seen fluttering and chattering in the reeds. Harder to spot are the American Bitterns and various rails that come in the winter. Flying overhead are Laughing Gulls, Caspian and Forster's Terns, and Roseate Spoonbills. Franklin Gulls are often seen over the park during migration.

Farther down the trail is the Palapa Grande, an open-air gazebo that also looks out over Gator Lake. In the winter, you could use this vantage point to spot American Shovelers and Northern Pintails. In the summer, you may see Ruddy or Black-bellied Whistling-Ducks. At this point, the trail leads out onto the 500-foot Wetlands Boardwalk. All of the water features in the gardens are dependent on rainfall, and this is especially true of the water in the wetlands area. In the summer, it can become quite dry, although these particular wetlands have not completely dried up in several years. A Texas Prairie Wetlands Project recently culminated with the construction of a levee to help maintain water for the wetlands portion of this site.

The trail above the boardwalk leads away from the wetlands and into more scrubland and meadows. Master naturalists are working as volunteers to enhance the habitat here. This portion of the trail is a little more challenging. Look here for sparrows and thrashers. It would also be a good area to try for Pyrrhuloxia, Olive Sparrows, and Groove-billed Anis.

Proceed right from the boardwalk to reach the wetlands. The map shows a trail leading around the wetlands, but this is sometimes impractical. Your best bet is to go as far as the birding blind and return by the same way. This should give you a fine opportunity to see Canadian and White-fronted Geese and Sandhill Cranes in the winter. Black-necked Stilts, Willets, Killdeer, Black Skimmers, Greater and Lesser Yellowlegs, White Pelicans, American Avocets, sandpipers, and plovers can be spotted much of the time. I was chased out of this area by breeding Least Terns. I didn't spot the nest, but I must have been very close, as the nesting pair were quite angry.

Return down the boardwalk and continue onto another boardwalk that leads to the Arid Garden, where many examples of cactus are planted. Along the way, you get a different view of the wetlands. Continue through the gardens and return to the parking lot. Plan to spend at least two hours here. Carry water with you.

General information: The 180-acre gardens are open year-round from 9:00 A.M. to 5:00 P.M. Tuesday to Sunday; closed Monday (entrance fee). There are a gift shop and restrooms. This is CTC#67. It is wheelchair accessible.

DeLorme: Texas Atlas & Gazetteer: Page 85 7G.

Elevation: 35 feet.

Hazards: There is heavy traffic on Staples Street.

Nearest food, gas, lodging: Staples Street.

For more information: Corpus Christi Botanical Gardens and Nature Center, 8545 South Staples, Corpus Christi, TX 78413-5900; (361) 852-7875.

⑨ J. C. Elliot Landfill

Habitats: City dump.

Specialty birds: White-tailed Kite, White-tailed Hawk.

Other key birds: *Resident*—Crested Caracara. *Fall/Winter*—Peregrine Falcon, Lesser Black-backed Gull, California Gull, Thayer's Gull, Kelp Gull, Western Gull. *Migrating*—Sabine's Gull.

Best times to bird: Fall and winter.

Directions: The J. C. Elliot Landfill is located at 7001 Ayers Street. The entrance is 2.4 miles south of the intersection of South Padre Island Drive and Ayers Street (Highway 286). There is no sign at the entrance, but you will have no trouble finding it.

The birding

Inform the guard at the entrance to the landfill that you are there to bird-watch. You will be directed to the office, where you will receive an orange safety vest and instructions. Surprisingly, there are some grassy areas where you can park. Of course, that is not where you will find the birds. They are where the garbage is, so get out and walk around. I recommend using a spotting scope.

You probably have already figured out that the only reason to go to the Corpus Christi landfill is to see gulls. This can be a challenging place to visit. First, it smells terrible. Second, you must be careful to avoid the activity and heavy machinery. Finally, there are so many gulls that at times it can be overwhelming. Laughing, Ring-billed, and Herring Gulls are always feeding. Other gulls that show up here may actually be very common in other parts of the United States but are seldom seen on the Gulf Coast. Within the past several years, local and visiting bird-watchers have listed Mew Gull, Yellow-legged Gull, a possible Asian "Vega" Herring Gull, Black-tailed Gull, Glaucous Gull, Nelson's Gull, Franklin's Gull, Lesser Black-backed Gull, Slaty-backed Gull, California Gull, Thayer's Gull, Kelp Gull, and Western Gull.

You will also find some raptors, such as Swainson's Hawks, Peregrine Falcon, and Crested Caracaras.

General information: The J. C. Elliot Landfill is open Monday to Friday from 7:00 A.M. to 6:00 P.M., Saturday from 7:00 A.M. to 5:00 P.M. Closed Sunday. There is no fee for bird-watchers.

The landfill is scheduled to close in 2007. Cefe Valenzuela Landfill, near the intersection of Old Brownsville and Staples Roads, will replace it. J. C. Elliot will continue to be open on a limited basis for residential dumping.

DeLorme: Texas Atlas & Gazetteer: Page 85 7G.

Elevation: 35 feet.

Hazards: Dangerous machinery.

Nearest food, gas, lodging: Corpus Christi.

For more information: City of Corpus Christi, 1202 Leopard, Corpus Christi, TX 78401; (361) 880-3211.

Corpus Christi: Northwest

The Nueces River dominates the northwest section of Corpus Christi. Pollywog Pond, Hazel Bazemore County Park, and Labonte Park are all located along the river. Although Tule Lake isn't actually in the northwest and has much in common with coastal sites, it is very near the Nueces River.

Historically, the Nueces River had a large flood plain, and frequent floods benefited wildlife. Now the river is dammed at Choke Canyon Dam and Wesley Seale Dam. The state does require water releases to ensure healthy salinity levels in the Nueces estuary. Consequently, the river is kept at more of a constant level. However, in times of heavy rainfall, the lower Nueces does experience flooding, which certainly affects these parks as well. The sites in this section, not including Tule Lake, demonstrate marginal riparian habitats. The trees along the river bottom are not large, but they are welcoming to many species of birds, especially migrating land birds.

10. Tule Lake

11. Pollywog Pond

12. Hilltop Community Center

13. Hazel Bazemore County Park (IBA)

14. Labonte Park (formerly Nueces River Park)

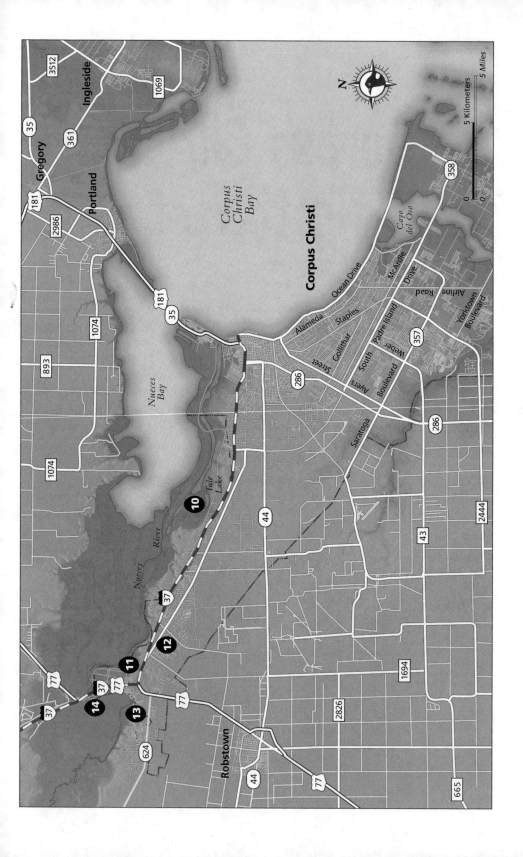

⑩ Tule Lake

Habitats: Secondary bay.

Specialty birds: *Resident*—Brown Pelican, Black-bellied Whistling-Duck, Reddish Egret, White-faced Ibis. *Spring/Summer*—Wood Stork. *Fall/Winter*—Peregrine Falcon, Piping Plover. *Migrating*—Hudsonian Godwit.

Other key birds: *Resident*—Neotropic Cormorant, Mottled Duck, Fulvous Whistling-Duck, Little Blue Heron, Roseate Spoonbill, Gull-billed Tern. *Spring/Summer*—Wilson's Plover. *Fall/Winter*—Marbled Godwit. *Migrating*—Shorebirds

Best times to bird: Year-round; best in the spring and fall for shorebird migration.

Directions: Tule Lake is located north of downtown Corpus Christi. From Corpus Christi, take the Corn Products Road exit (Exit 5) off Interstate 37 North. Turn right on Corn Products Road and travel ½ mile to Valero Way (formerly Up River Road). Turn left on Valero Way and travel 1.2 miles. The lake is on the 7200 block of Valero Way. If coming into Corpus Christi, take the Suntide exit (Exit 7). Turn left and travel down Suntide until you reach Valero Way. Turn right and travel only a few blocks. Park with care on the shoulder of the road.

The birding

There really is no reason to go to Tule Lake except for the quality and quantity of birds to be found there. It can be an uncomfortable place to bird. There is almost no place to park. On weekends, however, you can safely park at one of the businesses located on the other side of Valero Way. The road is narrow and full of potholes. Eighteen-wheelers plow down this small road at a nice clip. The lake is trashy, with abandoned tires and other debris visible in the water. It is impossible to walk around any part of the lake. Texas Parks and Wildlife has not listed Tule Lake on the Great Texas Coastal Birding Trail. Recently, the Coastal Bend Bays and Estuaries Program spearheaded a move to build a boardwalk at the edge of the lake. Birders are now able to walk out over the lake and use the two covered viewing areas with benches to more comfortably look for birds.

So why do people bird Tule Lake? They come because the birds, at certain times of the year, linger there in huge numbers. There are a few small trees on the edge of the lake. Occasionally you may see a Yellow-rumped Warbler, a sparrow, or another migrant. But no one comes to Tule Lake for the passerines. They come for the spoonbills, egrets, herons, gulls, terns, shorebirds, pelicans, cormorants, and ducks.

Look along the water's edge in the grass for Killdeer. A little farther out you may spot Piping, Snowy, Wilson's, American Golden, Semi-palmated, or Black-bellied Plovers. Also, in the mudflats look for Greater and Lesser Yellowlegs, Marbled Godwit, American Avocets, Black-necked Stilts, and a mix of sandpipers. Even Hudsonian Godwits are found during spring migration. Now is when a scope will come in handy; there should be enough space to set it up in one of the pavilions.

Marbled Godwit. PHOTO: TONY BAYLIS.

Floating in the middle of the lake are often White Pelicans and various species of ducks. Cormorants, both Neotropic and Double-crested, prefer to dry out on the debris. Wading birds such as Great Blue Herons, Roseate Spoonbills, and Great Egrets wander up and down the bank opposite the traffic. Reddish Egrets and Wood Storks are sometimes spotted here. Look overhead for Laughing Gulls, Least Terns, and Gull-billed Terns.

Another draw here are the hawks. Usually around is a Northern Harrier or a Red Tail Hawk. I have also listed a Peregrine Falcon here. You will know when the harrier or falcon is on the move as the peeps will fly off or flatten against the mud-flats. Be sure to check the utility poles on either side of the road for these birds.

General information: Tule Lake is a brackish, shallow water wetland area and a habitat for several State Listed Threatened Species. Tule Lake flows into Corpus Christi Inner Harbor, which in turn flows into Corpus Christi Bay. At one time a salt brine removal dump was present in the area. This site is now on the State Superfund List. Hazardous substances have migrated into Tule Lake, and the State of Texas and Flint Hills Resources monitor the levels.

The word *tule* most likely refers to the marsh reeds and rushes that typify this habitat. Tule leaves were used locally to thatch roofs of small *jacals,* or huts.

DeLorme: Texas Atlas & Gazetteer: Page 84 6E.

Elevation: 30 feet.

Hazards: Narrow road, traffic, mosquitoes.

Nearest food, gas, lodging: At the corner of I-37 and Corn Products Road.

For more information: City of Corpus Christi, 1202 Leopard, Corpus Christi, TX 78401; (361) 880-3211.

⑪ Pollywog Pond

Habitats: Freshwater ponds, transitional riparian forest.

Specialty birds: *Resident*—Least Grebe, Black-bellied Whistling-Duck, White-tipped Dove, Buff-bellied Hummingbird, Golden-fronted Woodpecker, Great Kiskadee, Couch's Kingbird, Green Jay. *Spring/Summer*—Cave Swallow. *Fall/Winter*—Vermilion Flycatcher.

Other key birds: *Resident*—Neotropic Cormorant, Mottled Duck, Fulvous Whistling-Duck, Inca Dove, Ladder-backed Woodpecker. *Spring/Summer*—Anhinga. *Migrating*—Neotropic Migrant Trap.

Best times to bird: Year-round, especially in spring.

Directions: From Corpus Christi, travel north on Interstate 37, and take the Callicoate Road exit (Exit 13B). Travel west on the access road for 0.7 mile and turn right just before you reach Sharpsburg Road. You will be turning onto a caliche road that is unmarked. The road is about 1 block long, and you should be able to see the entrance for Pollywog Pond from the access road. There is a yellow gate at the entrance. You will have to park there and walk around the gate.

If you are coming from north of Corpus Christi, take the same exit (13B) and travel back across the interstate on an overpass.

The birding

Pollywog Pond is actually part of the O. N. Steven Water Treatment Pond and Sludge Drying Beds, which are operated by the City of Corpus Christi. This area has a collection of lakes and pools that are used to settle the sediment from raw drinking water. You can also walk to the Nueces River here. The Pollywog Pond area consists of three ponds: the East Pond, the Northwest Pond, and the North Pond. You can enter and exit the area from the east or west entrance, but because a ditch runs between the ponds all the way to the Nueces River, you must use a bridge to cross over. Be aware that the area is very rugged and quite wild, except for the mown trails. The mown trails are not mowed often, and even when they are, they are still difficult to travel because the cut grasses may hide fallen limbs or depressions. Expect to do a lot of walking, and be aware that this is not wheelchair accessible.

The ponds are lined by willow and mulberry trees, which are known to attract migrants and songbirds. You should be able to find Common Yellow-throated, Yellow-rumped, Wilson's, and other migrating warblers. Both Great Kiskadees and Vermilion Flycatchers are common here, as are Couch's Kingbirds. All species of swallows, except the Blue-green, have been listed here. In the trees leading to the ponds, look for Titmouse, Red-shouldered Hawk, White-winged and White-tipped Doves, and the Groove-billed Ani. Watch in the grasses for LeConte's, Lincoln's,

Entrance to Pollywog Pond.

Swamp, Field, and Savannah Sparrows. A Green Kingfisher has used this canal from time to time. Look under the bridge for this very secretive bird. A Barred Owl is also known to inhabit this area. Not too far from the bridge is a photo blind looking out over one of the ponds. There are benches near the bridge also.

At the ponds you can expect to see a number of water-related birds. I have witnessed an American Bittern doing his "reed dance" at the edge of one pond. Least Bitterns are known to visit Pollywog in the summer. In the winter you may see King, Virginia, and Sora Rails. You may encounter ibis and herons, but you are more likely to see grebes and ducks. Least Grebes visit one of the clearer ponds. This is a good place to see Mottled Ducks, Ring-necked Ducks, and Lesser Scaups in the winter. You should also find Black-bellied Whistling-Ducks. On one of the dikes, Sedge Wrens have been spotted. There are several ponds, and each usually has a different group of birds, so take your time and carefully examine each location.

General information: The Audubon Outdoor Club of Corpus Christi helps to maintain this area for the use of bird-watchers. The Coastal Bend Bays and Estuaries and the Texas Commission on Environmental Quality are involved here as well. There is a nice sign at the east entrance explaining the habitat and which birds you can expect to find, as well as several interpretive signs along the trails. There are no restroom facilities. This is CTC#77.

DeLorme: Texas Atlas & Gazetteer: Page 84 5E.

Elevation: 30 feet.

Hazards: Snakes, poison ivy, fire ants, mosquitoes, poor trail conditions.

Nearest food, gas, lodging: Violet Road (Exit 11B) and I-37.

For more information: City of Corpus Christi, 1202 Leopard, Corpus Christi, TX 78401; (361) 880-3211.

⑫ Hilltop Community Center

Habitats: Transitional riparian forest, Tamaulipan thorn scrub.

Specialty birds: *Resident*—Groove-billed Ani, Common Pauraque, Buff-bellied Hummingbird, Golden-fronted Woodpecker, Great Kiskadee, Green Jay, Long-billed Thrasher, Olive Sparrow. *Spring/Summer*—Brown-crested Flycatcher, Scissor-tailed Flycatcher. *Fall/Winter*—Vermilion Flycatcher.

Other key birds: *Resident*—Inca Dove. *Fall/Winter*—Rufous Hummingbird.

Best times to bird: October through June.

Directions: From central Corpus Christi, take Interstate 37 North toward San Antonio about 9 miles, and take the Violet Road exit (Exit 11B). At the end of the exit lane turn left on Violet Road and travel for 0.3 mile. Turn right (north) at the first stoplight onto Leopard Street and go 2 blocks. On the right will be the Bill Bode County Building. The Hilltop Community Center will be on the left. There is a small sign that is difficult to see.

If you are traveling to Corpus Christi from the north, take I-37 to the Callicoate Road exit (Exit 13A). At the end of the exit lane turn right onto Callicoate and travel 2 blocks to Leopard Street. Turn left (south) onto Leopard for ½ mile; the center will be on your right. The birding trail starts behind the little red schoolhouse and the parking lot. It is open from sunrise to sunset.

The birding

Amble past a collection of historical buildings until you reach the trailhead. There is a nice wide, paved trail leading down into the ravine of a drainage creek. Joggers, who usually will not disturb the birder or the birds, use this path heavily. You may start near a busy street, but those noises will soon dissipate as you go deeper into the ravine.

Most of this area is covered in native brush, with only a few introduced species, such as Chinese tallow. There are several tall hackberry trees and dense underbrush. Most birds will be observed near the bottom of the slope. However, this is not always dependable, as the creek is often dry. Olive Sparrows and Pyrrhuloxia can be tricky to spot in the thick brush and understory. This is a good spot for thrushes, orioles, painted buntings, and tanagers during their migration.

In the early summer, it is often cool here, unlike more exposed parks, which heat up. In June I saw a pair of Yellow-billed Cuckoos mating. They were there for the tent caterpillars, or webworms as we call them in South Texas, which were abundant. I also observed a Least Flycatcher chasing a female American Redstart from his area. Stop for a while on the two bridges that cross the creek and listen for mockingbirds and sparrows, such as Clay-colored, Field, Vesper, Grasshopper, LeConte's, and Swamp. The trail is ½ mile long and makes for a short stroll. The grounds of the community center are sometimes productive for cardinals, mockingbirds, and Eastern phoebes.

Renovations are under way at Hilltop Community Center to lengthen the nature trail. Two freshwater ponds with viewing overlooks will also be added as will a bird-watching tower. The work is slated to be completed by the spring of 2007.

General information: The Hilltop Community Center is within the Corpus Christi city limits and is used by area residents for various group activities. The historical buildings were originally a tuberculosis sanitarium. Three wooden structures have been moved to the area to create a historical village. The birding trail was developed by a Boy Scout working to become an Eagle Scout. The trail drops into a natural drainage ravine. This is CTC#76. It is wheelchair accessible.

DeLorme: Texas Atlas & Gazetteer: Page 84 5E.

Elevation: 35 feet.

Hazards: Snakes, a steep incline, mosquitoes.

Nearest food, gas, lodging: There are several fast-food restaurants and gas stations at the corner of Violet Road and Leopard Street and two motels at the corner of I-37 and Violet Road.

Camping: Labonte Park.

For more information: Hilltop Community Center, 11425 Leopard Street, Corpus Christi, TX 78410; (361) 241-3754.

13 Hazel Bazemore County Park (IBA)

Habitats: Transitional riparian forest, freshwater pond, Tamaulipan thorn scrub.

Specialty birds: *Resident*—Least Grebe, Reddish Egret, White-faced Ibis, White-tipped Dove, Groove-billed Ani, Common Pauraque, Buff-bellied Hummingbird, Golden-fronted Woodpecker, Great Kiskadee, Couch's Kingbird, Green Jay, Long-billed Thrasher, Olive Sparrow, Cassin's Sparrow. *Spring/Summer*—Wood Stork, Brown-crested Flycatcher, Scissor-tailed Flycatcher. *Fall/Winter*—Vermilion Flycatcher. *Migrating*—Raptors, including rarities such as White-tailed Kite, Swallow-tailed Kite, Zone-tailed Hawk, Bald Eagle, Golden Eagle, Peregrine Falcon.

Other key birds: *Resident*—Neotropic Cormorant, Mottled Duck, Crested Caracara, Little Blue Heron, Roseate Spoonbill, Gull-billed Tern, Inca Dove, Ladder-backed Woodpecker, Bronzed Cowbird. *Spring/Summer*—Anhinga, Lesser Nighthawk, Painted Bunting. *Fall/Winter*—Rufous Hummingbird. *Migrating*—Raptors, shorebirds, Neotropic Migrant Trap.

Best times to bird: Year-round.

Directions: If you are coming from Interstate 37 North, take Exit 14 to U.S. Highway 77. Then take the first exit to Farm-to-Market 624. Travel north on FM 624 for 0.8 mile. After you pass the Calallen football stadium, turn right on County Road 69. Travel ½ mile to the park entrance. The park is open daily from sunrise to sunset.

The birding

There are not enough superlatives to describe Hazel Bazemore County Park. It is a small park covering 77.6 acres and located along the Nueces River just outside the city limits of Corpus Christi. It is maintained by the Nueces County Parks and Recreation Department. But the size and atmosphere of the park do not reveal, at first, the wonderful birding that takes place here. The park's bird list numbers 305 species. This is more than many national parks.

On the drive down CR 69, be sure to watch the high-line wires for Couch's Kingbirds. On the south side of the road, there is a drainage canal, which entices these colorful birds to wait and flycatch there. As you enter the park, look along the ground in the high grasses for Groove-billed Anis. These birds can be deceptive, as they look like grackles on first glance. But their unusual thick bill will soon give them away. Also, unlike grackles, they like to perch low and seldom fly much higher than shoulder height.

This park is great for drive-by birding if you live nearby. The road circles in the park for 1.9 miles. The serious, first-time visitor will want to park at the headquarters building, which is to the left as you enter at the main gate. The park is free to the public, but you may want to stop at the headquarters and pick up a checklist of birds. Take your time and examine the trees around the parking lot for Northern

HAWK WATCH AT
HAZEL BAZEMORE COUNTY PARK

Hawk Watch mission: To monitor and promote the conservation of eagles, hawks, and other birds of prey and to strive to increase public awareness of and commitment to birds of prey and the ecosystems that support them.

Hawk Watch at Hazel Bazemore: The Corpus Christi Hawk Watch at Hazel Bazemore County Park is a Hawk Watch International (HWI) site. HWI is the only group that conducts full season counts in Texas. No other site in the United States can come close to listing the number of hawks or the number of species seen at Hazel Bazemore. The majority of the hawks are Broad-winged. However, since the inception of the Hazel Bazemore Hawk Watch, thirty species have been seen at this site. During the eight-day peak in September, an average of 575,000 raptors is usually counted.

To watch the hawks, you literally take a lawn chair and join the group on the bluff above the Nueces River. The hawks stream by overhead. This is one time that bird-watchers can sleep in. Hawks ride the thermals, and they don't fly over until 9:00 A.M. or until the air heats up. Visitors are encouraged to stay as long as they like. Hawk Watch staff and the volunteer watchers are excited to point out kettles of hawks and to line them up in scopes for others to view. On some weekends, as many as 200 hawk enthusiasts show up, and it is not unusual to find watchers from states such as Pennsylvania and Montana.

Mockingbirds, cardinals, Green Jays, and Blue-gray Gnatcatchers. Don't be surprised if a resident Greater Roadrunner scurries out of your way.

From the parking lot you can walk west along the road that separates the park from River Hills Golf Course (private). Be aware of what is going on at the course, because you really do have to watch in this area for the stray flying ball. This is not a new rare bird, but a true hazard in this part of the park. This is also a good place to see a number of birds from the flycatcher family, including Eastern Kingbirds and Scissor-tailed, Brown-crested, and Ash-throated Flycatchers. Look for White-eyed Vireos and Ruby-crowned Kinglets on the park side of the road.

I prefer to walk from the parking lot/golf course area down to the lower level of the park along the river. There are also parking spaces on the lower level if you would rather drive. Here you will find three lovely surprises: the Nueces River, a nature trail, and a freshwater pond and marshy area with two photo blinds.

Anglers love the easy access to the river here. There is a boat ramp as well. If you walk here, you may spot American White Pelicans, Anhingas, Wood Storks,

In conjunction with the watch, Swarovski Optics, the Corpus Christi Convention and Visitors Bureau, and local businesses sponsor A Celebration of Flight the last full weekend in September. During the event, mini-programs on topics such as raptor identification and the ecology of raptor migration are presented at the site. Bird walks and other workshops are provided.

When to come: The peak of hawk migration occurs between September 23 and 30, and there are usually two to three days of counts exceeding 100,000. Below is a list of raptor species and the best times to see them.

Swallow-tailed Kite	August 15–September 10
Mississippi Kite	August 15–September 10
Broad-winged Hawk	September 15–October 10
Osprey	September 15–October 10
Peregrine Falcon	September 20–October 15
American Kestrel	September 20–October 15
Cooper's Hawk	September 20–October 15
Sharp-shinned Hawk	September 25–October 15
Red-tailed Hawk	October 1–October 25
Swainson's Hawk	October 5–October 20
Turkey Vulture	October 15–November 10
Black Vulture	October 25–November 15

Great Egrets, and Black-crowned Night Herons in or near the water. You are almost certain to see the Greater Kiskadee in the trees on either side of the river. This bird will call out its name and demand to be seen. This is a must-see for Hazel Bazemore Park. Look away from the river and back toward the park. Near the picnic tables look for Killdeer and Eastern Meadowlarks on the ground. And check the high-line wires and picnic tabletops for Vermilion Flycatchers. If they are present, these little gems are hard to miss. They stand out like hot burning coals among the browns and greens of the park. In the cooler months you may also see Eastern Bluebirds here. In the grassy areas around the picnic tables, watch for White-throated, Lincoln's, and Savannah Sparrows.

The residents of the pond and marsh area change with the seasons. You should be able to find a Belted Kingfisher. Listen for its rattle-like call, and you will spot it quickly enough. (Green Kingfishers and even Ringed Kingfishers have been listed on the Nueces River near the park.) Check the mudflats to the north and west of the pond for Common Snipe, Solitary Sandpipers, Greater and Lesser Yel-

Hawk watch location at Hazel Bazemore County Park.

lowlegs, Black-necked Stilts, and American Pipits. In the fall and winter, a Sedge Wren may cling to the reeds here. Check out the pond itself for ducks. Hooded Mergansers, Northern Shovelers, Blue and Green Winged Teal, Gadwall, and other dabbling ducks feed here, depending on the time of the year. Terns are also likely to be working the area. I have seen Forster's Terns here often. You can access the pond from the upper or lower area of the park.

Behind the upper picnic tables you will find a trail leading down to the photo blinds. This trail has two entrances, but neither is easily seen. They are in the area of the swing set. Be careful: The slope down to the boardwalk that connects the blinds is steep and can be slippery in wet weather or even in the morning with a heavy dew. When you get to the blinds, you have a great hidden view of the pond. These blinds are not large, but you can set up a scope or a camera on a tripod. Don't be surprised if you scare a Red-shouldered Hawk out of his favorite roosting area in the trees along the trail between the blinds. Enjoy the pond from this angle.

Located on the opposite side of the park is the Lucas Kimmel Memorial Nature Trail. The trailhead is marked with a nice sign. Quietly start down the path, paying close attention to the ground. In season, a Common Pauraque naps here. These nightjars are very difficult to locate due to their buff color, which blends in with dirt or limbs where they usually rest. You may find any number of passerines in this thickly wooded area. Green Jays tempt you by flitting across the way in front of you. They are another species of bird in South Texas that just won't be ignored. Look for Long-billed Thrashers and Olive Sparrows. This is a dirt trail that rises to a great vantage point above the Nueces River plain. Wooden timbers bolster the trail steps, and wooden bridges cross small ravines. To the left the trail arrives at a tower that places the birder above the trees and affords a nice look at the river and the wetlands. Visit this spot early in the morning and watch flights of Roseate Spoonbills making their way down the river. From here, watch Snow Geese going inland to feed each winter morning. The trail, which is loaded with ebony and mesquite and other native plants, circles back on itself.

It is impossible to think about Hazel Bazemore without thinking about hawks. How many hawks would you like to see in one day? On the way to work each winter day I see two Harris' Hawks, a Red-tailed Hawk, sometimes a White-tailed Hawk, and four or five American Kestrels. These birds never fail to excite me. I could tell you the route I take, or I could tell you where to set up a lawn chair and see 30,000 or more hawks in one day. Sound too good to be true? At Hazel Bazemore between September 23 to 30 each year, you will probably see even more.

General information: The park was named in 1956 for Hazel Bazemore, an assistant home demonstration agent who was killed in an automobile accident in 1955. She had worked for Nueces County from 1950 until the time of the accident.

The park is open sunrise to sunset. There is no fee. Picnicking and small fires are allowed in designated areas. Camping is not allowed. Pets are permitted on a leash. Fishing from the banks of the river is possible, as is swimming. A group pavilion is available by reservation. Sometimes the road to the lower level is closed due to river flooding. This is CTC#78.

DeLorme: Texas Atlas & Gazetteer: Page 84 5E.

Elevation: 40 feet.

Hazards: Snakes, poison ivy, fire ants, stray golf balls, steep incline.

Nearest food, gas, lodging: Corner of Highway 77 and FM 624.

Camping: Labonte Park.

For more information: Hazel Bazemore County Park, P.O. Box 4343, County Road 69, Corpus Christi, TX 78410; (361) 387-4231.

14 Labonte Park (formerly Nueces River Park)

Habitats: Transitional riparian forest.

Specialty birds: *Resident*—Harris' Hawk, Buff-bellied Hummingbird, Golden-fronted Woodpecker, Great Kiskadee, Couch's Kingbird. *Spring/Summer*—Scissor-tailed Flycatcher.

Other key birds: *Resident*—Inca Dove, Ladder-backed Woodpecker. *Migrating*—Raptors.

Best times to bird: October to June.

Directions: If you are traveling from Corpus Christi toward San Antonio on Interstate 37, take Exit 16, which leads directly into the park. If you are coming from San Antonio, you will also take Exit 16. The road circles near the river from either direction.

Nueces River at Labonte Park.

The birding

Labonte is a small city park used mainly as a visitor center for people traveling into the Corpus Christi area. At the center of this flat park are numerous soccer fields. The road that circles the park is 1 mile long. There is a boat ramp, and many locals come to fish for catfish. The Nueces River changes from fresh to saltwater at the southern edge of the park. The park is subject to flooding with the slightest rise of the river.

So why bird here? Well, it is rather easygoing, for one thing. Labonte is almost nude of any significant vegetation or trees. But the Nueces River is narrow here, and you can look across to the trees and brush that line the river on the opposite shore. Expect to see spring and fall migrants such as flycatchers and warblers. You should spot a Belted Kingfisher on one of the low overhanging branches.

At the upper end of the park (actually, this is not in the park boundaries) is a small dam. It is a good place to look for wading birds. However, anglers like the wade fishing possibilities also. It is possible to walk farther upriver along the shore into a roughly wooded area for a chance to see more passerines.

General information: This park was recently renamed to honor Bobby and Terry Labonte, NASCAR drivers, who are natives of Corpus Christi. This is a city park that allows free camping for three days a month. A permit is required, but it is free. There are no hook-ups and only one restroom. Pits and tables are available. Tent camping is permitted. The visitor center is open from 9:00 A.M. to 5:00 P.M. daily. This is CTC#75. It is wheelchair accessible.

DeLorme: Texas Atlas & Gazetteer: Page 84 5E.

Elevation: 30 feet.

Hazards: Snakes, fire ants.

Camping: Labonte Park.

Nearest food, gas, lodging: Corner of Highway 77 and Farm-to-Market 624.

For more information: Labonte Park Visitor Center, 1433 IH37, Corpus Christi, TX 78410; (361) 241-1464.

Corpus Christi: Flour Bluff and Padre Island

P adre Island is part of the complex of barrier islands that border the Gulf of Mexico. The Laguna Madre, which separates the island from the mainland, is also very important to the diversity of this region. The sites in this section are situated on beaches, dunes, grasslands, marshes, and mudflats. Even though Flour Bluff is on the mainland, sea breezes and saltwater also influence the sites here.

This rich habitat should provide the birder with a glimpse into the life of sand-pipers, plovers, gull, terns, pelicans, and ducks.

15. Caribbean/Ramfield/Yorktown (Flour Bluff)
16. Redhead Pond Wildlife Management Area
17. JFK Causeway Wetlands
18. Packery Channel Park
19. Padre Island National Seashore (IBA)
20. Mollie Beattie Coastal Habitat Community

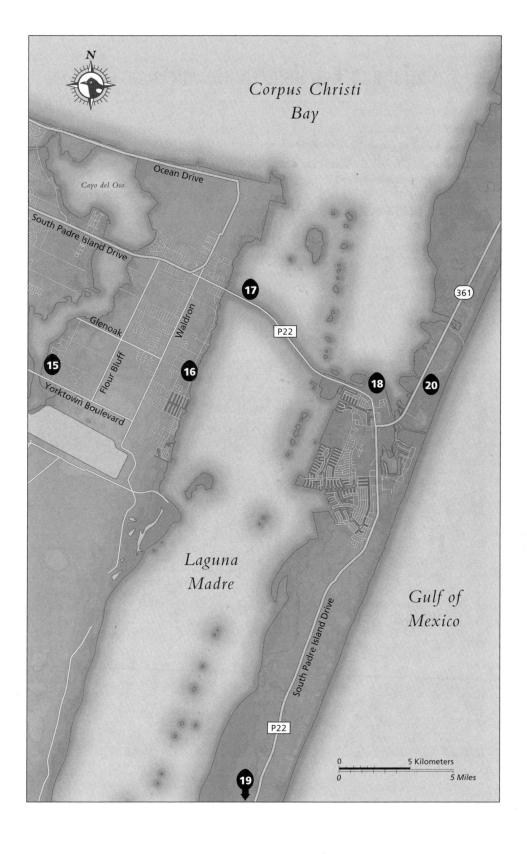

15 Caribbean/Ramfield/Yorktown (Flour Bluff)

Habitats: Freshwater ponds.

Specialty birds: *Resident*—Least Grebe, Black-bellied Whistling-Duck, White-faced Ibis, Groove-billed Ani, Golden-fronted Woodpecker, Couch's Kingbird. *Spring/Summer*—Wood Storks, Brown-crested Flycatcher, Scissor-tailed Flycatcher.

Other key birds: *Resident*—Mottled Duck, Roseate Spoonbill. *Spring/Summer*—Anhinga, Painted Bunting.

Best times to bird: Fall and winter.

Directions: Leave Corpus Christi on South Padre Island Drive/Highway 358 East toward Padre Island. Take the Flour Bluff Drive exit. Turn right on Flour Bluff and travel 1 mile. The next three right turns will lead to three differ-ent freshwater ponds. The first is Caribbean Street, next is Ramfield Road. The last is York-town, where Flour Bluff Drive finally comes to a dead end. These three streets are each ½ mile apart. Caribbean and Ramfield are 1 mile each and end at Roscher Road. Yorktown goes back into Corpus Christi.

Least Grebe. PHOTO: TONY BAYLIS.

The birding

This residential loop on Padre Island is well known among local birders. The size of these ponds is surprisingly large, considering they are in a housing subdivision. The pond at Yorktown is some distance from the road and will probably require the use of a scope. This is the pond where you are most likely to see Sandhill Cranes. At the other two ponds, the birder can get a little closer to the action. These are excellent sites for a variety of ducks in the winter and Black-bellied Whistling-Ducks and Least Grebes year-round. Also look for Anhinga in migration. You might be surprised to find breeding Eastern Bluebirds and Pyrrhuloxia here. Try to get a glimpse of Cedar Waxwings, Olive-sided Flycatchers, Couch's Kingbirds, and Painted Buntings in the nearby brush.

General information: These ponds are on private property, and there is very little space to park along Ramfield and Caribbean. During serious drought periods, these ponds can be dry.

DeLorme: Texas Atlas & Gazetteer: Page 85 7G.

Elevation: 30 feet.

Hazards: Traffic.

Nearest food, gas, lodging: South Padre Island Drive.

Camping: Padre Island National Seashore.

16 Redhead Pond Wildlife Management Area

Habitats: Freshwater (brackish) pond.

Specialty birds: *Resident*—Least Grebe, Black-bellied Whistling-Duck, White-faced Ibis, Groove-billed Ani, Golden-fronted Woodpecker. *Spring/Summer*—Scissor-tailed Flycatcher.

Other key birds: *Resident*—Mottled Duck, Roseate Spoonbill, Gull-billed Tern.

Best times to bird: Fall and winter.

Directions: Leave Corpus Christi on South Padre Island Drive/Highway 358 East toward Padre Island. Cross the Cayo del Oso and into the Flour Bluff suburb and exit at Waldron Road. Stay on the access road and cross over Waldron Road. Go ½ mile to Laguna Shores Road. This street is not marked, but a sign warns you that Laguna Shores is within 500 feet. Do not go up on the causeway. Turn right. Go down Laguna Shores for 2 miles. Redhead Pond is on the right. There is room for one car to park at the gate.

The birding

The ten-acre freshwater pond for which Redhead Pond Wildlife Management Area is named dominates this thirty-seven-acre site. The area is closed to vehicles, but the birder is able to follow the path around the gate and go a short distance to a boardwalk that leads to an observation deck over the pond. Obviously, Redhead Ducks use this pond, but so do Hooded Mergansers, Common Goldeneye, and other ducks. Black-bellied Whistling-Ducks breed here in the spring and early summer. The pond also entices such diverse species as Black-crowned Night Herons, Black-necked Stilts, Great Blue Heron, Pied-billed Grebes, Groove-billed Anis, and Golden-fronted Woodpeckers.

On the way to the pond, you drive along beside the Laguna Madre. In fact, sometimes the water will come up over Laguna Shores Road. You should have little trouble spotting a variety of gulls, terns, wading birds, and shorebirds.

General information: Texas Parks and Wildlife developed this site with the help of The Nature Conservancy. This is CTC#66.

DeLorme: Texas Atlas & Gazetteer: Page 85 7G.

Elevation: 30 feet.

Hazards: Traffic, water on the road, no place to park.

Nearest food, gas, lodging: South Padre Island Drive.

Camping: Padre Island National Seashore.

For more information: Texas Parks and Wildlife Department, 4200 Smith School Road, Austin, TX 78744; (800) 792-1112.

⟨17⟩ JFK Causeway Wetlands

Habitats: Shallow laguna.

Specialty birds: *Resident*—Brown Pelican, Reddish Egret, White-faced Ibis. *Fall/Winter*—Peregrine Falcon, Piping Plover. *Migrating*—Hudsonian Godwit.

Other key birds: *Resident*—Neotropic Cormorant, Little Blue Heron, Roseate Spoonbills, American Oystercatcher, Gull-billed Tern. *Spring/Summer*—Wilson's Plover, Sandwich Tern, Common Tern. *Fall/Winter*—Common Loon, Marbled Godwit. *Migrating*—Shorebirds.

Best times to bird: Year-round.

Directions: Take South Padre Island Drive (SPID)/Highway 358 toward Padre Island.

Continue on Park Road 22 to the JFK Causeway. Once on the causeway, watch for the sign that reads BEACH ACCESS. This will allow you to drive along the beach next to the causeway out of the flow of the traffic that is headed to the beach. You could easily just bird from your automobile. Parking here will definitely depend on the tide. You will have a chance to return to the causeway before the Intracoastal Waterway. There is no access like this on the opposite side. However, there is an Intracoastal Waterway turnabout going either way, and it would be possible to use these two exits to continue your bird watching.

The birding

This area is very salty, with little freshwater inflow. On some days, the birder can experience shorebird overload here. On other days, no bird will be in sight. Likely sightings include herons, egrets, pelicans, plovers, gulls, and terns, including Least Terns. Even after all of the new construction, Black Skimmers continue to nest at the end of this road in a protected area.

General information: The original causeway was just a few feet above the level of the laguna. This new raised causeway was completed in 2005. This is CTC#65.

DeLorme: Texas Atlas & Gazetteer: Page 85 7F.

Elevation: 25 feet.

Hazards: High tides.

Nearest food, gas, lodging: Park Road 22.

For more information: City of Corpus Christi, 1202 Leopard, Corpus Christi, TX 78401; (361) 880-3211.

18 Packery Channel Park

Habitats: A pass between the Gulf of Mexico and bays, oak woodland.

Specialty birds: *Resident*—Brown Pelican, Reddish Egret, White-faced Ibis, Groove-billed Ani, Buff-bellied Hummingbird, Golden-fronted Woodpecker, Couch's Kingbird. *Spring/Summer*—Scissor-tailed Flycatcher, Cave Swallow. *Fall/Winter*—Peregrine Falcon, Piping Plover. *Migrating*—Hudsonian Godwit.

Other key birds: *Resident*—Neotropic Cormorant, Mottled Duck, Little Blue Heron, Roseate Spoonbill, American Oystercatcher, Gull-billed Tern, Inca Dove. *Spring/Summer*—Wilson's Plover, Sandwich Tern, Common Tern, Lesser Nighthawk, Painted Bunting.

Fall/Winter—Common Loon, Marbled Godwit. *Migrating*—Shorebirds, Neotropic Migrant Trap.

Best times to bird: Fall and spring.

Directions: Take South Padre Island Drive (SPID)/Highway 358 toward Padre Island. Continue on Park Road 22 and cross the JFK Causeway and the Intracoastal Waterway Bridge. After the bridge, take the second left (about 1 mile). If this street has a name, no one seems to know what it is. A sign will lead you to the turn. The bright blue Padre Island Visitor Center is on the right after the turn. The center has restrooms and tourist information, including maps. A parking lot is on the right.

The birding

As you will see, there isn't much of a park here; however, this often proves to be one of the best Corpus Christi birding spots. Drive past the visitor center for several blocks; you will see Packery Channel. This pass connects Corpus Christi Bay with the Gulf of Mexico. It is usually full of silt, but it occasionally opens up with a storm surge. Currently a project is under way to dredge the pass and reconnect it with Laguna Madre and the gulf. The project includes a 2,000-foot jetty, with 700 feet atop the beach at Padre Island and the remaining 1,300 feet out into the gulf. Development of the area, with increased boat traffic, is planned. How this development will affect marine, bird, and plant life is still being argued. It appears that in the future access to the laguna by automobile traffic will be possible here.

At the channel you see shorebirds and waterfowl. This is a good place to use a spotting scope. Pelicans, cormorants, wading birds, gulls, and terns are usually here. In the winter look for loons, grebes, and ducks.

Opposite the parking lot for the visitor center, notice a large live oak motte surrounded by a fence. Such mottes were once the norm. Walk around this one to look for migrants, especially in the spring. Here you are likely to see warblers such as Bay-breasted, Black-throated Green, Chestnut-sided, Magnolia, Nashville, Tennesse, Mourning, and Pine.

When you leave the motte sanctuary, walk down to the corner of residential roads Maria Isabela and Sand Dollar. Notice a boardwalk that leads out to a viewing platform. This is part of the sanctuary owned by the Audubon Outdoor Club (AOC). This section of the sanctuary is known as Sandy's Pond. The AOC owns eighteen undeveloped lots in the subdivision. These lots are not all connected to each other. Future enhancements are planned for the sanctuary. It is permissible to walk through the rest of the sanctuary, but it is very wild, without planned trails. At Sandy's Pond and back at the motte, Ruby-throated and Black-chinned Hummingbirds are attracted to the many coral bean bushes. Eastern Kingbirds, Scissor-tailed Flycatchers, and Tree or Barn Swallows are often seen on the utility lines or whizzing overhead. If the drip is working at the pond, passerines such as Painted Buntings can stop by for a drink.

Now walk through this neighborhood, making a loop using Playa del Rey, Verdemar, Ave San Nico, and Sand Dollar Streets. I'm not sure the residents like this invansion of bird-watchers, but they are surely used to it. In spring, the area may have as many bird-watchers as birds. Please be considerate of private property.

Here is the only area with bay laurels and scrub oaks on the island and the last stand of trees for 130 miles. This migrant trap is especially productive in March, April, and May, right after the passage of a norther or cold front. Bad weather and heavy winds can cause dramatic fallouts in this little community. Even without these forced groundings of birds, you can spot Baltimore and Orchard Orioles, Yellow-billed and Black-billed Cuckoos, Blue and Rose-breasted Grosbeaks, Indigo and Painted Buntings, Yellow-headed Blackbirds, Groove-billed Anis, Veery, Hermit and Swainson's Thrush, and many, many species of warblers. At the corner of Maria Isabela and Playa del Rey, there is a lot with rather large trees against a small bluff. Search here during the day for Yellow-crowned Night Herons.

Building continues to go on in this area. However, at the time this was written, there were still large prairie areas between the neighborhood and the main highway. Be on the lookout for Mississippi Kites and Northern Harrier.

General information: The Padre Island Visitor's Center is open daily from 9:00 A.M. to 5:00 P.M. Packery Channel was named for the beef-processing plant that was built at the mouth of the pass a few years after the Civil War. When the beef-processing business slumped, the packing house was converted to a plant that processed feathers for women's hats and stuffed birds, such as Roseate Spoonbills, for ornamentation and wildlife displays.

Sandy's Pond was donated by AOC member Tom Schall in memory of his daughter. This is CTC#62 and CTC#64.

DeLorme: Texas Atlas & Gazetteer: Page 85 7F.

Elevation: 25 feet.

Hazards: Mosquitoes.

Nearest food, gas, lodging: Park Road 22.

Camping: Padre Island National Seashore.

For more information: City of Corpus Christi, 1202 Leopard, Corpus Christi, TX 78401; (361) 880-3211; Audubon Outdoor Club of Corpus Christi, Inc., P.O. Box 3352, Corpus Christi, TX 78463.

19 Padre Island National Seashore (IBA)

Habitats: Prairie, gulf beaches, Laguna Madre.

Specialty birds: *Resident*—Brown Pelican, Black-bellied Whistling-Duck, Harris' Hawk, White-tailed Hawk, Reddish Egret, White-faced Ibis. *Spring/Summer*—Wood Stork, Scissortailed Flycatcher. *Fall/Winter*—Peregrine Falcon, Piping Plover. *Migrating*—Hudsonian Godwit.

Other key birds: *Resident*—Neotropic Cormorant, Mottled Duck, Crested Caracara, Roseate Spoonbill, Clapper Rail, American Oystercatcher, Gull-billed Tern. *Spring/Summer*—Magnificent Frigatebird, Wilson's

Plover, Sandwich Tern, Common Tern, Lesser Nighthawk. *Fall/Winter*—Common Loon, Northern Gannet, Marbled Godwit. *Migrating*—Shorebirds, Neotropic passerines.

Best times to bird: Year-round.

Directions: Leave Corpus Christi on South Padre Island Drive/Highway 358 East toward Padre Island. The highway will eventually continue as Park Road 22. After traveling on the park road for 15.8 miles, you reach the entrance sign to the national seashore. It is another 1.3 miles to the toll booth.

The birding

Padre Island National Seashore is the longest remaining undeveloped stretch of barrier island in the world. It encompasses 130,434 acres. This is an Important Bird Area (IBA) for good reason, and you will find many opportunities to birdwatch. In its mission statement, the park has included ten goals. Most of these affect the bird-watching community. For instance, the park plans to provide appropriate types and levels of recreational use, consistent with long-term protection of the ecosystem. Another goal vows to protect threatened and endangered species, native wildlife, plants, and their associated habitats.

At the toll booth you will be given a map of the location, and you can ask for information about birding. Just a few yards from the entrance and on the right is the trailhead to the Grassland Nature Trail. Park and take the easy ¾-mile walk on the paved trail. Pick up a brochure that tells you about the numbered posts along the way. This is a good introduction to the "nonbeach" coastal prairie of this national preserve. In the spring and summer, wildflowers draw butterflies. Look for meadowlarks here, and perhaps Northern Harriers. Ephemeral ponds along the trail, if they are deep, are home to ducks and shorebirds in the fall and winter. This is not a long trail, and benches with shade covers along the way make for a pleasant walk. However, take water, wear a hat and sunscreen, and consider using insect repellent. There is a wheelchair accessible portable toilet at the head of the trail.

From the nature trail, travel another ½ mile down Park Road 22 to reach the right-hand turnoff for Bird Island Basin. About 0.3 mile down Bird Island Road, there is a permanent, rather large, freshwater pond on the left. In the winter, this pond teems with ducks. Recently, a Masked Duck was listed here. There are smaller, temporary ponds along the road. When shallow, they are used by wading birds such as egrets, herons, and spoonbills. It is permissible to walk through the coastal prairie here, but most visitors avoid this due to the threat of snakes. Grass lovers like Northern Bobwhite, Sprague's Pipits, sparrows, and larks hide here. In the winter, Sandhill Cranes are easily seen. At 0.6 mile there is a road to the right that leads to a large parking lot for the boat ramp. Continue on the main road for another ½ mile to reach the Bird Island Campground.

The Bird Island Basin area was renovated in 2005 to include spaces for forty-five recreational vehicles and twenty-five single vehicles. More important for the birder, there is now a day-use area at both the windsurfing park and the boat ramp. Both of these areas overlook Laguna Madre, where members of a breeding flock of White Pelicans often show up. Also look for Reddish Egrets, Tricolored Herons, Belted Kingfishers, osprey, gulls, and terns. There are a few willow trees at both sites where songbird migrants stop over in the spring. Horned Larks and Killdeer hang out in this area. In the late fall and winter, the laguna can be full of Northern Pintail, Redheads, Lesser Scaups, Red-breasted Mergansers, Buffleheads, Gadwalls, Mallards, and Ring-necked, Mottled, and Canvasback Ducks. At the windsurfing park, bird-watchers can rent kayaks to paddle out into Laguna Madre to get close to several spoils islands where waterbirds rest and nest. If you are not into kayaking, a spotting scope would be useful at this location.

Now return to Park Road 22. From Bird Island Road, it is another 2.8 miles to the Malaquite Beach Visitor's Center. This 3-mile area of beach, which is probably the most visited section of the park, is closed to beach vehicles. If you wish to drive on the beach, you must use the access roads either north or south of the visitor center. North Beach is only 1 mile long, whereas South Beach is about 60 miles long, ending at Mansfield Channel. The first 5 miles of South Beach accommodate two-wheel-drive vehicles. The remaining 55-mile stretch requires four-wheel-drive vehicles, and even that is some times questionable. Rangers at the visitor center keep abreast of all driving conditions. On South Beach, there is a primitive campground on the laguna side at Yarborough Pass. This pass at the 15-mile marker is well into four-wheel-drive territory.

Truthfully, most shorebirds can be seen by taking a walk on the beach at any access point. You know you will see gulls, terns, sandpipers, skimmers, and pelicans. Special sightings in the park include Ruddy Turnstones, Red Knots, Least Terns, Black Terns, Eared Grebes, Piping Plovers, Snowy Plovers, Wilson's Plovers, and American Oystercatchers. Pelagic birds such as Sooty Terns, Northern Gannets, boobies, shearwaters, and jaegers have occasionally stopped over on the island or been viewed off shore in migration using a powerful birding scope.

PADRE ISLAND NATIONAL SEASHORE
AND SEA TURTLES

Just as Aransas Wildlife Refuge is known for Whooping Cranes, Padre Island National Seashore is known for sea turtles, especially the Kemp's Ridley. The Gulf of Mexico is home to five of the world's sea turtles, and all of them have, at one time or another, nested on Padre Island. All five species—Leatherback, Hawksbill, Green, Loggerhead, and Kemp's Ridley—are now classified as either threatened or endangered.

The United States, Mexico, and Texas have joined together in a special effort to save the Kemp's Ridley sea turtle. These turtles nest in Tamaulipas, Mexico, on a beach called Playa de Rancho Nuevo. From 1978 to 1988, eggs were collected in Mexico, transported to Padre Island National Seashore, incubated, and released on the beach. After a short swim for the purpose of impression, they were recollected, taken to Galveston, and raised for another year before their permanent release.

The program finally saw some success in 1996, when two Kemp's Ridley sea turtles came ashore and laid eggs at Padre Island National Seashore. Since 1996, other turtles from this project have been found nesting on the island. In 2006, sixty-four nests were located at Padre Island National Seashore.

From March through September, Padre Island National Seashore employees and volunteers are on "Turtle Patrol" to search the beach for nesting sea turtles and their eggs. The patrol travels in well-marked vehicles. Please stay away from any turtles, but note their location and inform park authorities. Each year when young turtles are released, the public is invited to attend.

At the Malaquite Beach Visitor's Center, bird-watchers with disabilities can borrow special beach wheelchairs. From March through May, bird talks are given at the center. Plans are under consideration to construct a birding boardwalk that will begin on the west side of the road in front of the visitor center. The boardwalk will extend beyond the freshwater ponds and become a "back country" trail that will continue to Laguna Madre and Bird Island Basin. The trail will then go east across the Novillo Camp Line and onto the beach. This birding boardwalk is planned to cover various ecosystems within the park.

General information: There is a fee to enter the park. The park is open 24 hours a day, 365 days a year. The visitor center is open daily from 8:30 A.M. to 4:30 P.M. in winter, to 6:00 P.M. in summer. It is closed on January 1 and December 25. Beach wheelchairs may be borrowed from the visitor center.

Padre Island, and hence the national seashore, was named to honor Padre Nicolas Balli, who established the first permanent settlement on the island's southern tip around 1804. This is CTC#63.

DeLorme: Texas Atlas & Gazetteer: Page 85 7H.

Elevation: 0 to 50 feet.

Hazards: Mosquitoes, snakes, high tides, fog.

Nearest food, gas, lodging: Corpus Christi.

Camping: Padre Island National Seashore.

For more information: Padre Island National Seashore, P.O. Box 18130, Corpus Christi, TX 78401; (361) 949-8068.

Habitats: Tidal flats.

Specialty birds: *Resident*—Brown Pelican, Reddish Egret, White-faced Ibis. *Fall/Winter*—Piping Plover. *Migrating*—Hudsonian Godwit.

Other key birds: *Resident*—Neotropic Cormorant, Roseate Spoonbill, American Oystercatcher, Gull-billed Tern. *Spring/Summer*—Magnificent Frigatebird, Wilson's Plover, Sandwich Tern, Lesser Nighthawk, Black Tern. *Migrating*—Shorebirds.

Best times to bird: Year-round, with summer the least productive.

Directions: Once you arrive on Padre Island via Park Road 22, watch for Highway 361. At the intersection, turn left and travel for 1.5 miles. You will cross Packery Channel and 1852 Pass. The parking lot for Mollie Beattie is on the left, but a sign on the road does not warn you of the location, so pay attention.

Black Terns. PHOTO: TONY BAYLIS.

The birding

The Mollie Beattie Coastal Habitat Community will give you a different look at Corpus Christi Bay and the "back side" of Mustang Island. At first it appears that there isn't much to draw the bird-watcher to this location, but you may be pleasantly surprised. It is a featureless habitat dominated by sea grasses, saline soil, and oyster reefs. There are some ephemeral ponds, but high summer temperatures make short work of these.

There is a broad trail that leaves the parking lot. Small poles with a wire pulled through them mark the trail. After about ¼ mile, you arrive at a very small bluff overlooking the bay. Depending on the time of year, there could be a washover pass after you leave this bluff. Don't be afraid to walk through it. The area is very sandy, and you won't sink. This should put you closer to the shoreline and some small islands in the bay.

This habitat was set aside for the conservation of Piping and Snowy Plovers. They should be in residence in the fall and winter. Other plovers and sandpipers like this environment also. Ducks can be abundant in the bay at that time as well. At all times of the year, you will spot Great Egrets, Roseate Spoonbills, Laughing Gulls, Great Blue Herons, Tricolored Herons, and Killdeer. On the trail, watch for sparrows, Horned Larks, swallows, and nighthawks.

General information: In 1993 Mollie Beattie was named as the first woman to head the U.S. Fish and Wildlife Service. She served until her untimely death in 1996. This 1,600-acre property is named in her honor.

DeLorme: Texas Atlas & Gazetteer: Page 85 8G.

Elevation: 10 feet.

Hazards: Biting bugs, snakes.

Nearest food, gas, lodging: Intersection of PR 22 and Highway 361.

Camping: Mustang Island State Park; Padre Island National Seashore.

For more information: Coastal Bend Bays and Estuaries Program, 1305 North Shoreline Boulevard, Suite 205, Corpus Christi, TX 78401; (361) 885-6202.

Portland/Ingleside/ Bayside/Sinton

This region includes an odd mix of sites along Corpus Christi Bay and inland for habitats that typify Tamaulipan scrubland and oak woodland. The beach overlooks for Rincon Channel, Indian Point, Sunset Lake, and Violet Andrews Park are all located near the bay. Wading birds and shorebirds will be most prevalent at those parks.

Fred Jones and North Bay Sanctuaries, as well as the three Welder parks, are predominantly thorn scrub habitats. At those sites the birder should focus on thrashers, sparrows, wrens, and hawks. Live Oak City Park is an example of oak woodland habitat. Because it is a city park, the situation there is quite disturbed, but the birdwatcher should still look for titmice, flycatchers, and migrating thrushes, warblers, and vireos.

21. Corpus Christi Beach Wetlands Overlooks (Rincon Channel)

22. Indian Point Park

23. Sunset Lake Park

24. Violet Andrews Park

25. Fred Jones Nature Sanctuary

26. North Bay Sanctuary

27. Live Oak City Park

28. Whitney Lake

29. Park Welder

30. Rob and Bessie Welder Park

31. Rob and Bessie Welder Wildlife Foundation and Refuge

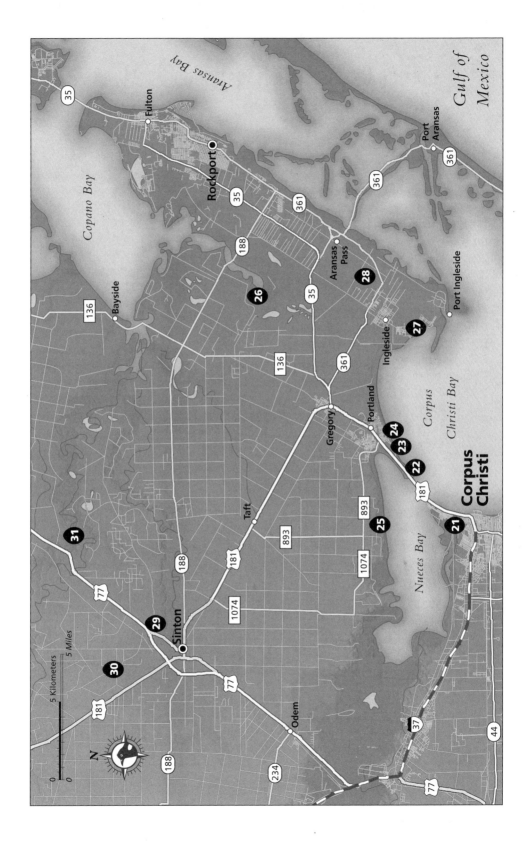

21 Corpus Christi Beach Wetlands Overlooks (Rincon Channel)

Habitats: Estuaries.

Specialty birds: *Resident*—Brown Pelican, Reddish Egret, White-faced Ibis. *Spring/Summer*—Wood Stork. *Fall/Winter*—Piping Plover. *Migrating*—Hudsonian Godwit.

Other key birds: *Resident*—Little Blue Heron, Roseate Spoonbill, Gull-billed Tern. *Spring/Summer*—Wilson's Plover. *Fall/Winter*—Marbled Godwit. *Migrating*—Shorebirds.

Best times to bird: Year-round.

Directions: When leaving Corpus Christi on Highway 35/U.S. Highway 181, the traveler will first cross the Harbor Bridge and then the Causeway before arriving in Portland. To get to these overlooks, take the Beach Avenue exit, which is between the bridge and the causeway.

There are two of these overlooks. The one on the bay side of Corpus Christi Beach is located at Timon Marsh. Once you exit, the access road will become Causeway Boulevard. At Beach Avenue turn right and travel 3 blocks to Gulf Breeze. Turn left and go until the road ends, about 4 blocks. Turn left onto Sandbar and go 1 block to the corner of Timon and Sandbar. (If this seems as if you are going around in a circle, you are. It must be done this way to avoid one-way streets.) Unfortunately, there is inadequate parking at this overlook.

The second overlook is on Rincon Channel. Continue south on Timon until it intersects Beach Avenue again. Turn right onto Beach and follow it under the causeway. It will come to a dead end at the overlook. There is a nice parking lot at this overlook.

From these two overlooks, it is very easy to return to Corpus Christi or travel north to Portland. There are excellent signs giving directions to either.

The birding

These two decklike observation overlooks provide an opportunity to study somewhat different habitats even though they are close together. The one at Timon Marsh is shallow, attracting small, short-legged shorebirds, such as Willets, Little Blue Herons, and Snowy and Piping Plovers, and numerous sandpipers. A sign at the site notes that plants in the salt marsh here are wolfberry, camphor daisy, glasswort, and salt grass.

The Rincon Channel boardwalk overlooks a deeper marsh that hosts Long-billed Curlew, Great, Snowy, and Reddish Egrets, and Great Blue Herons. The sign at this site mentions vegetation including silverleaf sunflower, Kleberg bluestem, and sea lavender.

It seems that these two overlooks could be covered in a matter of minutes. However, a lot of birds fly over this area, especially in the early morning. Other birds come and go in the marsh all day long. Take your time here.

General information: Wading anglers use the Rincon Channel area. The overlooks are wheelchair accessible.

Corpus Christi Beach Wetlands Overlook.

DeLorme: Texas Atlas & Gazetteer: Page 98 4A.

Elevation: 25 feet.

Hazards: Traffic.

Nearest food, gas, lodging: Corpus Christi Beach.

For more information: Texas State Aquarium, 2710 North Shoreline, Corpus Christi, TX 78402; (361) 881-1200, (800) 477-4853; Coastal Bend Bays and Estuaries Program, 1305 North Shoreline Boulevard, Suite 205, Corpus Christi, TX 78401; (361) 885-6202; Texas Coastal Management Program, 1700 North Congress Street, Austin Building, Austin, TX 78701 (512) 463-5054; Coastal Coordination Council, (800) 998-4GLO; United States Environmental Protection Agency, Region 6 Office, 1445 Ross Avenue, Suite 1200, Dallas, TX 75202; (214) 665-6444.

22 Indian Point Park

Habitats: Transition from a primary bay to a secondary bay.

Specialty birds: *Resident*—Brown Pelican, Black-bellied Whistling-Duck, Reddish Egret, White-faced Ibis. *Fall/Winter*—Peregrine Falcon, Piping Plover.

Other key birds: *Resident*—Neotropic Cormorant, Fulvous Whistling-Duck, Roseate Spoonbill, Clapper Rail, American Oyster-catcher, Gull-billed Tern. *Spring/Summer*—Wilson's Plover. *Migrating*—Shorebirds.

Best times to bird: Year-round.

Directions: When traveling from Corpus Christi to Portland, take Highway 35/U.S. Highway 181 over the Harbor Bridge, and then over the Nueces Bay Causeway. The causeway is about 1.5 miles long. Take the first exit after the causeway to Indian Point Park. Turn right at the end of the access onto the park road. The exit is well marked with a sign.

The birding

The road into Indian Point Park winds slowly toward the beach. Once parked, you may want to walk back this way. The road has wetlands on either side. Wonderful treasures wait here, including Roseate Spoonbills, Wimbrels, and Willets. On the utility wires in this area, look for a Belted Kingfisher. Forster's Terns often hover and dive over the pond on the west. Common Golden-eye and Red-breasted Mergansers feed in the pond. The bird population changes minute by minute. Likely found are Snowy Egrets, Great Blue Herons, and Long-billed Dowitchers. You might see Lesser Yellowlegs or Long-billed Curlews.

At the end of the road, there is a fishing pier and the parking lots. Parking is free, but there is a $1.00 charge to go on the pier. Birders shouldn't need the pier, as there are two boardwalks leading into the wetlands. However, be sure to scout around and under the fishing pier for plovers, Ruddy Turnstones, Red Knots, Sanderlings, Dunlin, and other sandpipers. Look out into the bay for Common Loons, Canvasbacks, and rafts of Redheads in the fall and winter.

One boardwalk angles out toward Corpus Christi. Wading birds inhabit the shallows aplenty as you go this way. At the end, look across the water into the grass for a Clapper Rail. This is an excellent place to find the Reddish Egret, including the white morph. Depending on the tides, your walk could also yield gulls, Snowy, Piping, Semipalmated, or Black-bellied Plovers, and a pair of American Oyster-catchers. White and Brown Pelicans often fly low over the park.

The other boardwalk juts out toward Portland closer to Nueces Bay. Here you may spot skimmers and ducks. On the mudflat side, look for sandpipers, such as Western, Semipalmated, Stilt, Pectoral, Spotted, and Least.

General information: Indian Point Park is owned and administered by the City of Portland, which was once a Native American village. As you enter the park, you will see a paved walking trail leading toward Portland. This is the back end of the Sunset Lake Park Hike and Bike Trail. See the Sunset Lake Park entry for directions to the head of this trail. This is CTC#73.

As you leave this site and head northeast down the access road, about ½ mile from Indian Point Park, you should notice two boardwalks. These boardwalks are actually on Sunset Lake. Though perhaps not in the best location, you may want to make a quick stop here to see what birds are available.

DeLorme: Texas Atlas & Gazetteer: Page 85 7E.

Elevation: 20 feet.

Hazards: Slippery walks.

Nearest food, gas, lodging: Portland.

For more information: Indian Point Pier, (361) 643-1600; City of Portland, 900 Moore Avenue, Portland, TX 78374; (361) 643-6501.

Boardwalk at Indian Point Park.

23 Sunset Lake Park

Habitats: Artificial lake, primary bay, Tamaulipan scrubland.

Specialty birds: *Resident*—Brown Pelican, Reddish Egret, White-faced Ibis, Couch's Kingbird. *Spring/Summer*—Wood Stork. *Fall/Winter*—Piping Plover.

Other key birds: *Resident*—Neotropic Cormorant, Little Blue Heron, Roseate Spoonbill, American Oystercatcher, Gull-billed Tern. *Spring/Summer*—Wilson's Plover. *Fall/Winter*—Marbled Godwit. *Migrating*—Shorebirds.

Best times to bird: Year-round.

Directions: As you are entering Portland from Highway 35/U.S. Highway 181, take the Farm-to-Market 8931/Moore Avenue exit. Turn right on Moore Avenue and travel 1 block to where the road curves onto Fifth Street. At the next corner, turn right on Houston. Go 1.3 miles to the main parking lot. This route is well marked with signs.

Sunset Lake Park.

The birding

Sunset Lake Park adjoins Indian Point Pier. There is a mile-long road leading to the main parking lot. The saltwater lake is on the passenger side of the road. Get ready to see birds right away. Be careful: The shoulder of this road is also a hike and bike trail, and no parking is allowed here. You will have to walk back or use one of the primitive parking spots along the other side of the road.

Shorebirds, gulls, sandpipers, and ducks frequent this lake and its shore. Try here for American Oystercatchers, Black-necked Stilts, and Marbled Godwits. There is a bluff with Portland residences on the east end of the lake. Scan the trees on this bluff for roosting Black-Crowned Night Herons. A Sharp-shinned Hawk may lurk here as well. Osprey often visit the lake.

At the parking lot and between the road and Nueces Bay there is woody brush used by songbird migrants in the spring and fall. You should be able to spot thrashers and Mockingbirds. Wintering sparrows can be found in the brushy grassland. On the other side of this brush is the bay. Ducks, such as Bufflehead and Northern Pintail, stop here.

From the parking lot, the hike and bike trail extends to Indian Point Pier. A portable toilet and trail benches are available.

General information: The park, which was opened in 2000, encompasses 333 acres and is heavily used by not only birders but also joggers and bikers. Wade fishing takes place on the gulf beach. This is CTC#73.

DeLorme: Texas Atlas & Gazetteer: Page 85 7E.

Elevation: 20 feet.

Nearest food, gas, lodging: Portland.

For more information: City of Portland, 900 Moore Avenue, Portland, TX 78374; (361) 643-6501.

24 Violet Andrews Park

Habitats: Primary bay.

Specialty birds: *Resident*—Brown Pelican, Reddish Egret, White-faced Ibis. *Fall/Winter*—Piping Plover.

Other key birds: *Resident*—Roseate Spoonbill, Gull-billed Tern. *Spring/Summer*—Sandwich Tern. *Migrating*—Shorebirds.

Best times to bird: Year-round.

Directions: Take the Harbor Bridge and causeway from Corpus Christi to Portland.

Use the Wildcat Drive exit and stay on the access road. Drive to the stoplight and turn right, then go 0.2 mile. Turn left on Broadway for ½ block, then turn right to return to Wildcat Drive. After 0.4 mile Wildcat dead-ends at Violet Andrews Park.

To get to the other parking lot, return on Wildcat for 1 block. Turn left on Second Street and travel 2 blocks to Elm Street. Turn left; the park is on the left.

The birding

This is actually two very small parks, totaling ten acres, which are connected by a ¼-mile sidewalk trail. The park on Wildcat Drive is used by windsurfers, as there is access to the water. Some beach exists when the tide is out, but most of the bird viewing will be of flyovers of terns, gulls, pelicans, ibis, egrets, herons, spoonbills, and ducks. The trail goes through some backyards. On the Nueces Bay side of the trail, some native habitat is intact, with windswept trees and grass–covered sand dunes. There is a short mowed trail through some of this native habitat. On the other side of the trail are manicured lawns. Two overlooks are equally spaced on the trail. Children and picnickers use the park on Elm Street.

General information: Tables and drinking water are available at both ends of the park. There is also an open shower on Wildcat and playground equipment at Elm.

Violet Andrews, an outdoor enthusiast, was the wife of former Portland school superintendent W. C. Andrews. The Andrews family gave money for the improvements to this park in her honor.

DeLorme: Texas Atlas & Gazetteer: Page 85 7E.

Elevation: 30 feet.

Hazards: Fog.

Nearest food, gas, lodging: Portland.

For more information: City of Portland, 900 Moore Avenue, Portland, TX 78374; (361) 643-6501.

25 Fred Jones Nature Sanctuary

Habitats: Tamaulipan thorn scrub, agricultural areas.

Specialty birds: *Resident*—Buff-bellied Hummingbird, Golden-fronted Woodpecker, Great Kiskadee, Couch's Kingbird, Long-billed Thrasher, Olive Sparrow. *Spring/Summer*—Brown-crested Flycatcher, Scissor-tailed Flycatcher, Hooded Oriole.

Other key birds: *Resident*—Pyrrhuloxia. *Spring/Summer*—Painted Bunting. *Migrating*—Neotropic Migrant Trap.

Best times to bird: Year-round, especially during spring or fall migration.

Directions: Leave Corpus Christi on Highway 35/U.S. Highway 181 going north toward Portland. Take the Moore Avenue exit, which is the first Portland exit. Turn left on Moore Avenue (which becomes North Farm-to-Market 893) and travel 6 miles. At the intersection, FM 893 goes to the right, and Farm-to-Market 1074 proceeds straight ahead. Turn left on County Road 3265 and travel ½ mile to the entrance to the Fred Jones Nature Sanctuary. The sign for the sanctuary is difficult to spot. There is room in front of the gate for two cars to park, or you may park parallel to the brush on the park side of the road. You will enter through a pedestrian gate.

The birding

On your way to the sanctuary, you will travel past miles of agricultural fields. Look on the wires for American Kestrel during the fall and winter. Also examine any newly plowed fields for Killdeer and Mountain Plovers.

The sanctuary is a small woody area with trails throughout. It is not tough going on the trails, but this is not a wheelchair accessible site. The paths are well maintained, but there is no special system for attacking this refuge. Just head out in one direction or the other. One path will circle back onto another. The area is relatively small, and getting lost is not likely. You can always look back and find the taller trees near the entrance. There is a large freshwater stream that winds through the sanctuary. A sturdy footbridge crosses it. This water, along with a drip by the park entrance, attracts many birds. Piles of cut limbs are left to entice wrens. Bewick's Wrens are a definite possibility here.

Throughout the year look for Northern Cardinals, Pyrrhuloxia, White-eyed Vireos, Northern Mockingbirds, and the resident Greater Roadrunner. In the winter, find Brown Thrashers, American Robins, and Goldfinches. In the spring and summer, search for hummingbirds, flycatchers, and Painted Buntings. Spring migrating vireos and warblers should be found here in sizable numbers. Throughout the summer, look overhead at dusk for Common Nighthawks.

Fred Jones is an excellent site for viewing wildflowers from early spring to midsummer. It is a great showcase for all South Texas specialties.

General information: Fred Jones, who in 1975 published *Flora of the Texas Coastal Bend,* donated the land for this sanctuary. The sanctuary is owned and maintained by the Audubon Outdoor Club. It is open daily from sunrise to sunset. There are several picnic tables and benches at key spots in the park. This is CTC#74.

DeLorme: Texas Atlas & Gazetteer: Page 85 7D.

Elevation: 45 feet.

Hazards: Snakes, mosquitoes, chiggers, ticks, thorns.

Nearest food, gas, lodging: Portland.

For more information: Audubon Outdoor Club of Corpus Christi, Inc., P.O. Box 3352, Corpus Christi, TX 78463.

26 North Bay Sanctuary

Habitats: Tamaulipan scrubland, Tamaulipan thorn scrub, freshwater pond.

Specialty birds: *Resident*—Least Grebe, Black-bellied Whistling-Duck, White-faced Ibis, Groove-billed Ani, Common Pauraque, Golden-fronted Woodpecker, Couch's Kingbird, Green Jay, Long-billed Thrasher, Olive Sparrow. *Spring/Summer*—Brown-crested Flycatcher, Scissor-tailed Flycatcher.

Other key birds: *Resident*—Neotropic Cormorant, Mottled Duck, Crested Caracara, Little Blue Heron, Gull-billed Tern, Inca Dove, Ladder-backed Woodpecker, Curve-billed Thrasher. *Spring/Summer*—Anhinga, Lesser Nighthawk, Painted Bunting.

Best times to bird: Year-round.

Directions: Leave Corpus Christi on U.S. Highway 181 North/Highway 35 and continue through Portland. The two highways split in Gregory. Take Highway 35 east toward Aransas Pass. At 4.5 miles after the split, look for the sign for County Road 93. Turn left. Once you turn, you will notice that you are actually on County Road 4343 (McCampbell Road). Continue on this narrow, curvy road for 4 miles. The road dead-ends. Turn right onto County Road 1432 (Johanson Road) and proceed for 1 mile. Go slowly, because the road abruptly turns into a gravel road. The North Bay Sanctuary is on the left at the end of the road. There is room to park along the roadside by the gate.

Groove-billed Ani. PHOTO: TONY BAYLIS.

The birding

Watch the utility lines and poles near the entrance for flycatchers and raptors. Once inside the gate of this seventy-five-acre sanctuary, you may take the path to the right through the thorn scrub or straight ahead for ½ mile to an observation tower. Either way, you will most likely see typical thorn scrub birds such as Northern Cardinals, Long-billed Thrashers, and Bewick's Wrens. North Bay Sanctuary would also be an interesting place to look for sparrows such as Savannah, Olive, Black-throated, Chipping, Clay-colored, and Vesper.

The viewing tower overlooks the adjoining Copano Ranch, a private, working ranch that stretches all the way to Copano Bay. Between the sanctuary and the ranch runs a freshwater stream. This stream is a creation of run-off from berms once used by the DuPont Company. The tower allows you to scan here for ducks and other water birds. The sanctuary is host to wildlife such as white-tail deer, bobcat, skunks, raccoon, and javelina.

General information: To access this sanctuary, you must contact one of the members of the board of directors of the Coastal Bend Audubon Society. The CBAS owns and operates the sanctuary on land donated by the DuPont Company in 1995. The tower was built in memory of Irene DeWese, longtime resident of the Coastal Bend.

DeLorme: Texas Atlas & Gazetteer: Page 85 7D.

Elevation: 15 feet.

Hazards: Snakes, thorns, fire ants.

Nearest food, gas, lodging: Gregory.

For more information: Coastal Bend Audubon Society, P.O. Box 3604, Corpus Christi, TX 78463.

27 Live Oak City Park

Habitats: Oak woodland, freshwater pond.

Specialty birds: *Resident*—Common Pauraque, Buff-bellied Hummingbird, Golden-fronted Woodpecker, Long-billed Thrasher. *Spring/Summer*—Brown-crested Flycatcher, Scissor-tailed Flycatcher.

Other key birds: *Resident*—Inca Dove, Ladder-backed Woodpecker. *Migrating*—Neotropic passerines.

Best times to bird: Spring.

Directions: Leave Corpus Christi on Highway 35/U.S. Highway 181 and go north through Portland on Highway 35. Watch the signs for Ingleside and take the exit for Highway 361. The main intersection in Ingleside is Highway 361 and Main Street. There is a stoplight at the intersection. Take a right on Main Street and stay on it for 2 miles. There is a large sign indicating the entrance of Live Oak City Park. It is actually 2 blocks off Main down Sherry Avenue, but there is no street sign, so watch for the park sign.

The birding

This city park has the feel of being out in the country, with its ninety acres of beautiful live oaks. This is a small remnant of an extensive oak forest that once covered the coast. The park has more potential for weekend picnickers than for the birder, but an observant bird-watcher should do quite well in the quieter sections of the park. The leaf litter is especially enticing to thrushes, thrashers, and other ground-dwelling birds. Try for Brown Thrasher, Gray Catbird, and Hermit Thrush.

You can drive around the paved park loop, but it is best to get out and walk. Golden-fronted and Ladder-backed Woodpeckers and Northern Mockingbirds should be easy to find. In the spring, warblers and vireos find this a nice resting place. Worm-eating Warblers and Ovenbirds have been listed here. There is a Frisbee golf course that runs through the park. Oddly enough, this may prove helpful to the birder. Some of the "holes" (which are represented in Frisbee golf as wire mesh baskets) are in the brush, so openings were cut that give access to the denser parts of the park. There is also a nature trail that proceeds into the section of the preserve that has not been cleared. In both cases, look for the Carolina Wren and Black-crested Titmouse.

The road on the north side of the loop road goes back to a small freshwater pond, which is used by waterfowl, herons, and egrets.

General information: Live Oak City Park has covered picnic tables, barbecue pits, restrooms, and a children's play area. It also has free tennis courts, a softball field, and a basketball court. This is CTC#055.

DeLorme: Texas Atlas & Gazetteer: Page 85 7E.

Elevation: 15 feet.

Hazards: Mosquitoes, ticks, chiggers.

Nearest food, gas, lodging: Ingleside.

Camping: Free overnight camping is permitted in the park. Call the Community Services Department at (361) 776-3438 to let them know you are camping.

For more information: City of Ingleside, P.O. Box 400, 2671 San Angelo, Ingleside, TX 78362; (361) 776-2517.

28 Whitney Lake

Habitats: Freshwater marsh and lake.

Specialty birds: *Resident*—Least Grebe, Black-bellied Whistling-Duck, White-faced Ibis, Golden-fronted Woodpecker, Great Kiskadee, Couch's Kingbird. *Spring/Summer*—Brown-crested Flycatcher, Scissor-tailed Flycatcher.

Other key birds: *Resident*—Mottled Duck, Inca Dove. *Migrating*—Shorebirds.

Best times to bird: Fall, winter, spring.

Directions: Enter Ingleside on Highway 361. At the first stoplight, take a left onto Main Street. Go 0.8 mile to Kenny Street. Turn right and go another 0.8 mile down Kenny. Whitney Lake is on your right.

The birding

This site was completed in 2005. It is so new that it is hard to tell what to expect of it in the future. Whitney Lake and surrounding lands cover a sixty-six-acre site. The lake and McCampbell Slough drain downstream into the Copano Bay system. The City of Ingleside acquired the property in order to protect this habitat and to provide public access.

There is a parking lot at the entrance. Picnic tables and interpretive signage enhance the preserve. Paved trails lead to two boardwalks that extend to observation platforms over the marshy edges of the lake. Waterfowl, shorebirds, and wading birds enjoy the area. Rails and Purple Gallinules would be a possibility here. Not far from this location a Masked Duck has been reported on several occasions. Some of the woodland was destroyed when designing the park. As the natural growth returns, it is hoped that passerines will return as well.

General information: This began as a drainage project for the City of Ingleside, but it has evolved into a wonderful destination for bird-watchers. The water levels depend on rainfall. Whitney Lake was named for Marvin Whitney, whose family owned the land for many years. The trails are wheelchair accessible.

DeLorme: Texas Atlas & Gazetteer: Page 85 8E.

Elevation: 25 feet.

Hazards: Mosquitoes.

Nearest food, gas, lodging: Ingleside.

Camping: Live Oak City Park.

For more information: City of Ingleside, P.O. Box 400, 2671 San Angelo, Ingleside, TX 78362; (361) 776-2517.

29 Park Welder

Habitats: Urban park, Tamaulipan scrubland.

Specialty birds: *Resident*—Golden-fronted Woodpecker, Couch's Kingbird, Long-billed Thrasher, Olive Sparrow. *Spring/Summer*—Brown-crested Flycatcher, Scissor-tailed Flycatcher, Cave Swallow. *Fall/Winter*—Vermilion Flycatcher.

Other key birds: *Resident*—Inca Dove, Pyrrhuloxia. *Spring/Summer*—Painted Bunting. *Migrating*—Neotropic passerines.

Best times to bird: Spring.

Directions: From Corpus Christi take Interstate 37 northwest toward San Antonio. After crossing the Nueces River bridge, take U.S. Highway 77 northeast to Odem and Sinton. Use the first exit into Sinton on U.S. Highway 77 Business. Travel 3 miles to the third stoplight at the intersection of US 77 and Sinton Street. Turn right toward Taft and go 5 blocks. Turn left onto Rachel Street and continue for 0.7 mile to 700 North Rachel. Because of a long-ago burned out bridge over Chiltipin Creek, the street stops at the park.

The birding

Park Welder, which covers less than twenty acres, was the first property donated by Rob Welder to the City of Sinton. Many years ago it had a small zoo. Today it is a charming spot to spend a quiet hour looking at birds.

Most of the trees in the park are ancient live oaks, with a few mesquites. The understory, however, is nicely manicured grass. The somewhat rolling terrain leads down to a meandering creek at the center of the park. This small creek, which empties into Chiltipin Creek, is fed by a free-running artesian well and always has water in it. All of the properties that border Park Welder are in a natural state.

In less than an hour, I saw Killdeer, Northern Mockingbirds, Northern Cardinals, White-winged and Inca Doves, Golden-fronted Woodpeckers, an Eastern Wood Pewee, Scissor-tailed Flycatchers, and Cave and Barn Swallows. Other birds common to this park are Blue-gray Gnatcatchers, Ruby-crowned Kinglets, and Bewick's Wren. In the spring the creek acts as a magnet for migrants, including warblers and water thrushes. In past years, a Barred Owl was known to inhabit the brushy area at the back of the park. Locals told me there is a trail into the brush, but I could not find it.

General information: The park has playground equipment and picnic tables, but there are no restrooms. This is CTC#45.

DeLorme: Texas Atlas & Gazetteer: Page 84 6C.

Elevation: 48 feet.

Hazards: Mosquitoes.

Nearest food, gas, lodging: Sinton.

Camping: Rob and Bessie Welder Park, Sinton.

For more information: City of Sinton, 301 East Market, Sinton, TX 78387; (361) 364-2381.

30 Rob and Bessie Welder Park

Habitats: Oak woodland, Tamaulipan scrubland, freshwater marsh.

Specialty birds: *Resident*—Least Grebe, Black-bellied Whistling-Duck, Golden-fronted Woodpecker, Great Kiskadee, Couch's Kingbird, Green Jay. *Spring/Summer*—Brown-crested Flycatcher, Scissor-tailed Flycatcher, Cave Swallow. *Fall/Winter*—Vermilion Flycatcher.

Other key birds: *Resident*—Neotropic Cormorant, Mottled Duck, Fulvous Whistling-Duck, Crested Caracara, Inca Dove, Ladder-backed Woodpecker, Curve-billed Thrasher. *Spring/Summer*—Anhinga, Painted Bunting. *Migrating*—Neotropic passerines.

Best times to bird: Winter, spring.

Directions: From Corpus Christi, take Interstate 37 north toward San Antonio. After crossing the Nueces River, take the exit for U.S. Highway 77 North. After about 15 miles you will pass through the town of Odem and bypass Sinton to the U.S. Highway 181 exit; turn left under the overpass. Stay on US 181 for 1.5 miles to the park entrance on the right.

The birding

Forty-five acres of the 300-acre Rob and Bessie Welder Park has been set aside as a nature preserve. The trail is an excellent place to bird. From the entrance to the park, take the first right and go past the baseball fields to a large parking lot. From this lot you can see the eighteen-hole public golf course. You can enter the walking/bike/nature trail from either end of the parking lot. I suggest that you take the entrance farthest from the golf course. The paved trail extends for about ⅓ mile, where it stops near a platform that goes out into the large freshwater pond. In South Texas this is large enough to be called a lake.

Once the paved trail ends, you will continue for another ⅔ mile or so on a wide, mowed trail. This trail makes a convenient loop through the brush and has cutbacks, so that you can return to the pond. It passes through thorn scrub habitat, but it also flanks a drainage ditch with water to draw in other types of birds. There are other mowed trails leading to bird-watching gazebos at either end of the lake. On the return trip, follow the trail in the opposite direction; you will end up at the parking lot. The trails, platforms, and gazebos are well kept. The mowed trail is marked in many places with bluebird boxes.

In the brush, expect to see Curve-billed and Brown Thrashers, Green Jays, Red-shouldered Hawks, Northern Mockingbirds, Northern Cardinals, Golden-fronted and Ladder-backed Woodpeckers, and perhaps Screech or Barred Owls. At the pond you will see Great Kiskadees, Couch's Kingbirds, Yellow-crowned and Black-crowned Night Herons, Anhingas, Clapper Rails, American Coots, Moorhens, Mottled Ducks, Least Grebe, and a Belted Kingfisher. Watch for a rare Wood Duck and the local alligator as well. In the more open areas near the rodeo arena and golf course, look for Loggerhead Shrikes, Scissor-tailed and Vermilion Flycatchers, White-winged and Inca Doves, and Meadowlarks. Along the drainage ditch and pond would be a great place to find migrating passerines such as Painted Buntings and Orchard Orioles in March and April.

General information: The park also has a swimming pool, basketball courts, baseball fields, party room, picnic tables, playground equipment, rodeo arena, and restrooms. There is no fee. This is CTC#46. Some of the nature trail is wheelchair accessible.

DeLorme: Texas Atlas & Gazetteer: Page 84 6C.

Elevation: 48 feet.

Hazards: Fire ants, snakes.

Nearest food, gas, lodging: Sinton.

Camping: There is a forty-five-site RV camp run by the City of Sinton within this park.

For more information: City of Sinton, 301 East Market, Sinton, TX 78387; (361) 364-2381.

31 Rob and Bessie Welder Wildlife Foundation and Refuge

Habitats: Tamaulipan scrubland, Tamaulipan thorn scrub, transitional riparian forest, freshwater lakes, prairie, mesquite savanna, oak savanna.

Specialty birds: *Resident*—Least Grebe, Black-bellied Whistling-Duck, White-tailed Kite, White-tailed Hawk, White-faced Ibis, White-tipped Dove, Common Pauraque, Buff-bellied Hummingbird, Golden-fronted Woodpecker, Great Kiskadee, Green Jay, Long-billed Thrasher, Olive Sparrow, Plain Chachalaca (introduced). *Spring/Summer*—Wood Stork, Scissor-tailed Flycatcher. *Fall/Winter*—Vermilion Flycatcher, Sprague's Pipit. *Migrating*—Hudsonian Godwit.

Other key birds: *Resident*—Neotropic Cormorant, Mottled Duck, Fulvous Whistling-Duck, Crested Caracara, Little Blue Heron, Roseate Spoonbill, Ladder-backed Woodpecker, Bronzed Cowbird, Pyrrhuloxia, Anhinga. *Spring/Summer*—Painted Bunting. *Fall/Winter*—Tundra Swan, Greater White-fronted Goose, Ross's Goose.

Best times to bird: October through May.

Directions: From Corpus Christi take Interstate 37 north toward San Antonio. After crossing the Nueces River, take the exit for U.S. Highway 77 North. After about 15 miles you will pass through the town of Odem and bypass Sinton. The entrance to the Rob and Bessie Welder Wildlife Foundation and Refuge is just off US 77, about 7.5 miles from Sinton, or about 20 miles from the exit at I–37. The Aransas River is the refuge's northern boundary, so should you cross the Aransas River, you have just passed the refuge entrance.

The birding

The habitat for birds at Welder Wildlife Refuge is superb. The refuge is mainly used for research; therefore, birders are mostly limited to once-a-week guided tours. The tour starts with the small museum at the foundation headquarters. The museum focuses on the animals of the refuge and has excellent examples of bird life. The foundation recently acquired a 400+ item collection from premier taxidermist Don Bowman. Plans for a new museum to highlight this collection are under way. The design for displaying the specimens includes showing the birds grouped into dioramas of the habitats in which they would normally be found. Such a museum would be a boon for visiting birders.

After touring the museum and hearing a short history of the foundation and refuge, visitors tour the Welder Wildlife Refuge by van. Often graduate students guide these tours. Although these students are not necessarily ornithologists, they are wildlife experts with degrees in wildlife science and are quite knowledgeable about South Texas wildlife. They will answer questions pertaining to wildlife ecology and habitat management. The tour makes a loop through parts of the ranch

Common Pauraque. PHOTO: TONY BAYLIS.

(see General Information), including Moody Creek, Lagarto Tank, Pollita Lake, and Big Lake. You will travel through upland live oak scrubland, mesquite thorn scrub, and grassland habitats, as well as riparian and freshwater wetland habitats. On these short afternoon tours, you stop at various locations to get a better look at birds and other wildlife, but due to the short duration of the tours, all birding is done from the van. Expect to see alligators, white-tailed deer, javelina, feral hogs, raccoons, and an occasional bobcat, as well as many of the abundant bird species that have been documented at Welder Wildlife Refuge. A bird list of the 380 bird species recorded at the refuge is available. The refuge participates in the Coastal Bend Wildlife Photo Contest sponsored by the Coastal Bend Wildlife Habitat Education Program.

General information: Tours, which last about two hours, are given every Thursday at 3:00 P.M., except on major holidays. No appointment is necessary, and the tours are free. You should wait at the main gate off US 77 for a tour guide. No private birding is allowed on the grounds of the refuge, but a small number of special guided half-day tours are scheduled annually on Monday through Friday for eight to fourteen people. Appointments for these tours must be scheduled well in advance of the trip. Call for scheduling and fee information. Educational programs for K–12 and university groups for up to thirty-six people are free of charge and can be arranged with advance reservations. Overnight facilities are available for education groups. Additionally, the foundation offers many programs for landowners, nature enthusiasts, and public school teachers. Please call for additional information.

Rob Welder ranched on lands in South Texas that had been passed down through the family from a Spanish land grant given to Welder's ancestors in 1834. The Welders amassed great wealth through cattle ranching and oil and gas production on their properties. Rob Welder's visionary and philanthropic nature created the Rob and Bessie Welder Wildlife Foundation and Refuge through his will in 1954. The 7,800 acre refuge was the first of its type in North America and most likely is one of the largest private refuges in the United States. It was created to promote research and education in the fields of wildlife science, conservation, and management. It is still a working cattle ranch and active oil and gas field.

The Welder Wildlife Foundation's primary mission is wildlife research and education. The foundation's focus is the annual funding of about fifteen graduate research students, who are known as Welder fellows. These students receive fellowships to attain graduate degrees in wildlife science and management and attend universities throughout the United States.

DeLorme: Texas Atlas & Gazetteer: Page 84 6C.

Elevation: 15 feet.

Hazards: Africanized bees, fire ants, snakes.

Nearest food, gas, lodging: Woodsboro for food and gas, Sinton for lodging.

Camping: Rob and Bessie Welder Park, Sinton.

For more information: Welder Wildlife Foundation, P.O. Box 1400, Sinton, TX 78387; (361) 364-2643.

Aransas Pass/ Port Aransas

Their names, their bay, and their ferry system link Aransas Pass and Port Aransas. Both are picturesque coastal towns. Aransas Pass is home to a large fleet of shrimp boats. Port Aransas is a typical resort coastal town. Both towns love anglers, beach-goers, shoppers, tourists, and bird-watchers.

Port Aransas has gone out of its way to provide two prime birding spots: the Leonabelle Turnbull Birding Center and Joan and Scott Holt Paradise Pond. Both of these sites, though near the Gulf of Mexico, are really influenced more by freshwater. Ducks, grebes, herons, egrets, ibis, and spoonbills are likely, but so are migrating passerines. The Whooping Crane Festival takes place in Port Aransas each February.

The Port Aransas Jetties and Mustang Island State Park are two more beach sites.

32. Aransas Pass Community Park/Ransom Road Navigation District Park

33. Leonabelle Turnbull Birding Center (formerly Port Aransas Birding Center)

34. Joan and Scott Holt Paradise Pond

35. Port Aransas Jetties (I. B. Magee Beach and Port Aransas Park)

36. Port Aransas Wetland Park

37. Mustang Island State Park

32 Aransas Pass Community Park/ Ransom Road Navigation District Park

Habitats: Prairie, saltwater channel, secondary bay, freshwater pond.

Specialty birds: *Resident*—Brown Pelican, Black-bellied Whistling-Duck, Reddish Egret, White-faced Ibis. *Spring/Summer*—Wood Storks, Scissor-tailed Flycatcher, Cave Swallow. *Fall/Winter*—Peregrine Falcon, Piping Plover. *Migrating*—Hudsonian Godwit.

Other key birds: *Resident*—Neotropic Cormorant, Mottled Duck, Fulvous Whistling-Duck, Little Blue Heron, Roseate Spoonbill, Clapper Rail, American Oystercatcher, Gull-billed Tern, Seaside Sparrow. *Sping/Summer*—Magnificent Frigatebird, Wilson's Plover, Sandwich Tern, Common Tern. *Fall/Winter*—Common Loon, Marbled Godwit. *Migrating*—Shorebirds.

Best times to bird: Year-round.

Directions: Leave Corpus Christi going north on Highway 35/U.S. Highway 181 and pass through Portland on Highway 35. Watch for signs for Ingleside and take the exit for Highway 361. Continue east through Ingleside on Highway 361 toward Aransas Pass. After 3 miles, watch on your right for Johnson Avenue. There is no sign on the highway for the Aransas Pass Community Park, so watch carefully for Johnson. On leaving Aransas Pass Community Park, continue on Highway 361 for 0.3 mile to Ransom Road on the right. Again, there is no sign marking the turn to the Navigation District Park, so watch carefully. Turn right again and go down Ransom Road for 0.8 mile. The road dead-ends at the park.

The birding

Aransas Pass Community Park and Ransom Road Navigation District Park are quite close to one another, yet they are very different. Together they make a wonderful birding experience.

The place that truly impressed me was Aransas Pass Community Park. I was reluctant to go there, as I knew it had a large aquatic center. I thought the swimming pool was the only highlight of this park. I was very wrong. The pool is nice and so are the baseball fields located here. At the end of the pool parking lot is a paved trail that leads to a freshwater wetland area.

The trail ends with a boardwalk that allows the bird-watcher to traverse most of the artificial ponds. Interpretive signs give information about the area. Water from treated wastewater effluent is pumped in here. There are shallow areas with unvegetated shorelines, deeper areas of water, and islands covered with grasses. There are many birds using the habitat. Look for gulls, ibis, plovers, stilts, Sandwich Terns, Least and Western Sandpipers, Roseate Spoonbills, Tricolored Heron, Great and Snowy Egrets, Willets, and Great Blue Heron. Least Tern and Black Skimmers nest here. Prairie habitat covers the remainder of the park. Look for Marsh Wren, Grasshopper Sparrows, and Seaside Sparrows. In the winter, ducks will be abundant

Clapper Rail. PHOTO: TONY BAYLIS.

here. Raptors such as Northern Harrier, Peregrine Falcon, and Osprey can be expected.

At the other end of the pool parking lot, there is a small beach with access to a saltwater marsh. This is a kayak launching area. Kayakers can reach Redfish Bay from this boat launch.

The City of Aransas Pass acquired this property in 1989. The nature park was realized after a grant from the Texas Coastal Management Program and the Coastal Coordination Council.

Ransom Road Navigation District Park, next door to Hampton's Landing Marina, is really for anglers. Also, this park is heavily used during duck-hunting season as a boat launch. There is a public boat ramp, covered picnic tables with barbecue pits, playground equipment, a small beach, and restrooms. The bird-watcher will find it a productive birding spot.

There are two boardwalks leading out over the edge of Redfish Bay. One walk ends at a covered gazebo; the other is a longer walk used for fishing. Each gives a good view of nearby spoils islands where wading and shorebirds feed and breed. Birders get a look at both deep water and vegetated marshland. In a short time, I saw Brown Pelicans, Double-crested Cormorants, Laughing Gulls, Great Blue Herons, and a Forster's Tern. Near the parking lot, I saw Red-winged Blackbirds and Mourning Doves. In the winter, look for grebes, loons, and ducks.

General information: Both parks are wheelchair accessible. A list of fifteen birds seen and $3.00 will earn you an Aransas Pass birding patch from the Chamber of Commerce. Ransom Road Navigation District Park is CTC#53, and Aransas Pass Community Park is CTC#54. CTC#52, Newbury Park Hummingbird Garden, is also in Aransas Pass. Since its listing on the Great Texas Coastal Birding Trail, the park has not been well cared for, and I would not recommend a stop there.

DeLorme: Texas Atlas & Gazetteer: Page 85 8D.

Elevation: 20 feet.

Hazards: Mosquitoes.

Nearest food, gas, lodging: Aransas Pass.

For more information: City of Aransas Pass, 600 West Cleveland Boulevard, Aransas Pass, TX 78336; (361) 758-5301.

33 Leonabelle Turnbull Birding Center (formerly Port Aransas Birding Center)

Habitats: Estuaries.

Specialty birds: *Resident*—Least Grebe, Black-bellied Whistling-Duck, White-tailed Hawk, White-faced Ibis. *Spring/Summer*—Wood Stork.

Other key birds: *Resident*—Neotropic Cormorant, Mottled Duck, Little Blue Heron, Roseate Spoonbill, Clapper Rail, Seaside Sparrow. *Migrating*—Neotropic passerines.

Best times to bird: October to May.

Directions: There are two interesting ways to get to Port Aransas and the birding sites there, including the Leonabelle Turnbull Birding Center. Each way involves birding as you go. First, you can come from Aransas Pass on Highway 361 and continue east toward Port Aransas. Before crossing the bridge, consider going to Conn Brown Harbor. Turn left on Pacific Street and go 1 block to Wilson Street. Turn right and go 2 blocks to Huff Street. Stay on Huff for

Roseate Spoonbill. PHOTO: TONY BAYLIS.

1 mile, then turn right onto Bigelow Street and travel 1 more mile. Basically, you are curving around the harbor area. At the end of Bigelow is Harbor Park. It is open from 6:00 A.M. to 9:00 P.M. and provides restrooms, tables, benches, and two fishing piers. Conn Brown Harbor is part of CTC#56. Return as you came to Highway 361.

Highway 361, at this point, is the 4-mile Dale Miller Causeway, crossing several islands and open water. Mostly anglers use the dirt roads that border the causeway, but the birder may easily pull off and take time to scope the area for wading birds such as Reddish Egrets, shorebirds such as Willets and Sanderlings, gulls such as Ring-billed, and terns such as Caspian, Royal, and Forster's. This is one place to try for Snowy, Piping, or Wilson's Plovers. Known as Aransas Pass Wetlands, this is the other part of CTC#56.

If you continue on Highway 361, you come to the free ferry to Port Aransas. The Texas Department of Transportation runs the ferry, and multiple boats are used. However, during spring break and in the summer, the wait can be long. This ferry ride gives you a great opportunity to see pelicans, cormorants, gulls, and terns. Most ferry riders also spot bottle-nosed dolphins on the short trip across the ship channel. Once off the ferry, you are on Cotter Avenue. At the first stoplight, turn right onto Cut-off Road. After about 5 blocks you come to a stop sign with Ross Avenue to your right at an extreme angle, almost a U-turn. The Birding Center is on the right, 0.6 mile down Ross Avenue. A trolley stop is near the entrance to the parking lot of the Birding Center.

Another way to come into Port Aransas is to travel north up Padre Island from Corpus Christi on Highway 361. This highway leaves Corpus Christi and comes up Padre Island to Mustang Island. Actually, this highway should be classified as a birding site of its own. You will cross several channels and inlets, including Corpus Christi Pass, which is CTC#61. This is an outstanding chance to see wading birds, terns, gulls, and ducks. In the winter look for Piping Plovers and Long-billed Curlews. In the spring, expect Snowy Plovers. Also, pay attention to the large utility poles on the bay side of the road (particularly the poles farthest away from the road). These poles, especially closer to Corpus Christi, are a reliable place to see White-tailed Hawks. Northern Harriers, Crested Caracaras, Merlin, and Peregrine Falcons are also a possibility. Scan the prairie here for sparrows such as Lincoln, Grasshopper, Savannah, Chipping, and even Cassin's. If you come into Port Aransas by this way, look for Avenue G at the first stoplight. Take a left. After about 4 blocks Avenue G curves onto Cut-off Road, but you will want to continue straight onto Ross Avenue and the Birding Center. A sign clearly marks the way.

The birding

The City of Port Aransas has done a wonderful thing in creating the Leonabelle Turnbull Birding Center. The parking lot faces several tanks in a wastewater treatment plant. The tanks have been decorated with a mural depicting many of the birds you will spot at this site. At the entrance is a bulletin board where birders post their recent sightings.

Adjacent to the parking lot is a small garden of wildflowers, cacti, some native plants, and several trees. The plants, most of which are labeled, are maintained to attract hummingbirds and butterflies. Actually, this small park is very productive during migration for warblers and other passerines.

At the end of the garden walk is the boardwalk out into the cattails. This marsh is associated with the effluent from the wastewater plant. About halfway down the boardwalk is a two-level observation deck, and another lookout is located at the end of the walk. The birder has a great view of the water and the nearby mudflats.

At the Birding Center look for alligators, turtles, and nutria. As for birds, in fall and winter many species of ducks show up here—Black-bellied Whistling-Ducks, Mottled Ducks, Lesser Scaup, American Shovelers, Ruddy Ducks, Blue-winged Teal, Cinnamon Teal, Green-winged Teal, and more. This is a productive site for American Bittern and Least Bittern. Herons, such as Tricolored, Little Blue, Great Blue, and Green, will abound, as will all of the white egrets. Many waders are usually present, including Roseate Spoonbills, American Avocet, and Black-necked Stilts. So are Pied-billed Grebes, Common Moorhens, American Coots, and Neotropic and Double-crested Cormorants. You should hear rails. Lucky birders will spot Sora, Clapper Rails, and Virginia Rails. Forster's Terns gracefully dive for a meal here. White Pelicans loaf and feed at the Birding Center.

Watch the cattails for Yellow-rumped Warblers, Red-winged Blackbirds, and Swamp Sparrows. And be ever mindful of the sky over the flats: Northern Harrier, Osprey, and other hawks are on the prowl.

This is an ideal site for a scope. Birds come and go here quickly. Take your time and enjoy the center.

General information: Leonabelle Turnbull is a member of the Audubon Outdoor Club, and for many years she led bird walks at the Birding Center. Guided bird walks are given every Wednesday at 9:00 A.M., except in extreme weather. Check with the City of Port Aransas to be certain they are ongoing. This is CTC#57. It is wheelchair accessible.

DeLorme: Texas Atlas & Gazetteer: Page 85 8E.

Elevation: 20 feet.

Hazards: Slippery walks, alligator.

Nearest food, gas, lodging: Port Aransas.

Camping: I. B. Magee Beach Park, Mustang Island State Park.

For more information: City of Port Aransas Parks and Recreation Department, 710 West Avenue A, Port Aransas, TX 78373; (361) 749-4158.

34 Joan and Scott Holt Paradise Pond

Habitats: Freshwater pond.

Specialty birds: *Resident*—Least Grebe, Buff-bellied Hummingbird.

Other key birds: *Resident*—Mottled Duck. *Spring/Summer*—Painted Bunting. *Migrating*—Neotropic Migrant Trap.

Best times to bird: Spring.

Directions: When coming into Port Aransas from the free ferry, you will leave the landing on Cotter Avenue. At the first stoplight turn right onto Cut-off Road. After 3 blocks look for the sign for Paradise Pond. This is a congested area, and the signs are not easily spotted. The turnoff is more of a one-lane alley than a road. The parking lot is behind a restaurant and the Shark Reef Resort.

Bird-watchers at Joan and Scott Holt Paradise Pond.

The birding

migration

The Joan and Scott Holt Paradise Pond is a little jewel of a birding location. It is only two and a half acres in size, but don't be fooled. During spring migration, the birder could easily be tempted to spend hours here.

At the entrance to the park is a garden designated to attract butterflies and hummingbirds, and the design is highly effective. Benches here allow you to stop and see which hummers will show up. Signs and labels in the garden give information about the flowers and birds.

The sidewalk through this garden hugs the fence on the right. Follow it around the corner to a boardwalk and three observation decks over this unique freshwater pond. These walks and decks are in the willows, so to speak—black willows. You will be very close to the birds. There is room on the decks for scopes, but for the most part you won't need them. This is also an ideal spot to photograph birds.

You will see Yellow-crowned and Black-crowned Night Herons, as well as Green Herons. Ducks show up here. But this is a migrant trap, and most birders come in the spring for the warblers and other songbirds. Yellow-billed Cuckoos, Black-billed Cuckoos, and Summer Tanagers use this as a migrating stopover. But it is the vireos and warblers just above your head that will be most enchanting. I once saw a note posted on the bulletin board by the boardwalk that read, "Seventeen species of warblers today." I believe it. At Paradise Pond, I have seen Black and White Warblers, Chestnut-sided Warblers, Bay-breasted Warblers, Black-throated Blue Warblers, Cerulean Warblers, Hooded Warblers, Magnolia Warblers, Nashville Warblers, Tennessee Warblers, Worm-eating Warblers, MacGillivray's Warblers, Yellow Warblers, Yellow-throated Warblers, Black-throated Green Warblers, Blue-headed Vireos, Yellow-throated Vireos, and Philadelphia Vireos. Prepare to have your breath taken away when you first spot a Prothonotary Warbler perched on a reed right above the water. On a sunny day it is difficult to tell which is the bird and which is the reflection. Don't miss this spot.

General information: This site is wheelchair accessible. Joan and Scott Holt, for whom the park is named, are biologists working at the University of Texas Marine Science Institute at Port Aransas. They are longtime birding enthusiasts. This site was first developed as a result of a donation made by winners of the Great Texas Birding Classic. The money was used to purchase the land. Eventually other donations and grants led to the completion of this wonderful site.

DeLorme: Texas Atlas & Gazetteer: Page 85 8E.

Elevation: 20 feet.

Hazards: Mosquitoes and gnats.

Nearest food, gas, lodging: Port Aransas.

Camping: I. B. Magee Beach Park, Mustang Island State Park.

For more information: City of Port Aransas Parks and Recreation Department, 710 West Avenue A, Port Aransas, TX 78373; (361) 749-4158.

35 Port Aransas Jetties
(I. B. Magee Beach and Port Aransas Park)

Habitats: Gulf beach.

Specialty birds: *Resident*—Brown Pelican, Reddish Egret. *Fall/Winter*—Piping Plover.

Other key birds: *Resident*—Neotropic Cormorant, American Oystercatcher, Gull-billed Tern. *Spring/Summer*—Magnificent Frigatebird, Wilson's Plover, Sandwich Tern, Common Tern, Least Tern. *Fall/Winter*—Common Loon, Northern Gannet. *Migrating*—Shorebirds.

Best times to bird: Year-round.

Directions: When coming into Port Aransas via the ferry, you exit onto Cotter Street. Stay on this street for 2 miles and you will arrive at the beach. Some people get lost about halfway there because the road goes through a very residential area. Don't be fooled; just keep going.

If you travel to Port Aransas down the island on Highway 361, you intersect Cotter at the second stoplight. Turn right toward the beach.

The birding

Aransas Pass was noted on maps as early as 1528, but crossing the Aransas bar was always a problem for sailing ships. In the nineteenth century various attempts were made to create a deepwater channel, including the construction of jetties. However, all of these efforts failed to increase the depth of the channel. At the beginning of the twentieth century, work began to enhance the jetties so as to deepen the pass. By 1919 the South Jetty, which is attached to Mustang Island, was completed to 7,385 feet, and the Haupt Jetty, which is attached to St. Joseph Island, was to 9,241 feet. Finally the channel began to deepen, opening the way for ship traffic to Aransas Pass, Rockport, and Corpus Christi.

Today, anglers and birders use the South Jetty in pursuit of their hobbies. The jetty is constructed of large rock and concrete boulders arranged at irregular angles. *You must watch your footing at all times.* Also, it is especially slippery during rough seas. But, of course, the farther out you venture, the more likely you are to spot pelagic birds such as gannets, boobies, storm petrels, terns, jaegers, shearwaters, and frigatebirds. If you are up to carrying a spotting scope in this treacherous place, it could be put to good use.

Walk along the beach here for a look at terns, gulls, sandpipers, and plovers. This would be a good spot to test your ability to separate Caspian Terns from Royal Terns. Brown Pelicans and Black Skimmers often feed at this beach, as do American Oystercatchers. Practice your skills on Sanderlings and Dunlins as well.

On the way to or from the jetties, the birder should consider stopping at the University of Texas Marine Science Institute, which is on Cotter Street as you approach the beach. There is no fee. Marine Science personnel conduct research in

Least Tern. PHOTO: TONY BAYLIS.

ecology, biological oceanography, marine botany, and several other disciplines. The birder would most enjoy the visitor center. Self-guided tours and movies are offered Monday to Thursday from 8:00 A.M. to 5:00 P.M., self-guided tours only on Friday. Seven aquariums show typical coastal habitats and the organisms that live in them. In addition, there is an avian display depicting coastal and marsh birds that are expected in the area.

General information: The South Jetty is at the north end of Port Aransas Park. The southern end of the park is outfitted with the 1,240-foot-long Horace Caldwell Fishing Pier. Primitive camping is allowed on the beach, or you may rent one of the seventy-five RV hook-ups in the 167-acre park. This beach is in Aransas County, and no windshield sticker is required as it is for beaches in Nueces County. There is also a public bathhouse. This is CTC#58.

DeLorme: Texas Atlas & Gazetteer: Page 85 8E.

Elevation: Sea level.

Hazards: High tides, slippery walk.

Nearest food, gas, lodging: Port Aransas.

Camping: Port Aransas Park.

For more information: Nueces County Parks and Recreation Department, 15802 SPID, Corpus Christi, TX 78408; (361) 949-8122; Port Aransas Park, 321 North on the Beach, Port Aransas, TX 78373; (361) 749-6117; The University of Texas at Austin, Marine Science Institute, Cotter Street, Port Aransas, TX 78387; (361) 749-6805.

36 Port Aransas Wetland Park

Habitats: Tidal flats, sand dunes.

Specialty birds: *Resident*—Black-bellied Whistling-Duck, Reddish Egret, White-faced Ibis. *Spring/Summer*—Wood Stork. *Fall/Winter*—Piping Plover.

Other key birds: *Resident*—Mottled Duck, Little Blue Heron, Roseate Spoonbill, Gull-billed Tern. *Spring/Summer*—Sandwich Tern, Common Tern. *Migrating*—Shorebirds.

Best times to bird: Winter, year-round.

Directions: The Port Aransas Wetland Park is located south on Highway 361 as you are leaving Port Aransas. It is across from the Port Aransas Post Office. This park is ½ mile south of the stoplight at Avenue G on the bay side. A nice parking lot is available.

The birding

You leave the parking lot and walk out onto a short but nice boardwalk that culminates at an observation gazebo. Ahead you can scan a freshwater wetland; to the right and left you can inspect a dune reconstruction with sea oats and beach morning glories. The wetlands support ducks, herons, egrets, kingfishers, gulls, terns, and plovers. The dunes are shelter for Eastern or Western Meadowlarks, Savannah Sparrows, and other prairie birds. Watch the skies for hawks. It is wheelchair accessible.

General information: The Port Aransas Wetland Park was a joint project of the Texas Parks and Wildlife and the Texas Department of Transportation and the City of Port Aransas. It has been deeded to the city. This is CTC#59. It is wheelchair accessible.

DeLorme: Texas Atlas & Gazetteer: Page 85 8E.

Elevation: 20 feet.

Nearest food, gas, lodging: Port Aransas.

Camping: I. B. Magee Beach Park, Mustang Island State Park.

For more information: City of Port Aransas Parks and Recreation Department, 710 West Avenue A, Port Aransas, TX 78373; (361) 749-4158.

37 Mustang Island State Park

Habitats: Prairie, gulf beach.

Specialty birds: *Resident*—Brown Pelican. *Fall/Winter*—Piping Plover.

Other key birds: *Resident*—Neotropic Cormorant, American Oystercatcher, Gull-billed Tern. *Spring/Summer*—Magnificent Frigatebird, Wilson's Plover, Sandwich Tern, Common Tern. *Fall/Winter*—Common Loon, Northern Gannet. *Migrating*—Shorebirds.

Best times to bird: Year-round.

Directions: Once you arrive on Padre Island from Corpus Christi via Park Road 22, watch for Highway 361. At the intersection, turn left and travel north for 4.9 miles toward Port Aransas. The entrance to Mustang Island State Park is on your right. Stop at the entrance booth and request a park bird list.

The birding

Mustang Island State Park, which was opened in 1979, encompasses over 4,000 acres of grass-covered dunes and 5.5 miles of gulf beach. Corpus Christi Pass to the south and Fish Exchange Pass to the north are also included within the park. The park extends to the bay side of the island as well.

What the birder can see at any beach site in this book depends on the time of day, the time of year, the weather, including events out in the Gulf of Mexico, the tides, the number of tourists present, and who knows what else. However, you can be assured that you will always see birds. Those most likely seen are gulls and terns. If plovers and sandpipers are present, the birder can be challenged to name the species. Occasionally, pelagic birds come ashore here as the result of an offshore storm. On Mustang Island, I have always seen Brown Pelicans. I love to see a number of Brown Pelicans flying parallel to the beach, almost on patrol, in full breeding colors: yellow and rich brown, including the bump on their beak.

In the fall, during migration, hummingbirds such as Ruby-throated and Black-chinned flock to the morning glories that stretch out over the dunes. In the winter, prairie birds such as sparrows and Sandhill Cranes use the vegetated flats as places to look for food and as a respite from the wind.

The most productive section of the park is on the bay side. This, however, is the most difficult section to access. At present, three dirt roads allow visitors to enter. One is near Corpus Christi Pass. It is 1.7 miles before the entrance to the park. The other two roads, at 0.3 mile and 0.6 mile past the entrance, enter at either side of Fish Exchange Pass. These three roads are completely impassable with even the slightest rainfall. To make matters worse, vehicles that have gone in when the roads were wet have left deep tracks and holes. Future plans for this park include grading these roads and providing parking lots that could be used as starting points for hiking into this section.

So why bother going into the bay side section of the park? Well, as I said, this area has more birds. In addition to the two passes that are used by birds, the area is dotted with shallow wetlands and brackish marshes. If you can make it to Corpus Christi Bay, you see many more birds there. The birder can expect Black Skimmers, Long-billed Curlews, ibis, herons, egrets, and more gulls and terns. In the winter, ducks can be found.

The Peregrine Fund has installed an artificial nest site in this section of the park. They are hoping to attract a pair of Aplomado Falcons from the neighboring population at Matagorda Island National Wildlife Refuge. They feel that the population at the NWR is doing well enough and should be expanding their range. At this time, no known Aplomado Falcons reside on Mustang Island. You should be able to see White-tailed Hawks using the tall utility poles as roosts, and Merlins have been seen on fence posts along the park's boundary.

Come to Mustang Island State Park to camp, hike, swim, or beachcomb, or just bring a lawn chair and your binoculars.

General information: There is an entrance fee. The park is open daily from 7:00 A.M. to 10:00 P.M. Included are a public bathhouse, a small gift shop that also sells ice and drinks, many shade-covered picnic tables that are on the beach, and RV campsites. In the day-use area, portable toilets are provided. On the weekends, rangers offer interpretive programs from 2:00 to 4:00 P.M. Alcohol is not allowed on this section of beach. The island and this park are named for the wild horses that once roamed here. This is CTC#60.

There are other access points to the beach, all of which are plainly marked on Highway 361. At most times, driving on the beach from these access roads is safe. Just proceed slowly and pay attention. Parking on any beach in Nueces County requires an annual sticker that can be purchased at the city hall in either Port Aransas or Corpus Christi. These stickers can also be purchased at most convenience stores near the beach. It is not necessary to be a resident to purchase a sticker. Wooden post markers on the beach are used for location purposes. Sometimes bird-watchers use these markers when giving directions (for instance, "A group of Piping Plovers was spotted today at Marker 29"). These markers also remind you that the beach road is subject to all Texas state traffic laws.

If you are interested in experiencing the beach on horseback, try Mustang Riding Stables near here (361–991–7433).

DeLorme: Texas Atlas & Gazetteer: Page 85 8F.

Elevation: 8 feet.

Hazards: Fog, high tides, snakes.

Nearest food, gas, lodging: Port Aransas.

Camping: Mustang Island State Park.

For more information: Mustang Island State Park, P.O. Box 326, Port Aransas, TX 78373; (361) 749-5246.

Rockport

The bay side town of Rockport, which promotes itself as one of the "100 Best U.S. Small Art Towns," is very well known in the worldwide bird-watching community. Birders flock to this small coastal town in winter to get a glimpse of the Whooping Cranes at nearby Aransas National Wildlife Refuge, or they come in September to experience the unbelievable hummingbird migration. The sites in this region are typical of wetlands near or on primary and secondary bays. In addition to the Whooping Cranes and the hummingbirds, expect to see skimmers, gulls, terns, pelicans, ducks, cormorants, and perhaps a loon or frigatebird.

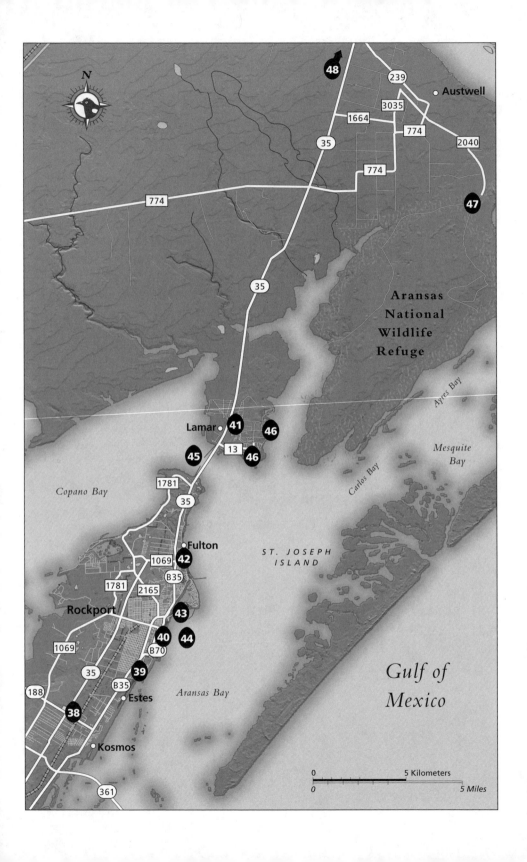

38 Aransas Woods

Habitats: Oak woodland, freshwater marsh.

Specialty birds: *Resident*—Black-bellied Whistling-Ducks, White-faced Ibis, Long-billed Thrashers. *Spring/Summer*—Scissor-tailed Flycatcher.

Other key birds: *Resident*—Mottled Duck, Crested Caracara, Little Blue Heron, Inca Dove, Ladder-backed Woodpecker.

Spring/Summer—Anhinga, Painted Bunting. *Migrating*—Neotropic passerines.

Best times to bird: October through April.

Directions: Take Highway 35 Bypass around Aransas Pass toward Rockport. Aransas Woods is on the right 1 mile past the exit for Highway 188. At the entrance to Aransas Woods, there is parking for three or four cars.

The birding

This thirty-two-acre preserve has intriguing bits of several habitats. Enter from the parking lot and follow the sidewalk around to the viewing platform that overlooks the wetlands/lake. This first portion is really the only part of the trail that can be considered wheelchair accessible. The birds here vary with the seasons and the depth of the lake. Actually, the lake always has some water. Did you notice the windmill at the front of the property? It pumps in water regularly. Try to find Mottled Ducks, American Shovelers, Blue-winged and Green-winged Teal, and Anhinga here. Waders such as Little Blue Herons and Tricolored Herons might pop up their heads. An Osprey works the water area, or you could glimpse a Sora in the grassy edges. Great Blue Herons have been known to nest in the trees at the rear of the lake.

From the platform follow mowed and marked trails through oaks and mesquite. There are several trails that cut back to the edge of the lake. On some trails you find benches, and on one near the lake there is a picnic table. If you become confused, a trail along the south fence line will return you to the entrance. Watch for Ladder-back Woodpeckers, Long-billed Thrashers, Northern Cardinals, Crested Titmice, Carolina Wren, and Scissor-tailed Flycatchers. You will notice many dead trees; they are the results of a fire several years ago.

The trail on the south side of the lake leads to a swamp. *Quiet, secluded, peaceful,* and *primeval* are but a few adjectives to describe the spot, especially in the spring. However, in some years, this wetland does dry up. It is a nice place to hunt out spring migrating warblers.

On the far side of the lake, near the windmill, birders have encountered Great Horned Owls and Screech Owls.

An additional ninety acres has recently been acquired for Aransas Woods. The new acreage not only includes additional wetlands but also some upland oak areas.

It seems probable that the stewardship of this new portion will further enhance the experience of the birder at Aransas Woods.

General information: This sanctuary was a joint project of the Texas Parks and Wildlife Department and the Texas Department of Transportation. It opened in 1997. Members of Aransas First serve as stewards of the preserve. The viewing platform is a memorial to Robert Latimer, outdoorsman and bird photographer. This is CTC#47.

DeLorme: Texas Atlas & Gazetteer: Page 85 8D.

Elevation: 25 feet.

Hazards: Mosquitoes, snakes.

Nearest food, gas, lodging: Rockport.

For more information: Aransas First, P.O. Box 266, Rockport, TX 78381; (361) 790-8384.

39 North Cove Harbor Wetlands Sanctuary

Habitats: Primary bay, saltwater marsh.

Specialty birds: *Resident*—Black-bellied Whistling-Duck, Reddish Egret, White-faced Ibis.

Other key birds: *Resident*—Neotropic Cormorant, Mottled Duck, Roseate Spoonbill, Clapper Rail, Gull-billed Tern, Seaside Sparrow. *Spring/Summer*—Wilson's Plover, Sandwich Tern, Common Tern. *Fall/Winter*—Nelson's Sharp-tailed Sparrow. *Migrating*—Shorebirds.

Best times to bird: Year-round.

Directions: From Corpus Christi, go north on Highway 35/U.S. Highway 181 and pass through Portland. When the roads split just north of Portland, stay on Highway 35. Be sure to stay on Business Highway 35 to Aransas Pass. Stay on this highway through Aransas Pass; the road will curve north toward Rockport. Do not go straight to Port Aransas. North Cove is a small development north of Aransas Pass on Business Highway 35. The North Cove Harbor Wetlands Sanctuary is 6.5 miles out of Aransas Pass and close to the Rockport city limits. If you get to the Loop 70 exit, you have gone too far. However, you should not miss it. It is very visible to the right of the highway.

Boardwalk at North Cove Harbor Wetlands Sanctuary.

The birding

This 109-acre sanctuary is very straightforward. There is a parking lot and an 800-foot elevated boardwalk over the wetlands. From the parking lot, birders really can't appreciate how special this site is. Go out to the end of the boardwalk before making up your mind about the North Cove Harbor Wetlands Sanctuary.

The water level here, as with so many sites, is dependent upon tides and rainfall. Viewing possibilities will vary with the weather. However, from the covered pavilion at the end of the walk, you can see an area that is more pondlike. You can also see across to Aransas Bay and North Cove Harbor. A spotting scope would be useful at this expansive vantage point.

The walk is just above the vegetation, and this makes spotting some birds much easier. For instance, I easily saw a Virginia Rail running in the grasses beneath the walk. A Tricolored Heron almost defied me to continue my walk and did not fly off until I was very close. Toward the bay was a pond that held about a dozen Roseate Spoonbills. Future plans call for another walk to extend toward this second pond. Terns and gulls continually flew overhead. All of this bird activity was impossible to predict from the parking lot.

General information: North Cove Harbor Wetlands Sanctuary is owned by Aransas County Navigation District but leased to Aransas First. Aransas First is a community-based group focusing on habitat protection. This site is wheelchair accessible.

DeLorme: Texas Atlas & Gazetteer: Page 85 8D.

Elevation: 20 feet.

Nearest food, gas, lodging: Rockport.

For more information: Aransas First, P.O. Box 266, Rockport, TX 78381; (361) 790-8384.

40 Connie Hagar Cottage Sanctuary

Habitats: Oak woodland.

Other key birds: *Resident*—Inca Dove, Ladder-backed Woodpecker. *Spring/Summer*—Painted Bunting. *Migrating*—Neotropic passerines.

Best times to bird: October through April.

Directions: When coming into Rockport on Highway 35, two exits are available. Take the first exit onto Market/Farm Road 1069. Turn right and travel for 1.8 miles to Church Street (also known as Loop 70). Go 0.8 mile to First Street. The Connie Hagar Cottage Sanctuary is on the right.

The birding

This small preserve in Rockport is the size of two very large city lots, or about six acres. The cottage is gone. The entrance to the property is dominated by a large viewing platform erected by the Friends of Connie Hagar. Most of the rest of the property is reverting to a wild state; however, there are new plantings of live oaks. Paths weave through the plot, and there is more of interest than you think at first. Keep your eyes out for Inca and Mourning Doves, Black-crested Titmice, Carolina Wrens, Northern Cardinals, and Ruby-throated and Black-chinned Humming-birds. This small preserve is good in the spring for migrating warblers, and the wildflowers and butterflies create an enchanting place. Sit for a spell on one of the benches, or wander around and enjoy the birds.

General information: The sanctuary is owned and maintained by the Friends of Connie Hagar. Connie and Jack Hagar lived on this property from 1935 until her death in 1973. Because of her love of bird watching and her studies of birds in the Rockport area, Connie was able to challenge long-held beliefs about birds of the Coastal Bend. In 1948 field guide originator Roger Tory Peterson visited her. In 1995 he returned to the site of the Hagar cottage to dedicate it as the first stop on the Great Texas Coastal Birding Trail. This is CTC#51.

To learn more about her life, read *Connie Hagar—The Life History of a Texas Birdwatcher* by Karen Hardin McCracken (Texas A&M University Press, 1986).

DeLorme: Texas Atlas & Gazetteer: Page 85 8C.

Elevation: 10 feet.

Nearest food, gas, lodging: Rockport.

Camping: Goose Island State Park.

For more information: Friends of Connie Hagar, P.O. Box 586, Rockport, TX 78381; City of Rockport, 622 East Market, Rockport, TX 78382; (361) 729-2213.

41 Crane House, St. Charles Bay Retreat

Habitats: Oak woodland, prairie, freshwater ponds, Tamaulipan thorn scrub, secondary bay.

Specialty birds: *Resident*—Brown Pelican, Black-bellied Whistling-Duck, Reddish Egret, White-faced Ibis, Common Pauraque, Long-billed Thrasher. *Spring/Summer*—Cave Swallow. *Fall/Winter*—Whooping Crane, Peregrine Falcon.

Other key birds: *Resident*—Neotropic Cormorant, Mottled Duck, Crested Caracara, Little Blue Heron, Roseate Spoonbill, Clapper Rail, Gull-billed Tern, Inca Dove, Ladder-backed Woodpecker, Pyrrhuloxia, Seaside Sparrow.

Spring/Summer—Painted Bunting. *Fall/Winter*—Common Loon, Marbled Godwit.

Best times to bird: November to April.

Directions: The Crane House ranch is located north of Rockport across the Copano Bay Causeway on the Lamar Peninsula. It is near Good Island State Park and the Big Tree. The owners meet first-time visitors at the corner of Highway 35 and Park Road 13.

This private ranch borders the Aransas National Wildlife Refuge, and the endangered Whooping Cranes regularly visit the property. Consequently, the owners have not made the exact location public, nor is it disclosed on their Web site.

The birding

Birders are used to roughing it: Christmas counts on cold and windy days, donning hip waders to flush secretive rails, or battling hordes of mosquitoes just to see that one special species. You could do all of that at the Crane House, or you could rest on the 400-square-foot screened-in porch and use the scope provided for bird watching. Bird feeders outside the porch are kept well supplied.

True, this is a unique situation. The wheelchair accessible ranch house and the entire ranch can be rented. "Ranch house" doesn't quite convey how modern or comfortable the bungalow is. It includes two bedrooms, two baths, a fully equipped kitchen, and a laundry room. Direct TV and all new appliances are provided. Bicycles, kayaks, and outdoor cooking equipment are included in the rental.

Why does the Crane House stay booked most of the year? It is very nice, but again that does not tell the whole story. The location and the habitat are exactly what Coastal Bend bird-watchers are seeking. Over one hundred birds are included on their bird list. The ranch covers about 800 acres, including 240 acres of saltwater marsh. The marsh acres have been sold to The Nature Conservancy, but the owners maintain the right to use the area. The other 600 acres are protected under a conservation easement.

The house sits in oak woodlands that cover most of the upper section of the property. You may wander the brush on foot or drive the ranch roads. Two freshwater ponds increase the desirability of the property. Look among the oaks and mesquites for Inca Doves, Common Pauraque, Ladder-backed Woodpeckers, Loggerhead Shrikes, Black-crested Titmice, Hermit Thrushes, Pyrrhuloxia, and Northern Cardinals. Thrashers and wrens enjoy this habitat as well.

Sloping below the house is a section of native coastal prairie. Although hunting is no longer allowed on the property, a couple of deer blinds remain that are used by birders. Near the house is a ground-level photography blind. Also in this prairie section are several deer feeders that dispense corn. Whooping Cranes come very near to the house in order to take advantage of the free food. A pair of Whoopers, usually with a chick, visits the ranch almost daily between November and April. Sandhill Cranes sometimes accompany them. Also in the coastal prairie section, look for sparrows—Field, Grasshopper, Vesper, Savannah, Song, Swamp, and Seaside. Coral bean bushes and wolfberries act as an additional draw for birds.

The prairie gives way to the marsh and eventually to the St. Charles Bay. Name a North American egret or heron; it has been listed at Crane House. So have ibis, sandpipers, plovers, terns, and gulls. The bird list includes seventeen species of ducks. Hawks, such as Osprey and Peregrine Falcon, patrol the area.

Also expect to see white-tailed deer, feral hogs, and the pet ranch horse. In the spring enjoy the plentiful wildflowers and butterflies. Not only birders, but writers, artists, and photographers find Crane House a productive place to visit. Early reservations are recommended.

General information: Fishing is allowed. Continental breakfast is available for an additional charge. The owners do not live on the ranch but in nearby Rockport.

DeLorme: Texas Atlas & Gazetteer: Page 85 9B.

Elevation: 10 feet.

Hazards: Snakes, mosquitoes.

Nearest food, gas, lodging: Rockport for food and gas; lodging at Crane House.

Camping: Goose Island State Park.

For more information: Crane House, 1401 North Terry Street, Rockport, TX 78382; (361) 729-7239; www.cranehouseretreat .com.

42 Rockport Demonstration Bird Garden and Wetlands Pond/Tule Creek Nature Center

Habitats: Garden, freshwater pond.

Specialty birds: *Resident*—Buff-bellied Hummingbird.

Other key birds: *Resident*—Clapper Rail, Inca Dove. *Fall/Winter*—Rufous Hummingbird. *Migrating*—Neotropic passerines.

Best times to bird: Spring and fall.

Directions: From Corpus Christi, take Highway 35/U.S. Highway 181 north. Stay on Highway 35 when the roads split just north of Portland. Travel north 34 miles to Rockport. Take the second Rockport exit onto East Farm-to-Market 1069 and drive about 2 miles. The road curves to the left at Rockport Harbor and continues toward Fulton. From the curve it is 1.5 miles to the Rockport Demonstration Bird Garden and Wetlands Pond. The five-acre garden is on the right side of the road.

The birding

Business Highway 35 is being widened through Rockport. Although construction is affecting this site, all of the local groups involved feel that the postconstruction Demonstration Bird Garden and Wetlands Pond will be improved. The front of the garden has picnic tables. Currently, there are many ornamental trees that will be replaced by native trees and plants. These natives produce nectar, fruits, and berries, and are expected to encourage passerines and hummingbirds to stop at the park. There is a nineteen-stop 0.8 mile nature trail that will be restored after Highway 35 is no longer a work zone. In the past, this site was known as a prime spot for bird and butterfly watching. Let's hope it returns to its glory days.

In addition to the garden area, Aransas First has secured another five acres of land that will be designated the Tule Creek Nature Center. Currently, there is a boardwalk that extends over a wet slough and through a willow grove and an area covered in wild trumpet creeper.

General information: This was originally a state roadside park. Today it is a joint project of Texas Department of Transportation, Texas Parks and Wildlife, the City of Rockport, and Aransas First. This is CTC#50. It is wheelchair accessible.

DeLorme: Texas Atlas & Gazetteer: Page 85 8C.

Elevation: 20 feet.

Hazards: Fire ants.

Nearest food, gas, lodging: Rockport.

For more information: Texas Department of Transportation Travel and Information Division, P.O. Box 5064, Austin, TX 78763; (800) 452-9292.

Buff-bellied Hummingbird. PHOTO: TONY BAYLIS.

㊸ Rockport Beach Park and the Connie Hagar Wildlife Sanctuary

Habitats: Primary bay, secondary bay.

Specialty birds: *Resident*—Brown Pelican, Reddish Egret. *Fall/Winter*—Piping Plover. *Migrating*—Buff-breasted Sandpiper, Hudsonian Godwit.

Other key birds: *Resident*—Neotropic Cormorant, Mottled Duck, Roseate Spoonbill, Clapper Rail, American Oystercatcher, Gull-billed Tern. *Spring/Summer*—Magnificent Frigatebird, Wilson's Plover, Sandwich Tern, Common Tern. *Fall/Winter*—Common Loon, Marbled Godwit. *Migrating*—Shorebirds.

Best times to bird: Year-round.

Directions: Use Highway 35/U.S. Highway 181 to leave Corpus Christi via the Harbor Bridge. Continue north on Highway 35 when the roads split just north of Portland. Stay on Bypass Highway 35 to Rockport. Take the second Rockport exit for Farm-to-Market 1069. Turn right and go 2 miles on FM 1069. When the road curves to the left at Rockport Harbor, turn right on Seabreeze Drive. You will immediately see a large seashell-shaped sign advertising the park.

Black Skimmer on eggs. PHOTO: TONY BAYLIS.

The birding

Rockport Beach Park is a small public beach that often is very crowded. It has also been designated a wildlife sanctuary. No pets are allowed in the park.

Though small and crowded, this park is well known for its nesting Black Skimmers. Hundreds of Black Skimmers choose to nest here. No one is quite sure why they are willing to put up with all of the people who use this park, but they do. In the summer, close-up looks at young chicks and fledglings can be exciting. Other colonial water birds nest and breed here or on the Rookery Islands in nearby Little Bay. These include Least Terns, Tricolored Herons, Roseate Spoonbills, Great Blue Herons, Great Egrets, and Snowy Egrets.

The beachfront along Aransas Bay is about 1 mile long at this point. But it is the lagoon and islands in Little Bay on the mainland side that will most interest birders. At the far end of the park is a bird observation deck. Use a spotting scope from this deck to scan the rookeries of Little Bay during breeding season. At all times of the year, gulls, terns, herons, and pelicans come and go. In the winter, look for ducks such as Bufflehead, Lesser Scaup, and Canvasback. In 2004 a Long-tailed Duck was reported here. Shorebirds such as Sanderlings, Willets, Long-billed Curlews, sandpipers, and plovers may be seen on any given day.

General information: Rockport Beach Park is open daily from 5:00 A.M. to 11:00 P.M. Sunday to Thursday, to midnight Friday and Saturday. There is a fee. This is the only Texas-certified Blue Wave Beach, a national certification program designating clean and safe destinations. The park has many covered picnic tables, barbecue grills, restrooms, showers, boat ramps, and fishing pier. No overnight camping is allowed.

While in the Rockport-Fulton area, consider visiting the Fulton Mansion State Historic Site (361–729–0386) and the Texas Maritime Museum (866–729–9938).

DeLorme: Texas Atlas & Gazetteer: Page 85 8C.

Elevation: 20 feet.

Hazards: Fog.

Nearest food, gas, lodging: Rockport.

For more information: City of Rockport, 622 East Market, P.O. Box 1059, Rockport, TX 78381; (877) 929-7977, (361) 729-2213.

44 Boat Trips

Habitats: Marine.

Specialty birds: *Resident*—Brown Pelican, Black-bellied Whistling-Duck, White-faced Ibis. *Fall/Winter*—Whooping Crane, Peregrine Falcon, Piping Plover.

Other key birds: *Resident*—Neotropic Cormorant, Mottled Duck, Fulvous Whistling-Duck, Little Blue Heron, Roseate Spoonbill, American Oystercatcher, Gull-billed Tern, Seaside Spar-row. *Spring/Summer*—Magnificent Frigatebird, Sandwich Tern, Common Tern. *Fall/Winter*—Common Loon, Northern Gannet. *Migrating*—Shorebirds.

Best times to bird: November through March.

Directions: Boats leave from Port Aransas, Rockport, and Fulton Harbors. Please see Appendix C for a list of boat operators and their locations.

The birding

If you are serious about seeing Whooping Cranes, this is your best bet. These boats travel in the Intracoastal Waterway, Copano Bay, and Aransas Bay. Some have enclosed cabins and exterior viewing decks, snack bars, restrooms, and narration.

Obviously, it is impossible to guarantee a crane sighting, but the boats come as close as possible to the nesting grounds at the Aransas National Wildlife Refuge. Many other birds should be seen on the trip. Some will be in the water, others will fly over, and many will be seen on small islands or in marshy areas on the nearby shore. Think loons, grebes, cranes, gulls, terns, herons, egrets, ducks, ibis, pelicans, plovers, stilts, Peregrine Falcon, Osprey, Willets, cormorants, and sandpipers.

Because these boat trips are offered from November to March, the weather may be cold and wet, but I have never found these trips to be anything but exciting and enjoyable.

There are other types of boat trips available for those interested. The Jetty Boat is a passenger ferry that leaves from Fisherman's Wharf in Port Aransas for ten daily trips to St. Joseph Island. This is a privately owned island with no vehicular access. Most people go there to fish or beachcomb, but bird-watchers often find the island attractive.

When the Whooping Crane season is over, boats such as the *Wharf Cat* and *Scat Cat* revert to deep sea fishing trips. These go at least 50 miles out into the gulf. Bird-watchers can leave the rod and reel at home, and find they are welcomed aboard with binoculars for a chance to spot pelagics. Just remember that these trips are still planned with fishermen in mind. Also, many smaller boats, and some larger ones, can be chartered for trips that you design. In most cases, you would act as your own guide.

Whooping Crane. PHOTO: TONY BAYLIS.

Finally, kayaking is becoming more and more popular in the Coastal Bend, and I see more bird-watchers using these small boats to get close to water birds. Several operators in the area rent kayaks, and some give lessons or provide tours.

General information: All of these boat trips charge a fee. Some of the operators have worked in the area for many years and have an outstanding reputation; others are new. This business can be transitory. It is always best to call ahead and make reservations.

DeLorme: Texas Atlas & Gazetteer: Page 85 8E or 8C.

Elevation: Sea level.

Hazards: Fog, uncertain weather conditions, seasickness.

Nearest food, gas, lodging: Port Aransas, Rockport.

Camping: Mustang Island State Park; Port Aransas Park; Goose Island State Park.

For more information: See Appendix C for a list of boat operators. The Rockport Chamber of Commerce keeps a current list of boat and tour operators.

45 Copano Bay State Fishing Pier

Habitats: Primary bay.

Specialty birds: *Resident—*Brown Pelican.

Other key birds: *Resident—*Neotropic Cormorant, Mottled Duck, Fulvous Whistling-Duck, Black-bellied Whistling-Duck, Little Blue Heron, Roseate Spoonbill, American Oystercatcher, Gull-billed Tern. *Spring/Summer—*Sandwich Tern. *Fall/Winter—*Common Loon, Marbled Godwit. *Migrating—*Shorebirds.

Best times to bird: Fall, winter, spring.

Directions: Take Highway 35 north from Rockport. Once you leave Rockport, it is about 3.5 miles to the Copano Bay Causeway. The pier is actually the old bridge that once crossed the bay. You can exit at the south or north end of the causeway to park for the pier.

Common Loon. PHOTO: TONY BAYLIS.

The birding

Copano Bay is an extension of Aransas Bay. It was named after the Copane Indians of the area. The main reason for stopping here is to look for Common Loons, Eared and Horned Grebes, and many species of diving ducks in the winter. Copano is a large bay and probably the deepest one within the scope of this book. It therefore is home to waterfowl such as loons that are seen in only a few other places in the Coastal Bend. Expect pelicans, cormorants, gulls, and terns also.

Before entering the south end of the causeway, exit Highway 35 to the roadside opposite the pier onto a shell road that leads to a marshy area. Fishing occurs on this site, and often there are just too many people and no birds. But it can be productive for Buffleheads and Common Goldeneyes, shorebirds, and wading birds. There is a similar situation at the north end of the causeway. A small pond just off the highway is a reliable place to look for Fulvous Whistling-Ducks.

General information: The pier is operated as a concession for the Texas Parks and Wildlife Department. The pier, which is open only to pedestrians, was built in 1931 as a causeway. It now extends 1.5 miles across the bay, with the original drawbridge section having been removed. There is a charge per fishing pole to use the pier, but birders can enjoy themselves for free. Restrooms and concession stands are available at each entrance. The pier is lighted at night and is open twenty-four hours a day. This is CTC#49. it is wheelchair accessible.

DeLorme: Texas Atlas & Gazetteer: Page 85 9B and 9C.

Elevation: 10 feet.

Hazards: Fog, slippery.

Nearest food, gas, lodging: Rockport/Fulton.

Camping: Goose Island State Park.

For more information: Copano Bay State Fishing Pier Concession Operation, P.O. Box 39, Fulton, TX 78358; (361) 729-7762.

46 Goose Island State Park/Big Tree

Habitats: Oak savanna, oak woodland, primary bay, secondary bay.

Specialty birds: *Resident*–Least Grebe, Brown Pelican, Black-bellied Whistling-Duck, White-tailed Hawk, Reddish Egret, White-faced Ibis, Common Pauraque, Buff-bellied Hummingbird, Golden-fronted Woodpecker, Long-billed Thrasher. *Spring/Summer*–Wood Stork, Scissor-tailed Flycatcher, Cave Swallow. *Fall/Winter*–Whooping Crane, Piping Plover, Vermilion Flycatcher.

Other key birds: *Resident*–Neotropic Cormorant, Mottled Duck, Fulvous Whistling-Duck, Crested Caracara, Little Blue Heron, Roseate Spoonbill, Clapper Rail, Amercian Oystercatcher, Gull-billed Tern, Inca Dove, Ladder-backed Woodpecker, Bronzed Cowbird, Seaside Sparrow. *Spring/Summer*–Magnificent Frigatebird, Wilson's Plover, Sandwich Tern, Painted Bunting. *Fall/Winter*–Common Loon, Greater White-fronted Goose, Marbled Godwit, Rufous Hummingbird, Nelson's Sharp-tailed Sparrow. *Migrating*–Shorebirds, Neotropic Migrant Trap.

Best times to bird: Year-round.

Directions: Take Highway 35/U.S. Highway 181 out of Corpus Christi and north over the Harbor Bridge. When the road divides just north of Portland, stay on Highway 35. Continue on Highway 35 as it bypasses Rockport. At the end of the bypass, return to Business Highway 35 and turn north to cross the Copano Bay Causeway. Once on the other side of the causeway, turn right at the first road, Park Road 13. Travel 1.3 miles to a stop sign. Turn left to go to the Big Tree section of Goose Island State Park. Travel 0.9 mile down Twelfth Street, take a right, and go 0.4 mile to the tree on the left.

When you reach the main section of Goose Island State Park, take a right at the stop sign and go 0.4 mile to the park entrance. Don't be fooled; it seems as though you are going into a residential area. There are plenty of signs to guide you.

The birding

Be sure to make one of your stops at Goose Island State Park to see the Big Tree. This live oak is at least 1,000 years old, and some say it could be 2,000 years old. At any rate, it is old and big. The tree is 44 feet high with a crown spread of 89 feet, and it is 35 feet in circumference. It is also known as the Lamar Oak (it is on Lamar Peninsula), the Bishop's Oak, and the Goose Island Oak. It is recognized as the Texas State Champion Coastal Live Oak. You really have to see it to believe it.

There can be good birding at the Big Tree. I've seen American Kestrels there, Northern Cardinals, Northern Mockingbirds, Black-crested Titmice, flycatchers, and migrants in the spring. This is an excellent place to seek out sparrows such as Vesper, Lincoln's, Savannah, Song, White-throated, and Field. In 2004 a White-breasted Nuthatch was seen at the tree, which is very rare for South Texas. You can continue on the road past the tree for a different look at St. Charles Bay. Occasionally, a Whooping Crane can be seen on the shoreline.

The main section of the park encompasses two very different habitats. The bayfront sites are on the island that divides St. Charles Bay from Aransas Bay. Of the 150 acres in this section of the park, only 17 are above sea level. The rest is marsh. Here the bird-watcher will see the typical shorebirds and wading birds. One of the best areas for these birds is the marsh to the left, just past the bait stand and bridge. Look for egrets such as the Reddish Egret, herons, and Roseate Spoonbills. In the marshes, Virginia and Clapper Rails and Sora have been noted, and this is a good site to try for the elusive Seaside Sparrow. From the bay shore, pelicans, gulls, terns, and cormorants can be seen. On a good day, you can spot American Oystercatchers and Black Skimmers. The park fishing pier is a fine place to use a scope to scan for birds that eschew the shore. In the winter, many dabbling and diving ducks can be seen, and perhaps Common Loons as well.

The wooded area of the park on the mainland presents a different bird picture. Here oak woodlands and savannas prevail. The park is laced with paved roads leading to numerous campsites. These make fine hiking paths for birders. One road is even called Warbler Way. Additionally, the ½-mile Turk's Cap Trail leads through typical habitat for Inca Doves, Painted Buntings, Bewick's Wrens, Brown Thrashers, and Gray Catbirds. Start this trail at the parking lot near campsite 157. The trail uses crushed shell for the pathway. Several benches are available along the way, but the walk is easy and pleasant.

A sign at the trailhead states that thirty species of warblers have been spotted on the trail. This would certainly be possible during spring migration. The trail is aptly named, as there is an abundance of Turk's caps. Hummingbirds are especially drawn to these plants.

Along the Turk's Caps Trail, you pass some very large and lovely live oaks as well as a cattail pond. Wildflowers blanket some areas in the spring and early summer. There are savannas where the birder should pay attention for sparrows. The trail ends at another parking lot on Lantana Loop. Be sure to walk down Warbler Way when returning to your car. First, it is the shortest way; second, it goes past the bird sanctuary operated by the Friends of Goose Island State Park. Sit and watch the seed lovers who stop by for a snack.

General information: Goose Island State Park is open daily from 6:00 A.M. to 10:00 P.M. for day use. There is a fee. The park has overnight camping in shade campsites on the water's edge and in the oak woodlands. There is a small gift shop, recreation hall, showers and restrooms, boat ramp, and a 1,620-foot lighted fishing pier. From January through April, guided bird walks are offered at the park.

The land for this park was acquired in the 1930s, and the Civilian Conservation Corp did the initial work at the park. Goose Island State Park has come a long way since those early days. It is one of five state parks involved in a pilot program that provides wireless Internet access in state park campgrounds. Another ongoing project is the construction of a 4,400-foot breakwater to stop the erosion on the island. Spoil from the construction of the containment levees will be used to increase the marsh. The area will be planted with native grasses. This work should benefit bird-watchers in the future.

No one knows for sure how the island got the name Goose Island. There are two theories. One theory relates to the abundance of geese in the area, the other considers the idea that from the air, the island resembles a goose. Take your pick. This park is CTC#48. Some parts of the park are wheelchair accessible. Call for details.

DeLorme: Texas Atlas & Gazetteer: Page 85 9B.

Elevation: 20 feet.

Hazards: Fire ants, mosquitoes, gnats, snakes, alligators, fog, high tides.

Nearest food, gas, lodging: Rockport.

Camping: Goose Island State Park.

For more information: Goose Island State Park, 202 South Palmetto Street, Rockport, TX 78382; (361) 729-2858.

47 Aransas National Wildlife Refuge (IBA)

Habitats: Prairie, oak savanna, oak woodland, primary bay, freshwater marshes and ponds.

Specialty birds: *Resident*—Least Grebe, Brown Pelican, Reddish Egret, White-faced Ibis, Groove-billed Ani, Common Pauraque, Buff-bellied Hummingbird, Cassin's Sparrow, Golden-fronted Woodpecker. *Spring/Summer*—Wood Stork. *Fall/Winter*—Whooping Crane, Peregrine Falcon, Piping Plover, Sprague's Pipit. *Migrating*—Swallow-tailed Kite, American Golden Plover.

Other key birds: *Resident*—Neotropic Cormorant, Mottled Duck, Black-bellied Whistling-Duck, White-tailed Kite, Crested Caracara, Little Blue Heron, Roseate Spoonbill, Clapper Rail, American Oystercatcher, Gull-billed Tern, Inca Dove, Seaside Sparrow. *Spring/Summer*—Anhinga, Wilson's Plover, Sandwich Tern, Common Tern, Scissor-tailed Flycatcher, Painted Bunting. *Fall/Winter*—Common Loon, Greater White-fronted Goose, Ross's Goose, Nelson's Sharp-tailed Sparrow, Marbled Godwit. *Migrating*—Raptors, shorebirds, Neotropic passerines.

Best times to bird: Fall, winter, spring.

Directions: From Rockport, take Highway 35 north for 19 miles. Turn right onto Farm-to-Market Road 774 and travel for 9 miles. Turn right and follow FM 2040 for 7 miles to the refuge entrance. There are signs at each turn.

The birding

The people of Texas, especially the birders of the Coastal Bend, are very fortunate to have access to the beautiful Aransas Wildlife Refuge, which encompasses over 58,000 acres. It is indeed a wonderful and exciting place to visit, and nature lovers from the United States and around the world avail themselves of the opportunity. The park opens at sunrise and closes at sunset. The visitor center is open from 8:30 A.M. to 4:30 P.M.

Start your adventure at the Wildlife Interpretive Center, where you pay the entrance fee and pick up a bird checklist. The list includes the 406 species recorded at the refuge. This is the second highest count of any national refuge. You also find bird specimens in a small museum, along with a 12-minute film, which gives information about the history of the refuge. The center houses a small gift shop and restrooms.

Begin your wildlife viewing right at the visitor center. Some water is nearby in a small reservoir. Across the road from the visitor center is Thomas Slough. Check it out for American alligators. The slough, lined in black willows, is fenced off, but you can easily sit at the nearby picnic area and scan the area for birds that like freshwater marsh habitat.

Not far from the center is the Rail Trail. It is a short, 0.3 mile trail beside a freshwater cattail marsh. Listen and look for rails, of course, American coots, Common Moorhens, Pied-billed Grebes, Purple Gallinules, and bitterns. In the spring,

From Dagger Point in the Aransas National Wildlife Refuge.

Yellow-billed Cuckoos and many songbirds stop here. The Rail Trail connects with the Heron Flats Trail at the beginning of the 16-mile auto loop.

Heron Flats Trail has a little of everything, including larger trees, scrub brush, freshwater marsh areas, a shell ridge, and saltwater tidal flats. The trail is 1.4 miles long and includes two observation platforms. If your time at the refuge is limited, give Heron Flats Trail serious consideration. In recent years, a Whooping Crane family has occasionally used the salt marsh area near this trail, and you can get a fine look at them. The park keeps a close eye on the cranes and passes along information to visitors. If you are interested specifically in the Whooping Cranes, check at the visitor center. On the tidal flats you will also see Roseate Spoonbills, White Pelicans, Willets, Dunlins, American Oystercatchers, gulls, terns, ducks, herons, and egrets. In the upland section of the Heron Flats Trail look for passerines such as Northern Cardinals, Brown Thrashers, White-eyed Vireos, Gray Catbird, Carolina Wren, and Northern Mockingbirds. Turk's cap with its red flowers draws in hummingbirds. During spring migration, vireos, warblers, and tanagers should be plentiful.

Next on the tour loop is Birding Trail 1. This short, 0.1-mile trail leads the birder in a loop through some oaks. Spring and fall migrating warblers and tanagers love these trees. You may also try for Yellow-billed Cuckoos, Inca Doves, Ladder-backed Woodpeckers, and Cassin's Sparrows at this site. Farther along the auto route and past the picnic area is the first bay overlook.

The bay overlook is Dagger Point, your next stop. The hike to this overlook is 1 mile. The shoreline is eroding here, and it is very interesting to see live oaks "sliding" over the edge. In the 1980s it became apparent that the refuge was losing as much as twenty-five acres a year to erosion. Projects are ongoing to stabilize the area. From Dagger Point, Eared and sometimes Horned Grebes can be seen. Willets, Dunlin, and various sandpipers feed near the shoreline.

Continuing the auto loop, the next 0.6-mile trail is called Bird Trail 2. The trail passes through mixed grasslands, where you should look for Loggerhead Shrikes, Savannah Sparrows, and White-throated Sparrows. Farther on you encounter oak woodlands and a small pond with a photo blind. Here is chance to find the rare Cassin's and Seaside Sparrows. Also watch for Ruddy Ducks, Merlin, Cooper's and Sharp-shinned Hawks.

A short distance from Birding Trail 2, on the other side of the road, is Jones Lake. A paved walk leads to a platform overlooking the lake. This lake can nearly dry up in drought conditions. If there is water in Jones Lake, the bird life has the potential to be abundant. Search for egrets and herons, especially Black-crowned Night Herons, Roseate Spoonbills, Purple Gallinules, American Coots, bitterns, and rails. If the lake is really full, White-faced Ibis and Least Grebe are possibilities. In the winter, ducks such as Blue-winged and Green-winged Teal, Mottled and Ring-necked Ducks use the lake.

Your final stop brings you to the parking lot of the Observation Tower. From there you may choose the boardwalk, which leads to the 0.7-mile Big Tree Trail, or you can cross the road to the 0.9-mile Hog Lake Trail.

The boardwalk leads you down to the salt marsh for water birds such as Great Blue Herons, White Pelicans, and Long-billed Curlews, and perhaps a flyover by a Magnificent Frigatebird. In late summer, expect Wood Storks. The Big Tree Trail proceeds into live oaks and a very large tree with a wonderful umbrella-like canopy. Watch for Brown-crested Flycatchers and Long-billed Thrashers.

If you choose Hog Lake, use the platform to look out over the alligators. American Bitterns have been noted around the lake edges. Check the brush around Hog Lake for Inca Doves, Scissor-tailed Flycatchers, and migrants like Blue Grosbeaks and Painted Buntings.

The 40-foot Observation Tower puts the birder in the perfect position to observe both San Antonio Bay and Mustang Lake. Everyone is here to see the Whooping Cranes. From November to April, your chances are good. While you are observing from the tower, look for Double-crested Cormorants, Brown Pelicans, Magnificent Frigatebirds, Redheads, Lesser Scaups, and Buffleheads.

ABOUT THE WHOOPING CRANES

Numbering about 450 worldwide, the Whooping Crane is the rarest crane. In 1941 there were only fifteen remaining birds. Their decline is mostly attributed to loss of habitat and uncontrolled hunting. Today, 128 Whooping Cranes are in captivity at various locations such as zoos. There are another seventy-nine or so cranes in a nonmigratory flock in Florida, and about forty-seven cranes in Wisconsin.

In 2005 an all-time high of 217 Whooping Cranes migrated to the Aransas National Wildlife Refuge from their summer home at the Wood Buffalo National Park in Canada (the number declined slightly to 214 in 2006). This Canadian nesting ground of the whoopers was only discovered in 1954 by a pilot of a fire crew. The birds are protected, while nesting, by the Canadian Wildlife Service (CWS). The CWS reported fifty-four nesting pairs that fledged forty chicks in 2004. When the cranes migrate the 2,500 miles from Canada to the Aransas National Wildlife Refuge, they do stop along the way to rest and feed.

Whooping Cranes stand nearly 5 feet tall, with a wing span of 7 feet. Their average weight is 15 pounds. They fly at a speed of 35 to 45 miles per hour. Whoopers live as long as twenty-five years. Cranes mate for life, with unusual rituals of calling, head bowing, and tremendous leaps.

Whooping Cranes eat crayfish, clams, frogs, grains, and berries. Their favorite food, however, is the blue crab. The population of blue crabs is greatly affected by the inflow of freshwater into marshy areas. Consequently, cranes thrive in wetter years, eating as many as eighty crabs a day. The availability of blue crabs directly influences the success of the following breeding season for the Whooping Cranes. At night, the cranes stand in shallow water for protection. It is now predicted that by the fall of 2020, the Whooping Crane flock wintering at Aransas will number over 400.

Beyond the tower parking lot, the auto loop turns into a one-way road and winds through wild country for another 11 miles. On your way out, if it is winter, look for Sandhill Cranes, Northern Bobwhites, Wild Turkey, Red-tailed Hawks, and Northern Harriers.

With the many bird possibilities, you should have no problem enjoying yourself. The refuge also has other animals: deer, feral hogs, javelinas, coyotes, bobcats, raccoons, alligators, turtles, frogs, snakes, and armadillo. There is no camping in the refuge, but there are several places to picnic. Most of the sanctuary is actually closed to the public in order to protect the Whooping Cranes. For the same reason, fishing is not allowed when the cranes are in winter residence.

There is a smaller detached unit of the refuge that you should not miss. Stop at this site on your way to the Aransas National Wildlife Refuge or as you return to Rockport. Tatton Wildlife Watching Trail is on Highway 35 north out of Rockport. At mile 16, look for a picnic area on the right after crossing Salt Creek. At the side of this picnic area is the entrance to the Tatton Wildlife Watching Trail. The 0.3-mile trail leads through the coastal prairie to a boardwalk and overlook. In this area, the U.S. Fish and Wildlife Service has reintroduced Aplomado Falcons. It is also a place to try for the elusive Cassin's Sparrow. White-tailed Kites and Short-eared Owls have been spotted here as well. Good luck in finding some of these rarities.

General information: There is no moving water on the Blackjack Peninsula; groundwater and rain provide the water for the lakes, marshes, and ponds that you encounter in the refuge. The peninsula juts out between San Antonio Bay and St. Charles Bay. It is named for the blackjack oaks that grow there. Many different types of trees are found at Aransas NWR, including black willow, live oak, mesquite, and hackberry.

As for the name *Aransas,* it is actually an anglicized version of the Basque phrase "Aranza zu," meaning "You are sitting in thorns." According to a legend, the Virgin Mary appeared to a Basque shepherd in 1740. The vision appeared in a thorn bush and became known as the Lady of Aranza zu, or Our Lady of Thorns. In 1746 Captain Basterra explored the coast of the Gulf of Mexico for Spain. The coastal natives used a word that sounded to Basterra like the Basque word *aranza.* This name was later given by Basterra's commander to an early fort on Live Oak Peninsula.

President Franklin Roosevelt signed the law establishing the 47,261-acre Aransas Migratory Waterfowl Refuge in 1937. The Tatton Unit addition in 1967 of 7,568 acres enlarged the refuge to 54,829. The Lamar Unit and the Whitmire Unit added 734 acres and 3,000 acres, respectively. Matagorda Island National Wildlife Refuge, covering 56,500 acres, is on the barrier island opposite Aransas NWR. The only way to reach Matagorda Island is via a pedestrian ferry from Port O'Conner, which is north of the scope of this book. Aransas National Wildlife Refuge is CTC#37. Some trails are wheelchair accessible. Call for details.

DeLorme: Texas Atlas & Gazetteer: Page 85 9B.

Elevation: Less than 150 feet.

Hazards: Mosquitoes, chiggers, poison ivy, snakes, fire ants, slippery walks.

Nearest food, gas, lodging: There is no food available at the refuge nor at the nearby town of Austwell. You will need to bring a picnic or plan to return to Rockport or Tivoli.

Camping: Goose Island State Park (there is no camping in the refuge).

For more information: Aransas National Wildlife Refuge, P.O. Box 100, Austwell, TX 77950; (361) 286-3559.

By appointment only

Guadalupe Delta Wildlife Management Area

Habitats: Estuaries, tall riparian forest, transitional riparian forest.

Specialty birds: *Resident*—Brown Pelican, Black-bellied Whistling-Duck, White-tailed Kite, White-tailed Hawk, Reddish Egret, White-faced Ibis, Long-billed Thrasher. *Spring/Summer*—Wood Stork, Brown-crested Flycatcher, Scissor-tailed Flycatcher, Cave Swallow. *Fall/Winter*—Whooping Crane, Peregrine Falcon, Piping Plover. *Migrating*—Buff-breasted Sandpiper.

Other key birds: *Resident*—Neotropic Cormorant, Mottled Duck, Fulvous Whistling-Duck, Crested Caracara, Little Blue Heron, Roseate Spoonbill, Clapper Rail, Gull-billed Tern, Ladder-backed Woodpecker, Seaside Sparrow. *Spring/Summer*—Anhinga, Wilson's Plover, Sandwich Tern, Lesser Nighthawk, Painted Bunting. *Fall/Winter*—Tundra Swan, Greater White-fronted Goose, Ross's Goose, Marbled Godwit, Nelson's Sharp-tailed Sparrow. *Migrating*—Shorebirds, Neotropic passerines.

Best times to bird: Year-round.

Directions: Take Highway 35/U.S. Highway 181 out of Corpus Christi and over the Harbor Bridge. When the highways divide just north of Portland, stay on Highway 35 all the way to the small town of Tivoli. It will be about an hour's drive north up the coast. Continue on Highway 35 through Tivoli for 4.8 miles to the Guadalupe Delta overlook on the right (east) side of the road. This overlook of the fresh-

water marsh is just the tip of the preserve. The Guadalupe Delta Wildlife Management Area consists of 7,200 acres in four units.

The Mission Bay Unit is near the overlook platform. Turn back on Highway 35 toward Tivoli and take the first dirt road to the left. This is about 0.1 mile from the platform. This unit consists of rich habitat from the freshwater flooding of the Guadalupe River and adjacent bayous.

Continue on Highway 35 toward Tivoli for 0.2 mile and cross Hog Bayou. The entrance to Hog Bayou Unit is another dirt road on the east side of Highway 35.

To reach the Hynes Bay Unit, return to Tivoli. At Highway 239 take a left onto Landgraph Road. Travel for 0.3 mile and turn right down Austwell Road for exactly 2 miles. The entrance to Hynes Bay Unit is a little hard to see, as it is off the road. Austwell Road curves, and on the left is a fenced area up on a mound. The entrance is to the side of this mound. It is marked, as are all of the entrances to the other units.

The San Antonio River Unit is west of Tivoli. At the intersection of Highway 35 and Highway 239 in Tivoli, there is a blinking light. Turn west onto Highway 239 and travel 0.6 mile to Bissett Street. Turn right. The road twists, turns, and narrows. At 0.3 mile it turns into a gravel road. Continue another 0.7 mile to the entrance.

The birding

Each of the four units offers different habitat, therefore different birds.

The Mission Bay Unit, sometimes referred to as the Buffalo Lake Unit (4,447 acres), on the north side of the Guadalupe River features beautiful freshwater wetlands created by overflow from the river. This area experiences natural flooding, as it must have been before Texas rivers were so heavily dammed. At this unit you see

Black-necked Stilts, American Avocets, Little Blue Herons, Lesser and Greater Yellowlegs, Tricolored Herons, Purple Gallinule, and Anhingas. Cattails hide Clapper Rails and Sora, while giving a place for Red-wing Blackbirds to land. In this unit, many species of ducks spend the winter. Peregrine Falcons and White-tailed Hawks thrive here. Several years ago there was a nesting pair of Bald Eagles at the Mission Bay Unit. This is most likely the only site mentioned in this book to spot Boat-tailed Grackles. Check for their darker eye and song that is much different from the Common and Great-tailed Grackle.

The Hog Bayou Unit (1,138 acres) on the south side of the Guadalupe River is made up of tall pecan and elm trees. This is also the place to keep a diligent eye open for poison ivy. Two nonnatives are finding some success at this site: the Chinese tallow and the Cherokee rose. Look in this tall riparian habitat for Red-bellied Woodpeckers, White-eyed Vireos, Brown and Long-billed Thrashers, Black-crested Titmice, Carolina Chickadees, Ruby-throated Hummingbirds, and migrating warblers.

The Hynes Bay Unit (1,007 acres), east of Tivoli, begins with mesquite in the uplands, drops into coastal prairie, and finally changes into saltwater marsh. Here

Fulvous Whistling-Ducks. PHOTO: TONY BAYLIS.

you'll find swallows, Seaside Sparrow, plovers, sandpipers, Brown Pelicans, Reddish Egrets, ibis, gulls, terns, and more ducks.

The San Antonio River Unit (700 acres) also includes riparian habitat but on a smaller scale. Birds you might find here include Belted Kingfishers, Barred Owls, Northern Mockingbirds, Loggerhead Shrikes, Eastern Wood-Pewees, Carolina Wrens, and Painted Buntings.

General information: Guadalupe Delta Wildlife Management Area is available by appointment only. Visitors must have either an annual public hunting permit or a limited public use permit.

Land was first purchased for this preserve beginning in 1985. The preserve is funded by the Pittman/Robertson Fund from a tax on sporting goods. Staff biologists use a variety of active management plans to increase usable habitats. However, there is not enough staff available to keep this wildlife area open on a full-time basis. In the fall, duck hunting is permitted on certain dates on a first come, first served basis. Limited hunting for deer, feral hogs, and alligator is through drawings. Birding tours for larger groups can be arranged through the Texas Parks and Wildlife Department. This is CTC#36.

DeLorme: Texas Atlas & Gazetteer: Page 79 10J.

Elevation: Less than 150 feet.

Hazards: Fire ants, snakes, poison ivy.

Nearest food, gas, lodging: Food and gas in Tivoli; return to Rockport for lodging.

For more information: Guadalupe Delta WMA-Texas Parks and Wildlife Department, 2601 North Azalea, Suite 31, Victoria, TX 77901; (361) 576-0022, (361) 790-0308.

Goliad/Refugio

Steeped in Texas history and characterized by tall riparian forests, this part of the Coastal Bend is like no other. The Mission, Guadalupe, and San Antonio Rivers have etched the landscape at these sites. Rich soils and gallery forests dominate this northern end of the Coastal Bend. The birds found at these ranches and parks are different from those in the other regions of this book. Bird-watchers can locate Amercian Crows, Tufted Titmice, Carolina Chickadees, and Downy Woodpeckers.

49. Egery Flats/Black Point/Mission River Flats
50. Fennessey Ranch
51. Womack Family Ranch
52. Lion's/Shelly City Park
53. Angel of Goliad Hike and Bike Trail
54. Goliad State Park
55. Coleto Creek Reservoir and Park

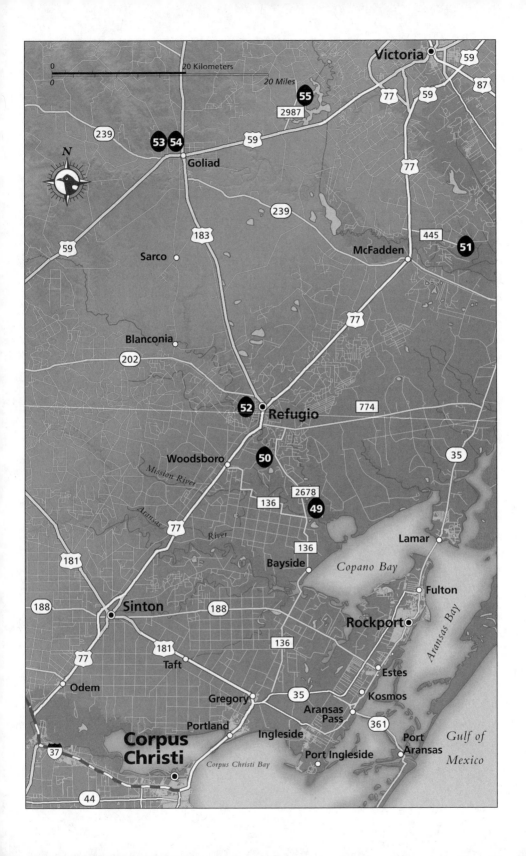

49 Egery Flats/Black Point/Mission River Flats

Habitats: Tamaulipan thorn scrub, prairie, estuary, secondary bay.

Specialty birds: *Resident*—Brown Pelican, Black-bellied Whistling-Duck, Reddish Egret, White-faced Ibis. *Spring/Summer*—Wood Stork, Cave Swallows. *Fall/Winter*—Peregrine Falcon, Piping Plover. *Migrating*—Buff-breasted Sandpiper.

Other key birds: *Resident*—Neotropic Cormorant, Mottled Duck, Fulvous Whistling-Duck, Crested Caracara, Little Blue Heron, Roseate Spoonbill, Clapper Rail, American Oystercatcher, Gull-billed Tern, Inca Dove, Seaside Sparrow. *Spring/Summer*—Magnificent Frigatebird, Sandwich Tern, Common Tern. *Fall/Winter*—Marbled Godwit, Nelson's Sharp-tailed Sparrow. *Migrating*—Raptors, shorebirds.

Best times to bird: Year-round.

Directions: From Corpus Christi, take Highway 35/U.S. Highway 181 north over the Harbor Bridge. When the two highways split, stay on Highway 35. The highway passes over Gregory. About 3 miles out of Gregory it intersects with Highway 136. Turn left toward Bayside/Refugio. It is 13 miles from this intersection to Bayside. Just before Bayside there is a causeway over Copano Bay. Turn right onto Egery Island Road just before the causeway. This road is 2 miles long.

On the north side of the causeway, drivers must exit to enter the town of Bayside. Following the exit, the first narrow road to the right is Black Point Road. This road is about ½ mile long. At the end of Black Point, turn right onto Salt Flat Road. This circles near the bay and ends at the Evans Bait Stand and RV Park.

Continue on Highway 136, which turns off to the left after 4 miles. Continue straight on Highway 2678 for another 2 miles to cross the Mission River.

The birding

These three birding sites are centered on the town of Bayside, and they are very similar to each other. The Egery Flats site follows a country road, with the Aransas River and Copano Bay to the left and prairie to the right. When it dead-ends, some of the habitat is Tamaulipan thorn scrub. Black Point takes you to the opposite shore of the river and the bay. The Mission River Flats site is on the bay north of Bayside.

All of these sites are good locations for a scope. If the tide is out, peeps, sandpipers, and plovers crowd the shore. Wading birds and shorebirds, such as egrets, Roseate Spoonbills, Marbled Godwits, Long-billed Dowitchers, American Avocets, Black-necked Stilts, Long-billed Curlews, and herons, are looking for a meal. At all three sites in the winter, you should see abundant species of ducks. In the summer, look for Wood Storks. The shallow waters encourage the terns to feed here. In early spring, look for migrating Black Terns. Later you should find Caspian, Royal, Sandwich, Gull-billed, and Least Terns. Laughing Gulls are ever present, as are Osprey.

In the marshes and prairie sections, watch for birds such as Seaside Sparrow and Nelson's Sharp-tailed Sparrow flying up from the grasses. Search the edges of the marshes for bitterns and rails.

Bayside sits on a bluff. This bluff acts as a conduit for updrafts. Hawks come this way in the fall to ride the air currents. Especially after an early October cold front, look for Cooper's and Sharp-shinned Hawks, as well as American Kestrel, Merlin, and Peregrine Falcons. Northern Harriers use the prairie areas for hunting. Even Harris and Red-tailed Hawks can be seen along the road.

General information: Egery Flats is CTC#44. Black Point, which was an old Spanish landing place, was the original name of the settlement that is now Bayside. Black Point is CTC#43. Be careful at the Mission River Flats site, as parking and access near the river are limited. The Mission River Flats is CTC#42.

DeLorme: Texas Atlas & Gazetteer: Page 85 7B and 7C.

Elevation: 15 feet.

Hazards: Traffic, fog.

Nearest food, gas, lodging: Food and gas in Bayside; lodging in Refugio.

For more information: City of Bayside, P.O. Box 194, Bayside, TX 78340; (361) 529-6520.

50 Fennessey Ranch

Habitats: Tamaulipan thorn scrub, tall riparian forest, freshwater lakes, prairie.

Specialty birds: *Resident*—Least Grebe, Black-bellied Whistling-Duck, White-tailed Kite, Harris' Hawk, Reddish Egret, White-faced Ibis, Groove-billed Ani, Common Pauraque, Buff-bellied Hummingbird, Green Kingfisher, Golden-fronted Woodpecker, Great Kiskadee, Couch's Kingbird, Green Jay, Long-billed Thrasher. *Spring/Summer*—Wood Stork, Brown-crested Flycatcher, Scissor-tailed Flycatcher, Cave Swallow. *Fall/Winter*—Piping Plover, Vermilion Flycatcher, Sprague's Pipit. *Migrating*—Buff-breasted Sandpiper, Hudsonian Godwit.

Other key birds: *Resident*—Neotropic Cormorant, Mottled Duck, Fulvous Whistling-Duck, Crested Caracara, Little Blue Heron, Roseate Spoonbill, Gull-billed Tern, Inca Dove, Ladder-backed Woodpecker, Bronzed Cowbird, Pyrrhuloxia, Seaside Sparrow. *Spring/Summer*—Anhinga, Wilson's Plover, Lesser Nighthawk, Painted Bunting. *Fall/Winter*—Tundra Swan, Greater White-fronted Goose, Marbled Godwit, Rufous Hummingbird, Nelson's Sharp-tailed Sparrow. *Migrating*—Raptors, shorebirds, Neotropic passerines

Best times to bird: Fall and spring.

Directions: From Corpus Christi, take Highway 35/U.S. Highway 181 north over the Harbor Bridge. When the two highways split, stay on Highway 35, which passes over Gregory. About 3 miles out of Gregory, it intersects with Highway 136. Turn left toward Bayside/Refugio. It is 13 miles from this intersection to the town of Bayside. Just past Bayside is a historical cemetery that is a quiet spot to look for songbirds. Five miles past Bayside, Highway 136 turns off to the left. The road that continues straight ahead is Farm-to-Market 2678. Stay on FM 2678 for another 5 miles, crossing the Mission River as you go. The Fennessey Ranch is on the left, with a sign at the entrance.

I prefer going through Bayside, which allows you to drive along the back side of Copano Bay and offers many chances to see birds. You could also take U.S. Highway 77 from Corpus Christi to Refugio. At the first stoplight upon entering Refugio, turn right on Farm-to-Market 774. After 1.5 miles turn right on FM 2678 and travel another 1.6 miles to the Fennessey Ranch gate on the right.

The birding

The Texas state motto is "Friendship." If you want to experience true Texas friendship and hospitality, then plan your birding trip for Fennessey Ranch, where the ranch guide encourages visitors to "have more fun."

The birding tours start at the ranch entrance, where participants leave their cars and ride on a specially outfitted trailer. A ranch guide and a birding expert accompany the group. The ranch guide is in contact with the truck driver by way of a walkie-talkie. The rig is stopped quickly when a bird is spotted. The driver also wears binoculars and will stop if he spots something ahead. Often the motor is turned off so birdcalls can be heard. At many locations, participants get off the trailer and walk to search out target birds. You'll be happy to know that several restroom breaks are planned. (Note: These tours are not planned with birders with handicaps in mind. However, if you are able to climb three steps onto the trailer, this trip would be feasible.)

The route of the tours on this 3,500-acre ranch varies depending on the weather and what bird life has previously been seen. Your first stop might be Kaiser Flats, a ninety-acre natural wetland/marsh. During droughts, the ranch pumps in water to maintain at least ten acres of wetland for use by birds and other wildlife. Here you should spot water-loving birds—swallows, herons, egrets, gulls, Roseate Spoonbills, Little Blue Herons, White and White-faced Ibis, and Anhingas. There is always a chance for a Glossy Ibis as well. Other wetlands and oxbow lakes on the ranch are more ephemeral.

Much of the ranch is Tamaulipan thorn scrub, with mesquite, huisache, and retama trees. Some of the area is leased for cattle ranching, and the ranch is also an active oil and gas field. To keep cattle in or out of certain areas, electric fences are used instead of barbed wire. This is done so that the flow of wildlife is not impeded. In the thorn scrub you should see fifty or sixty species of birds if the weather cooperates. Of course, there will be Northern Cardinals and Northern Mockingbirds. The symbol of the ranch, the Crested Caracara, will most likely be seen as well as heard giving his "prehistoric" call. Look for Carolina Wrens, Scissor-tailed Flycatchers, Brown-crested Flycatchers, Green Jays, and Long-billed Thrashers. The trip will cross some prairie land. Eighteen species of sparrows have been listed on the Fennessey Ranch, including Grasshopper, Le Conte's, White-crowned, and Song. You might even surprise a Sprague's Pipit. In or near the wetlands, Seaside and Swamp Sparrows also have been seen.

The driver stops at a location that allows easy viewing of the Mission River. This 26-mile river is the second shortest in Texas. Nine miles of the river run through the ranch. Mission River does occasionally flood. During spring migration, here would be a fine spot to search the tall trees for colorful birds such as Blue Grosbeak, Indigo Bunting, Baltimore and Orchard Oriole, Summer Tanager, Yellow-headed Blackbird, Great Kiskadee, Green Kingfisher, and the seven vireos and thirty-one warblers on the ranch list. At the river stop, a mid-morning snack is offered.

The ranch runs a separate wildflower tour. On the birding trips, however, there are enough flowers to satisfy even the most diligent horticulturist. You will notice bluebonnets, spider lilies, prickly poppies, lantana, black-eyed susans, scarlet sage, spiderwort, wine cups, huisache daisies, rattlesnake master, and Mexican hats. In places with deep sand, the wildflowers really flourish. You see many varieties of trees as well: hackberry, cedar elm, box elder, and pecan.

For lunch, the group takes a break at McGuill Lake. Enjoy the meal, especially the dessert from Crofutt Sandwich Shop and Bakery in Bayside. Be sure to check the lake for waterbirds, including Purple Gallinules and Least Bitterns.

In September the ranch offers a hawk and hummer tour. In the spring, look for encounters with Ruby-throated, Black-chinned, and Buff-bellied Hummingbirds and Cooper's, Swainson's, and Red-shouldered Hawks or even a Northern Harrier.

In addition to birds, butterflies, and wildflowers, the visitor may startle turtles, rabbits, raccoons, snakes, alligators, armadillo, bobcats, feral hogs, deer, and cougar.

Recently, three photo blinds have been constructed. Photographers are encouraged to lease the ranch for daily photo shoots. The ranch participates in the Elderhostel program, and other groups are welcome by special arrangements.

General information: The birding tours are by reservation only, and a fee is charged. Rained-out trips are rescheduled. Other available activities on the ranch include kayaking, night campouts, and photo workshops. As of 2006, the fee was $48.50 for a full day, including a fabulous lunch.

Brien O'Connor Dunn, who owns the ranch, won the National Wetland Award for Land Stewardship in 1997. The ranch participates in the Coastal Bend Wildlife Photo Contest sponsored by the Coastal Bend Wildlife Habitat Education Program. The original owner, a Mexican land grant recipient, was named Fennessey. McGuill Lake was named for another Mexican land grantee from Ireland. This is CTC#41.

DeLorme: Texas Atlas & Gazetteer: Page 85 7B.

Elevation: 20 feet.

Hazards: Thorns, snakes.

Nearest food, gas, lodging: Refugio.

Camping: Lion's/Shelly Park and Jeter RV Park.

For more information: Fennessey Ranch, P.O. Box 99, Bayside, TX 78340; (361) 529-6600.

51 Womack Family Ranch

Habitats: Tall riparian forest, prairie, freshwater ponds and marshes, agricultural areas.

Specialty birds: *Resident*—Least Grebe, Brown Pelican, Black-bellied Whistling-Duck, White-tailed Kite, White-tailed Hawk, White-faced Ibis, Green Kingfisher, Great Kiskadee, Couch's Kingbird. *Spring/Summer*—Wood Stork, Scissor-tailed Flycatcher, Cave Swallow. *Fall/Winter*—Peregrine Falcon, Vermilion Flycatcher. *Migrating*—Swallow-tailed Kite, Zone-tailed Kite, Buff-breasted Sandpiper.

Other key birds: *Resident*—Neotropic Cormorant, Mottled Duck, Crested Caracara, Little Blue Heron, Roseate Spoonbill, Inca Dove, Ladder-backed Woodpecker. *Spring/Summer*—Anhinga, Wilson's Plover, Painted Bunting. *Fall/Winter*—Greater White-fronted Goose, Ross Goose, Marbled Godwit. *Migrating*—Raptors, shorebirds, Neotropic passerines.

Best times to bird: Year-round.

Directions: From Corpus Christi, take U.S. Highway 77 85 miles north toward Victoria. Three miles past the exit for Highway 239 there is a turnoff for the small town of McFaddin. Turn right onto Farm-to-Market 445. Two miles on this road will take you to the town of McFaddin; continue through the town. When the road forks just past the post office, stay to the left. This is a gravel road. It crosses Kuy Creek over a narrow bridge. After about 5.5 miles the road ends at the Womack Family Ranch.

The birding

At present, this ranch is open to groups by appointment and for a fee. But I am telling you, get a group together, go there, and pay whatever is asked. The property is so beautiful, I wept the first time that I saw it. The owners are always working to do "the right thing." In 2002 Jess and Lou Womack were the statewide winners of the Texas Lone Star Land Steward Award for innovative and ecologically sound management of wild habitats. As Lou said, "We think it is right to leave it better than we found it for our children and for future generations of Texans."

The ranch is situated at the confluence of the Guadalupe and San Antonio Rivers. In the early 1900s ancestors of the Womacks built levees to drain the land for cotton farming. Today the levees are used to hold in water in an effort to restore the wetlands. A conservation easement covers 4,500 acres of land in the Wetlands Reserve Program. Another 1,800 acres are managed as part of the Texas Prairie Wetlands project. According to Gary Homerstad, a biologist for Texas Parks and Wildlife, "The ranch contains some of the most important freshwater wetlands in the Guadalupe River drainage."

So what does all of this mean to the bird-watcher? It means you aren't likely to find a more beautiful or more productive ranch along the Central Texas coast. The upland property is covered with large oak mottes, pecan trees, some mesquite and

Yellow-crowned Night Heron. PHOTO: TONY BAYLIS.

huisache. Birders are free to walk the property or drive on existing roads to look for passerines. Vermilion and Scissor-tailed Flycatchers, Carolina Chickadees, Tufted Titmice, Bewick's Wrens, Northern Mockingbirds, Savannah Sparrows, and Meadowlarks are there in abundance. In the spring, vireos and warblers migrate through the ranch. Even during the Christmas count, when only Yellow-rumped Warblers should be present, the observers on the ranch noted seven other species of warblers.

Raptors are present in this part of the ranch as well. Owls such as Barred, Barn, Western Screech, and Great Horned are known to live here. Other prominent raptors include Red-tailed Hawks, Northern Harriers, White-tailed Hawks, Crested Caracaras, Merlin, Cooper's, and Sharp-shinned Hawks, and Red-shouldered Hawks. In the winter, Bald Eagles use the wetlands for feeding grounds.

Also common are a number of woodpeckers. Be prepared to identify Red-bellied, Ladder-backed, Downy, and even Pileated Woodpeckers. If you are a sparrow aficionado, try for LeConte's, Grasshopper, Vesper, Lincoln's, Swamp, White-throated, and White-crowned.

Starting to get a picture of the Womack Family Ranch? Wait until we discuss the wetlands. The levels of these flooded areas depend on the annual rainfall. Some areas do dry out occasionally, but most retain some water year-round. In the late fall and winter, the area is overrun with ducks and geese, including Canvasbacks, Wood Ducks, Blue-winged and Green-winged Teal, Northern Shovelers, Ring-necked Ducks, and Snow Geese. In times of lower water levels, wading birds and shorebirds come into the picture. Ibis, herons, egrets, sandpipers, plovers, Purple Gallinules, and Sora are all well known here. In May and June, the ranch supports three colonial wading bird rookeries. Two small boats are available to take bird-watchers for a close-up look at hundreds of nests of Yellow-crowned Night Heron, Anhinga, Cattle Egret, Roseate Spoonbill, White Ibis, Great Blue Heron, Snowy Egret, and others. Jesse Womack, the ranch manager, told me that "this will knock your socks off," and it did. The boat was able to go in a deep channel right under all of the birds.

The owners do not live on the property; however, there is a main house that is still used by the family. There is a camp house with kitchen, which can sleep up to ten people for overnight groups.

General information: The land was originally part of the 34,000-acre McFaddin Ranch, which was founded about 1870. Jess and Lou Womack took these 8,500 acres in 1991, when the ranch was partitioned. Jess recently passed away, and management of the land has reverted to Lou and the couple's oldest son, Jesse. Boy Scouts and other youth groups are invited to the ranch for fishing days and youth hunts. To remain financially viable, the ranch does run cattle, maintains some oil and gas holdings, allows hunting leases for deer, alligator, and duck hunters, and harvests large numbers of blue crabs and crayfish as a commercial fishing venture.

In nearby McFaddin be sure to stop in at the McFaddin Cafe, housed in the 1910 McFaddin Mercantile.

DeLorme: Texas Atlas & Gazetteer: Page 79 9J.

Elevation: Less than 150 feet.

Hazards: Alligators, mosquitoes, snakes.

Nearest food, gas, lodging: Food in McFaddin; gas and lodging in Refugio or Victoria.

For more information: Womack Family Ranch, c/o Jesse Womack, 711 Navarro, Suite 404, San Antonio, TX 78205; (361) 570-4796.

52 Lion's/Shelly City Park

Habitats: Tall riparian forest.

Specialty birds: *Resident—Green Kingfisher.*

Other key birds: *Migrating—Neotropic passerines.*

Best times to bird: Spring and fall.

Directions: Enter Refugio after driving north from Corpus Christi 40 miles on U.S. Highway 77. At the first stoplight take a left onto Empresario Street and travel for 2 blocks to the entrance to the park. The city-owned Jeter RV Park is on the left. Go straight ahead for the Lion's/Shelly City Park.

Green Kingfisher. PHOTO: TONY BAYLIS.

The birding

Lion's/Shelly is a nice city park in the town of Refugio. There are restrooms and a large pavilion with sports equipment and picnic tables. Many people use this park; consequently, it is not exactly a prime birding spot. There are two good reasons, though, to go visit and bird.

First, much of the habitat surrounding Refugio has been given over to agriculture. Therefore, spring and fall migrants look upon this slice of riparian woodlands as a much-needed resting spot. The Mission River flows through the park, and you can walk along the bank to search for birds in the bottomland trees. To the right of the pavilion are two nature trails. One winds along just across Little Creek and ends up at the fishing pier on the Mission River. Keep your eyes open for Painted Buntings, Carolina Chickadees, and American alligators. The other trail goes through a wooded area and also ends at the fishing pier. Try here for American Robins, Wilson's Warblers, Golden-fronted Woodpecker, or maybe a Merlin. The two trails make a loop of about ½ mile. A large sign at the trailhead can help you decide which way to start. White-tailed deer, racoons, and wild hogs have also been spotted along these trails in the early morning or early evening hours.

The second reason to bird here is that this historically has been an excellent place to look for Green Kingfishers. The park entrance road dead-ends at the pavilion. Go left to find a restroom at the far end of the park. Overlooking the river is a platform with benches. There is a sign declaring that you have arrived at Green Kingfisher Point. Ringed and Belted Kingfishers are tenacious birds that often sit in plain sight. The Green Kingfisher is different and very shy. Be patient and carefully scan the opposite bank, where they are likely sitting on a branch so as to blend in with the surrounding foliage.

General information: The Lion's Club was a major sponsor of this park when it was first built, hence the name. In 1998 a project to upgrade the park was completed. During that project, the Shelly family donated land for a nature trail and fishing pier. The Jeter family donated land for the RV park. This is CTC#38.

DeLorme: Texas Atlas & Gazetteer: Page 85 7A.

Elevation: 43 feet.

Hazards: Steep banks of river, snakes, alligators.

Nearest food, gas, lodging: Refugio.

Camping: Jeter RV Park.

For more information: City of Refugio, 613 Commerce Street, P.O. Box 1020, Refugio, TX 78377; (361) 526-5361.

53 Angel of Goliad Hike and Bike Trail

Habitats: Tall riparian forest, Tamaulipan scrubland, prairie.

Specialty birds: *Resident*—Black-bellied Whistling-Duck, Buff-bellied Hummingbird, Green Kingfisher, Golden-fronted Woodpecker, Couch's Kingbird, Long-billed Thrasher, Olive Sparrow. *Spring/Summer*—Brown-crested Flycatcher, Scissor-tailed Flycatcher. *Fall/Winter*—Vermilion Flycatcher.

Other key birds: *Resident*—Crested Caracara, Inca Dove, Ladder-backed Woodpecker, Pyrrhuloxia. *Spring/Summer*—Anhinga, Painted Bunting. *Fall/Winter*—Greater White-fronted Goose. *Migrating*—Neotropic passerines.

Best times to bird: Year-round.

Directions: From Corpus Christi, take Interstate 37 north to the U.S. Highway 77 exit. Travel north 40 miles on US 77 to Refugio, then take U.S. Highway 183 for 27 miles to Goliad. Immediately after you pass Goliad State Park the highway dips near an old railroad overpass. Once the highway crests upward again, turn left onto End Street. You will notice two signs to help you know when to turn. One sign has GOLIAD HISTORIC DISTRICT; another reads HISTORIC DOWNTOWN. If you get to the intersection with U.S. Highway 59, you have gone too far.

You will spot the tower of the courthouse the moment you make the turn at End Street. Go 2 blocks on End Street to Market Street. Take a left on Market and continue 2 blocks to the entrance of the Angel of Goliad Hike and Bike Trail. Market Street narrows and makes a small jog to the left, but you will notice that it stops at the trailhead.

The birding

This trail was built for hike and bike enthusiasts, but it is also perfect for bird watching. Much of the trail is paved; the remainder comprises boardwalks and switchbacks. There are many switchbacks, I suppose, to make it easier for bikers and those in wheelchairs. The trail takes you up, down, and near the San Antonio River. At the entrance to the trail, much of the underbrush has been cleared, giving it a parklike effect. It is beautiful here. Look for Red-bellied and Downy Woodpeckers, doves, and thrushes. In most spots, the understory is intact. Listen for thrashers such as the Northern Mockingbird and Brown Thrasher.

In some places, as the trail edges along the river, birders can peer straight into the tops of trees. This makes it easier to find White-eyed Vireos, Northern Cardinals, Blue Jays, Carolina Chickadees, Indigo Buntings, and Black-crested Titmice.

At other locations, stop along the trail for a nice look at the river. This is where you can check for herons, egrets, shorebirds, ducks, and even raptors that use the river as a travel guide. A bridge takes the birder over a drainage creek that empties into the river. Look here for water-loving passerines. There are many native plants, such as mustang grape and dewberry, that tempt birds with their fruits.

Finally, the trail enters the front edge of Goliad State Park. (If you continue on the trail through the state park, you are not required to pay the entrance fee.) Here

Bird watchers on the Angel of Goliad Trail.

the path levels out and continues through a section of terrain that is more like thorn scrub. Look here for the Long-billed Thrasher. The trail leads under the river bridge, up the other side, and back near Highway 183. At this point native habitat is left behind, and the area is open and flat. The trail continues in front of the presidio, past the birthplace of Ignacio Zaragoza, and winds around to end at Fannin Monument. A statue honoring the Angel of Goliad guards the final part of the course.

The trail is 2¼ mile long. The only drawback is that it does not make a loop. You return the way you came, or you must decide to turn back earlier. In my opinion, the best birding habitat is at the beginning of the trail. If you are looking for a shorter route, turn back when the walk enters Goliad State Park.

General information: At the trailhead, there is a mailbox, where you can find a bird and butterfly list. There are no restrooms or water fountains on the trail, but you can use the facilities at the state park or at a public restroom at the city park on End Street. The trail is wheelchair accessible. This joint project for the City of Goliad and Goliad County was begun in 1984. It was completed in 1996 with the help of multiple grants and various partners. The vision included the idea of linking the historic downtown with Goliad State Park, the presidio, and the grave site of Colonel James Fannin's Texas revolutionary forces.

The town of Goliad has a charming courthouse square with antiques and gift shops, museums, and quaint cafes. It also has numerous monuments and references to Texas's revolutionary past.

Goliad State Park now protects the Spanish mission that was built there in the 1700s. The replica of Presidio La Bahia is owned and managed by the Catholic Diocese of Victoria, Texas. The original was built as a fort to house Spanish soldiers employed to protect several missions in the area. Consider taking the tour. This is the only example of a presidio east of the Rocky Mountains.

Near the presidio is a small house that was the 1829 birthplace of Ignacio Zaragoza. On May 5, 1862, General Zaragoza led the Mexican army to victory over a French expeditionary force at the Battle of Puebla. Today this victory is celebrated in Mexico as Cinco de Mayo. The house, which has a few artifacts, is owned and operated by the State of Texas.

In March 1836 about 400 Texans under the command of Colonel Fannin occupied the presidio during the Texas Revolution against Mexico. A battle occurred at what is now Fannin Battleground State Historic Site. The Texans surrendered to Mexican forces led by General Jose Urrea and were returned as prisoners to the presidio. One week later, on Palm Sunday, they were marched out onto the prairie and massacred by orders of General Antonio López de Santa Anna. The wife of a high-ranking Mexican officer begged that the lives of the Texans be spared. Señora Francisca "Panchita" Alavez did indeed save at least twenty-eight men. Today she is remembered as the Angel of Goliad. Later, the remains of the dead were collected and buried in a mass grave behind the presidio. Three hundred and forty-one names are engraved on the monument marking the grave site.

DeLorme: Texas Atlas & Gazetteer: Page 79 7I.

Elevation: 185 feet.

Nearest food, gas, lodging: Goliad.

Camping: Goliad State Park.

For more information: City of Goliad, 152 West End Street, Goliad, TX 77963; (361) 645-3454; Presidio La Bahia, Friends of the Fort, P.O. Box 57, Goliad, TX 77963; (361) 645-3752; Goliad State Park, 108 Park Road 6, Goliad, TX 77963; (361) 645-3405.

54 Goliad State Park

Habitats: Tall riparian forest, Tamaulipan scrubland, prairie.

Specialty birds: *Resident*—Black-bellied Whistling-Duck, Common Pauraque, Green Kingfisher, Golden-fronted Woodpecker, Long-billed Thrasher, Olive Sparrow. *Spring/Summer*—Wood Stork, Brown-crested Flycatcher, Scissor-tailed Flycatcher. *Fall/Winter*—Vermilion Flycatcher, Sprague's Pipit. *Migrating*—Buff-breasted Sandpiper.

Other key birds: *Resident*—Mottled Duck, Fulvous Whistling-Duck, Crested Caracara, Little Blue Heron, Inca Dove, Ladder-backed Woodpecker, Curve-billed Thrasher, Bronzed Cowbird, Pyrrhuloxia. *Spring/Summer*—Anhinga,

Lesser Nighthawk, Painted Bunting. *Fall/Winter*—Greater White-fronted Goose, Rufous Hummingbird.

Best times to bird: Year-round.

Directions: From Corpus Christi, take Interstate 37 north to the U.S. Highway 77 exit. Travel north 40 miles on US 77 to Refugio, then take U.S. Highway 183 for 27 miles to Goliad. The first large structure you encounter on the right upon entering Goliad is the Presidio La Bahia. You will cross the San Antonio River. On the left is the entrance to Goliad State Park. A short Park Road 6 takes the visitor to the tollbooth.

The birding

There are many excellent opportunities for bird watching at the 188-acre Goliad State Park. Perhaps the first place to try would be the Aranama Nature Trail, named for the Native Americans in this area. Stay to the left of the mission chapel (see General Information) on the path until you come to an iron gate toward the back of the compound. Just past the gate is the trailhead, where a container holds booklets that include a trail map and descriptions of the plants and animals along the way. Pick one up to use as you walk. This is a dirt path trail, and parts of it are moderately challenging. Wooden stairs lead down to drainage areas in two places. They are safe but somewhat steep. A bridge crosses a creek that flows into the San Antonio River. There are benches along the way. The 0.3-mile trail loops around to shorten the return trip. You may spot woodpeckers, thrushes, or thrashers along this trail.

Another trail to consider is River Trail. This is another dirt path that follows the San Antonio River for approximately 1 mile. It is shown on the park map available to visitors as a hiking trail. But hey, the birds don't know that. They just like to be close to the water. Although not plentiful, herons, egrets, and even sandpipers show up here. Many species of ducks stop over during the winter. The Belted Kingfisher is common along the river, but Green Kingfishers have been listed as well. What you are apt to see along this wooded trail are passerines such as Eastern Phoebe, Great Crested Flycatchers, Carolina Chickadees, Tufted Titmice, White-eyed, Red-eyed, or Solitary Vireos, and Spotted Towhees. Woodpeckers should be there, too.

This is an excellent place to look for a Downy Woodpecker, and even Pileated Woodpeckers have been seen in this park. The park hosts an extremely large Turkey Vulture roost. During spring migration, warblers stream through the park. And watch on picnic tables and other low perches for Eastern Bluebirds.

At the camping areas, the land has been cleared and looks more like prairie land. Look for sparrows such as White-crowned, Black-throated, and Lincoln's. Although they are hard to find, this is one place to try for the Cassin's Sparrows. Raptors, such as Mississippi Kites, Northern Harriers, and Red-shouldered Hawks, are well represented in the park. The bird checklist, available from the visitor center, includes seven species of owls.

In the spring, the park is covered with wildflowers. It becomes a butterfly haven at that time. The campers who use the park consider it beautiful, quiet, and safe. They have also tried to keep it a secret. I have always found it a relaxing yet exciting place to bird.

There is one drawback to this park: It floods. Even mild flooding will cover up some of the primitive campsites and the River Trail. At these times, walking on the park roads can still provide you with a good bird show. In fact, flooding brings different birds that are drawn to the water.

General information: There is an entrance fee. Gates open at 7:00 A.M. and close at 10:00 P.M. The park has campsites, RV hook-ups, and shelters. For day use, there are picnic tables and pits, playground equipment, and restrooms. Across the highway from the park entrance is a swimming pool that is operated by the City of Goliad. This is CTC#39. Parts of the park are wheelchair accessible.

More Texas history: Goliad State Park is the site of the Mission Nuestra Señora del Espiritu Santo de Zuniga. Spanish Franciscan monks built the present structure in 1749. Not only was this a missionary church for the conversion of Native Americans, it was also a community, with native cooks, potters, weavers, ranch hands, and farmers. The mission closed in 1830.

In 1931 the Texas State Park system acquired the site. The Civilian Conservation Corps worked to restore the buildings. Today the visitor can tour the chapel, granary, Native American apartments, and workshops.

The rangers at this park also manage the Mission Nuestra Señora del Rosario ruins west of Goliad on Highway 59, the Fannin Battleground State Historic Site, and the Zaragoza Birthplace.

DeLorme: Texas Atlas & Gazetteer: Page 79 7I.

Elevation: 187 feet.

Hazards: Poison ivy, snakes, mosquitoes, flooding.

Nearest food, gas, lodging: Goliad.

Camping: Goliad State Park.

For more information: Goliad State Park, 108 Park Road 6, Goliad, TX 77963; (361) 645-3405.

55 Coleto Creek Reservoir and Park

Habitats: Tall riparian forest, prairie.

Specialty birds: *Resident*—Least Grebe, Black-bellied Whistling-Duck, Common Pauraque, Golden-fronted Woodpecker, Couch's Kingbird, Long-billed Thrasher, Olive Sparrow. *Spring/Summer*—Wood Stork, Cave Swallow. *Fall/Winter*—Vermilion Flycatcher.

Other key birds: *Resident*—Neotropic Cormorant, Crested Caracara, Roseate Spoonbill, Inca Dove, Ladder-backed Woodpecker, Curve-billed Thrasher, Bronzed Cowbird. *Spring/Summer*—Anhinga, Lesser Nighthawk, Painted Bunting, Scissor-tailed Flycatcher. *Migrating*—Raptors.

Best times to bird: Fall, winter, spring.

Directions: From Corpus Christi, travel north on U.S. Highway 77. Go north 40 miles on US 77 until you reach Refugio. Go north 27 miles on U.S. Highway 183 to Goliad. At Goliad, turn right (east) on U.S. Highway 59. Continue 13½ miles to the Coleto Creek Reservoir and Park. Signs will direct you to the park entrance, which is actually 0.3 mile off US 59. From Victoria, travel west on US 59 for about 12 miles. If you are interested in touring the Fannin Battleground State Historic Site, the turnoff from US 59 is about 4 miles before the Coleto Creek Park entrance if you are coming from Goliad.

The birding

This park, which was opened in 1981, covers 190 acres; the reservoir is about 3,100 acres in size, with 60 miles of shoreline. The main focus of the park is family recreation. The most productive birding will be around the reservoir. In all seasons, look for gulls, terns, and cormorants. See if you can spot an Anhinga perched on a low limb, its wings spread out to dry. There is a small flock of White Pelicans who act more like residents than migrants.

In the winter, the reservoir can be thick with diving ducks such as Ring-necked Ducks, Canvasbacks, Lesser Scaups, and Redheads, or dabbling ducks such as Northern Pintails, Green-winged and Blue-winged Teal, and American Wigeons. Osprey will easily be seen here. Also, Bald Eagles winter here. There are two known eagle nests, both of which are out of the public view. However, the eagles can be seen fishing over the lake, and a dead tree near the dam is often used as an eagle perch. September is a good time to look for migrating raptors, especially Broad-winged Hawks.

Wading birds and shorebirds show up depending on the level of the lake. You should see Great Blue Herons, Roseate Spoonbills, and Great Egrets. More rare would be the sighting of Black-necked Stilts, American Avocets, and Spotted Sandpipers. Expect Wood Storks wading about in the summer.

Around the camping areas, the underbrush has been cleared completely. Finding passerines may prove to be a little difficult. However, there is plenty of natural habitat left, including some along the Hiking and Nature Trail. These are actually two mowed trails that come together and weave around the brush for about 1½

Scissor-tailed Flycatcher. PHOTO: TONY BAYLIS.

miles. The trail has numbered markers. At the visitor center, pick up a guide that explains the trees and plants along the trail. In trees near the reservoir, look for resident birds such as Northern Mockingbirds, Eastern Bluebirds, Red-bellied Woodpeckers, Carolina Chickadees, and Tufted Titmice. In brush and grassy areas, look for sparrows such as Chipping, Savannah, Vesper, Grasshopper, Field, Lincoln's, and Song. In wetter spots, you may notice Sedge Wrens and Swamp Sparrows. On high lines and fences, watch for Couch's Kingbirds and Vermilion Flycatchers.

Spring migration should add to the possibilities for successful bird sightings. If conditions are good, warblers, vireos, orioles, tanagers, and other traveling Neotropics could be seen in the lovely live oaks scattered throughout the park.

General information: There is a fee. This park is owned and operated by the Guadalupe–Blanco River Authority. The lake is a cooling reservoir for the Coleto Power Plant. Camping, RV sites, cabins, day-use areas, boat ramps, playground equipment, lighted pier, lake swimming, and restrooms are all provided. This is CTC#40.

DeLorme: Texas Atlas & Gazetteer: Page 79 8H.

Elevation: 121 feet.

Hazards: Poison ivy, snakes.

Nearest food, gas, lodging: Goliad and Victoria.

Camping: Coleto Creek Reservoir and Park.

For more information: Coleto Creek Reservoir and Park, P.O. Box 68, Fannin, TX 77960; (361) 575-6366.

North and West of Corpus Christi

L and north and west of Corpus Christi is used for a number of agricultural purposes, mainly dry land farming. Lake Corpus Christi and Choke Canyon Reservoir, both on the Nueces River, are of major importance to the people and habitat of these locations. Smaller artificial lakes and ponds dot the region. Tamaulipan thorn scrub dominates here, but in many western sites it fades into Tamaulipan scrubland. Away from the influence of the Gulf of Mexico, these sites are even drier and hotter than others listed in the book.

Look in these locales for birds that thrive in prickly pear cactus and honey mesquite. Birds typical of these sites are Harris' Hawk, Caracara, Painted Buntings, Scissor-tailed Flycatchers, and Long-billed Thrashers.

56. John J. Sablatura Nature Park
57. Lake Findley (formerly Lake Alice)
58. San Patricio de Hibernia Preserve
59. Knolle Farm Area
60. San Patricio La Fruta Park
61. Tecolote Creek Ranch
62. Wesley Seale Dam and the City of Corpus Christi Wildlife Sanctuary
63. Pernitas Point/Carmel Hills
64. Lake Corpus Christi State Park and Recreation Area
65. Highway 624–McMullen County
66. La Ramireña Ranch
67. Veteran's Memorial Park
68. Berclair Loop
69. Barnhart Q5 Ranch
70. Choke Canyon State Park
71. James E. Daughtrey Wildlife Management Area

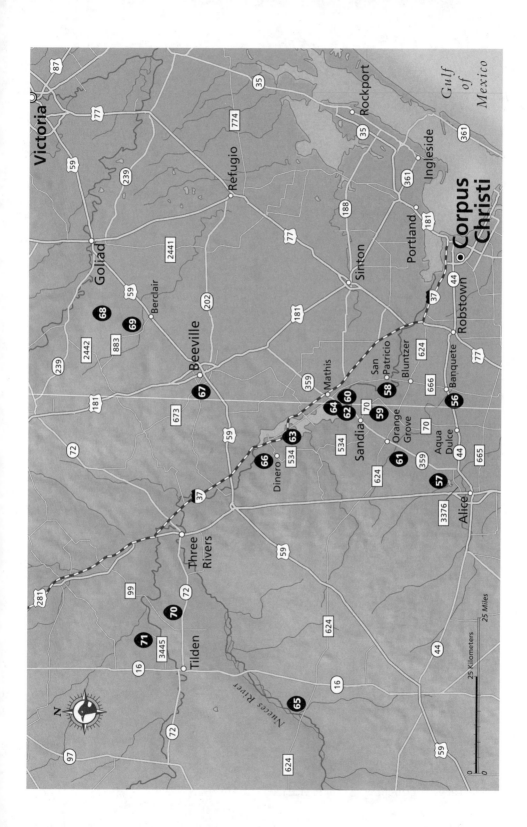

56 John J. Sablatura Nature Park

Habitats: Tamaulipan thorn scrub, transitional riparian, agricultural areas.

Specialty birds: *Resident*—Harris' Hawk, White-tipped Dove, Common Pauraque, Golden-fronted Woodpecker, Couch's Kingbird, Green Jay. *Spring/Summer*—Brown-crested Flycatcher, Scissor-tailed Flycatcher.

Other key birds: *Resident*—Inca Dove, Ladder-backed Woodpecker, Pyrrhuloxia. *Spring/Summer*—Painted Bunting.

Best times to bird: Winter, spring.

Directions: From Corpus Christi, take Highway 44 west through Robstown and on toward Alice. Nine miles west of Robstown on Highway 44 is the small town of Banquete. John J. Sablatura Park is 1 mile west of Banquete on Highway 44. If you get to Agua Dulce, you have gone too far.

The birding

This twenty-acre county park does not have true Tamaulipan scrub habitat. There are many beautiful mesquite trees in the park, however; the underbrush has been removed and the area manicured to accommodate picnicking and family get-togethers. The Agua Dulce Creek runs through the park. The chances of finding water in the creek, though, are slim to none. Nevertheless, this is a fine stopover where you can stretch your legs if you are driving west of Corpus Christi.

Expect to see resident birds typical of this habitat, such as Mockingbirds, White-winged Doves, Green Jays, Northern Cardinals, and Golden-fronted Woodpeckers. In the spring, some migrants use this park. In the fall and winter, check for American Robins, Eastern Blue Birds, Goldfinches, Chipping Sparrows, and Lark Sparrows.

All of the surrounding fields are dedicated to agriculture. Look there for Meadowlarks and on the power lines for American Kestrels. If there are any newly plowed fields in the late fall or winter, inspect them for Mountain Plovers. Occasionally, migrating Broad-winged Hawks and Swainson's Hawks show up.

General information: John J. Sablatura was the mayor of Agua Dulce from 1940 until 1944. He served as a Nueces County commissioner from 1944 until 1966. Commissioner Sablatura was instrumental in establishing this county park, which was dedicated on September 8, 1962.

The park is open daily from 7:00 A.M. to 7:00 P.M. There are restrooms, picnic tables, barbecue pits, playground equipment, a basketball court, and a baseball field. This is CTC#84.

DeLorme: Texas Atlas & Gazetteer: Page 84 4E.

Elevation: 40 feet.

Hazards: Snakes.

Nearest food, gas, lodging: Banquete can provide fast food. You will have to return to Robstown for lodging.

For more information: Hazel Bazemore County Park, P.O. Box 4343, County Road 69, Corpus Christi, TX 78410; (361) 387-4231; Nueces County Parks and Recreation Department, 15802 South Padre Island Drive, Corpus Christi, TX 78408; (361) 949-8122.

57 Lake Findley (formerly Lake Alice)

Habitats: Transitional riparian, Tamaulipan scrubland, freshwater lake.

Specialty birds: *Resident*—Least Grebe, Black-bellied Whistling-Duck, White-tipped Dove, Groove-billed Ani, Golden-fronted Woodpecker, Great Kiskadee, Couch's Kingbird, Green Jay, Long-billed Thrasher, Olive Sparrow, Audubon's Oriole. *Spring/Summer*—Wood Stork, Scissor-tailed Flycatcher, Cave Swallow. *Fall/Winter*—Vermilion Flycatcher, Sprague's Pipit.

Other key birds: *Resident*—Crested Caracara, Inca Dove, Ladder-backed Woodpecker, Curve-billed Thrasher. *Spring/Summer*—Anhinga, Lesser Nighthawk.

Best times to bird: Fall, winter, spring.

Directions: From Corpus Christi, take Highway 44 west. You will pass through Robstown, Banquete, and Agua Dulce. As you approach Alice (45 miles from Corpus Christi), watch for the exit to Highway 369. Turn right and travel north on Highway 369 for 0.8 mile to Farm-to-Market 3376. Turn left and stay on FM 3376 for about 4 miles until you reach Texas Boulevard in Alice. Turn right and travel 1.5 miles. The road ends at Lake Findley. Note: A permit is required to enter the park, and it must be obtained at the Alice City Hall, 500 East Main Street. The permit is free.

Ladder-backed Woodpecker. PHOTO: TONY BAYLIS.

The birding

Lake Findley (formerly Lake Alice) is the water source for the City of Alice. The water is pumped through a pipeline from Lake Corpus Christi. The park is simple, but the addition of water always draws interesting birds.

The Texas Parks and Wildlife Department stocks the lake with fish, and local anglers enjoy the benefits, as do kayakers and canoers. The park has many covered picnic tables and several barbecue pits, but there are no restrooms.

The tree-lined road leading into the park is especially beautiful. Drive slowly or walk here, and look for Golden-fronted Woodpeckers, Northern Mockingbirds, Green Jays, Couch's Kingbirds, and Scissor-tailed Flycatchers on the wires, and Mourning and White-winged Doves on the ground. There are two baseball fields, and Sprague's Pipits are reported to favor the area in the winter. Meadowlarks may be here, too. Look in the taller grasses for sparrows such as Grasshopper.

There is a fishing pier on the lake. This would be a nice place to set up a scope and look for water-loving birds. The opposite lake shore is heavily wooded. Try for egrets, herons, and Anhingas resting there. In the fall and winter, ducks and even Sandhill Cranes could surprise you. Check along the lake's edge for Least Grebe. Great Kiskadee sometimes act almost like kingfishers and dive for fish. Salt cedars and willows have been planted near the water, and a Yellow-billed Cuckoo has been listed at this site.

There is only one road that parallels the lake. If you go in either direction, you will notice signs stating that you cannot continue without a permit. As mentioned, these permits are free and can be obtained at Alice City Hall. The city has future plans to develop a nature trail through part of the unmanicured sections of the area.

General information: This 800-acre park was dedicated on July 4, 1990. It is a joint project of the City of Alice and the Texas Parks and Wildlife Department. It was first named Lake Alice and recently renamed to honor W. E. "Bill" Findley Jr., who is the chairman and longtime member of the Alice Water Authority.

The park opens daily at 7:00 A.M. and closes at 10:00 P.M. This is CTC#83.

While in Alice, why not consider visiting the Tejano R.O.O.T.S. Hall of Fame and Museum, which highlights the Tejano culture. See Appendix A for the museum's address and phone number.

DeLorme: Texas Atlas & Gazetteer: Page 84 3F.

Elevation: 205 feet.

Nearest food, gas, lodging: Alice.

For more information: City of Alice, 500 East Main Street, P.O. Box 3229, Alice, TX 78333; (361) 668-7210.

58 San Patricio de Hibernia Preserve

Habitats: Transitional riparian, Tamaulipan scrubland.

Specialty birds: *Resident*—Black-bellied Whistling-Duck, White-tailed Kite, Harris' Hawk, White-tipped Dove, Common Pauraque, Green Kingfisher, Golden-fronted Woodpecker, Great Kiskadee, Couch's Kingbird, Green Jay, Long-billed Thrasher, Olive Sparrow. *Spring/Summer*—Brown-crested Flycatcher, Scissor-tailed Flycatcher. *Fall/Winter*—Vermilion Flycatcher.

Other key birds: *Resident*—Crested Caracara, Inca Dove, Ladder-backed Woodpecker. *Spring/Summer*—Lesser Nighthawk, Painted Bunting.

Best times to bird: Year-round.

Directions: From Corpus Christi, take Interstate 37 north toward San Antonio. Get off at Exit 14 (U.S. Highway 77 South/Robstown). Once on US 77, take the first exit on US 77 to Valero Way (formerly Up River Road) and Farm-to-Market 624. Turn right onto FM 624. Stay on FM 624 for 10 miles to the small community of Bluntzer and the intersection of Farm-to-Market 666. Turn right (north) on 666 and travel for 4 miles. This will take you into the old town of San Patricio. Turn left on County Road 60. A sign at that intersection will indicate that you are heading toward the McGloin Homestead and Dougherty House. Stay on CR 60. At 1.5 miles the road forks; stay to the right. The road ends at 1.8 miles at the McGloin Homestead. Just before the road ends and on the left is the entrance to the San Patricio de Hibernia Preserve. There is limited parking near the locked gate.

The birding

The drive alone down tree-lined CR 60 to get to this site is worth the trip. The 786-acre preserve at the end of the road is in a very natural state. Evidence suggests that in the 1800s there was a wagon trail to Fort Lipantilan that ran along the river here. There was limited grazing in the past, and today it is a lovely riparian forest. The area is fenced, and in addition to a dirt road, there are some paths through the property. However, there are no serious improvements, and none are planned. San Patricio County owns the property, and the hope is that mainly youth and nature groups will make use of the area. There is access to the Nueces River after a hike of more than a mile.

This is certainly a "birdy" place. Just by looking over the fence, I saw Cattle Egrets, Black-bellied Whistling-Ducks, Northern Mockingbirds, Northern Cardinals, a Golden-fronted Woodpecker, a White-eyed Vireo, and Couch's Kingbirds. In late spring, I watched a Swallow-tailed Kite making lazy circles overhead.

Birdwatchers on the Nueces River. PHOTO: K. KASTNER PHOTOGRAPHY.

General information: Access is limited and by reservation only. This property is managed jointly by San Patricio County and the Coastal Bend Bays and Estuaries Program.

In 1828 John McMullen and James McGloin were awarded an empresario contract by the Mexican government. They brought in Irish settlers and founded the town of San Patricio de Hibernia, named for the patron saint of Ireland. The original McGloin Homestead, which is not part of the preserve, is open for tours February to October on the second Sunday of each month from 3:00 to 5:00 P.M.; November to January, second Tuesday from 3:00 to 5:00 P.M. There is a fee. Contact the Corpus Christi Area Heritage Society at (361) 882–8691.

DeLorme: Texas Atlas & Gazetteer: Page 84 4D.

Elevation: 150 feet.

Hazards: Snakes, fire ants, mosquitoes, poison ivy.

Nearest food, gas, lodging: Mathis.

Camping: Lake Corpus Christi State Park.

For more information: San Patricio County Judge, 400 West Sinton, Sinton, TX 78387; (361) 364–6120; Coastal Bend Bays and Estuaries Program, 1305 North Shoreline Boulevard, Suite 205, Corpus Christi, TX

59 Knolle Farm Area

Habitats: Agricultural areas, Tamaulipan scrubland.

Specialty birds: *Resident*—Black-bellied Whistling-Duck, Harris' Hawk, White-tailed Hawk, Great Kiskadee, Green Jay, Olive Sparrow. *Spring/Summer*—Wood Stork, Brown-crested Flycatcher, Scissor-tailed Flycatcher. *Fall/Winter*—Vermilion Flycatcher. *Migrating*—Buff-breasted Sandpiper.

Other key birds: *Resident*—Mottled Duck, Crested Caracara, Roseate Spoonbill, Inca Dove, Ladder-backed Woodpecker, Bronzed Cowbird, Pyrrhuloxia. *Spring/Summer*—Wilson's Plover. *Fall/Winter*—Greater White-fronted Goose, Ross's Goose.

Best times to bird: Fall and winter.

Directions: U.S. Highway 77 intersects with Farm-to-Market 624 in the 5 Points area of Corpus Christi. From the intersection, take FM 624 west for 16.5 miles. Turn right on North Farm Road 70. From this point it is 4.2 miles to Knolle Farms. You should not consider Knolle Farms as your destination, but more as a starting point. At the farm, which is marked with a large, noticeable sign, FM 70 makes a ninety-degree turn to the left. Continue instead on the narrow Jim Wells County Road 360. If you follow this road to its end, you come to the town of Sandia on Highway 359. Turn south on Highway 359 and go 5.5 miles to Orange Grove. You will see FM 70 about 0.3 mile after you turn onto Highway 359. You thus can use CR 360, Highway 359, and FM 70 to create a loop of this area.

About 1 mile before FM 70 makes the ninety-degree turn, County Road 58 intersects it. If you follow CR 58 for 1.2 miles to its dead end, you come to CTC#81, Fort Lipantitlan State Historic Park. I do not recommend this site. It is only five acres, and it is not well cared for. There are no facilities whatsoever.

The birding

The main reason for taking this drive in the winter is to see the thousands of geese, mainly Snow, Ross's, and Greater White-fronted. These geese spend their days in or near the cow feed lots and pastures. It is an impressive site. Sandhill Cranes also feed in the fields. There are water holes that come and go depending on the weather. If present, the water holes host various species of ducks, some shorebirds, and some wading birds. Killdeer will be present and perhaps other plovers. Black-bellied Whistling-Ducks, Roseate Spoonbills, and Wood Storks may be an extra surprise, depending on the time of year and the amount of water standing.

The grazing fields also are home to Northern Harriers and Red-tailed Hawks. A Ferruginous Hawk has been listed in this area. Brush along the road shelters Mockingbirds, Northern Cardinals, and Pyrrhuloxia. Also watch for sparrows such as the Lark Sparrow and Lark Bunting. Keep your eyes open for Bobwhite Quail, Vermilion Flycatchers, Bronzed Cowbirds, and Green Jays.

Knolle Farm operates a bed-and-breakfast (Knolle Farm and Ranch Bed, Barn, and Breakfast). Guests of the B&B who are interested in birding are invited to roam the ranch freely, or staff will arrange for an experienced guide. Knolle has numerous flooded wetlands that are managed for waterfowl habitat. Staff can even arrange birding by canoe on the Nueces River. Knolle Farms participates in the Coastal Bend Wildlife Photo Contest sponsored by the Coastal Bend Wildlife Habitat Education Program.

General information: Knolle Farm and Ranch Bed, Barn, and Breakfast offers not only lodging but also many outdoor activities. Canoeing and kayaking, fishing, hiking, biking, and horseback riding, as well as skeet shooting and hunting, are available. It is also known for great food.

DeLorme: Texas Atlas & Gazetteer: Page 84 4C.

Elevation: 180 feet.

Nearest food, gas, lodging: Orange Grove, Knolle Farm and Ranch Bed, Barn, and Breakfast.

For more information: Knolle Farm and Ranch Bed, Barn, and Breakfast, FM Road 70, Route 1, Box 81, Sandia, TX 78383; (361) 547-2546.

Habitats: Transitional riparian, Tamaulipan scrubland.

Specialty birds: *Resident*—Black-bellied Whistling-Duck, White-tailed Kite, Harris' Hawk, White-tipped Dove, Common Pauraque, Green Kingfisher, Golden-fronted Woodpecker, Great Kiskadee, Couch's Kingbird, Green Jay, Long-billed Thrasher, Olive Sparrow. *Spring/Summer*—Brown-crested Flycatcher, Scissor-tailed Flycatcher. *Fall/Winter*—Vermilion Flycatcher.

Other key birds: *Resident*—Crested Caracara, Inca Dove, Ladder-backed Woodpecker, Pyrrhuloxia. *Spring/Summer*—Lesser Nighthawk, Painted Bunting.

Best times to bird: Year-round.

Directions: Take Interstate 37 north out of Corpus Christi toward San Antonio. Exit at the town of Mathis, which is about 30 miles west from Corpus Christi. Take Exit 34 for West Spur 459. Merge onto Highway 359 West and travel for 3.8 miles. Turn left onto County Road 1092. Follow CR 1092 for 0.3 mile. When it forks, follow the left fork to its end at the gate to San Patricio La Fruta Park.

Long-billed Thrasher. PHOTO: TONY BAYLIS.

The birding

This is a wonderful piece of property along the Nueces River. The forty-seven acres are semideveloped, but there are plans that would further enhance accessibility for river enthusiasts, scouts, and bird-watchers. This is perhaps the only public approach to the river below the Wesley Seale Dam, since most property along the river is privately owned. San Patricio County envisions this as a launching place for kayakers, canoers, tubers, and anglers.

The riparian habitat, as well as the mesquite in the uplands, should make for prime birding. At the river, look for Great Blue Herons, Green Kingfishers, and Great Kiskadees. In the scrubland, look for thrashers and sparrows.

General information: Currently, access is by reservation and permission of the San Patricio County Judge. San Patricio County runs the site. Plans include a visitor center and an RV park.

La Fruta was a small town in the late 1800s. It derives its name from the vegetables and fruits shipped from there. Beginning in 1871, Calvin Wright operated a hand-pulled ferry across the Nueces River. In 1915, a bridge was completed nearby.

DeLorme: Texas Atlas & Gazetteer: Page 84 4C.

Elevation: 160 feet.

Hazards: Snakes, fire ants, mosquitoes, poison ivy.

Nearest food, gas, lodging: Mathis.

Camping: Lake Corpus Christi State Park.

For more information: San Patricio County Judge, 400 West Sinton, Sinton, TX 78387; (361) 364-6120.

61 Tecolote Creek Ranch

Habitats: Tamaulipan scrubland, Tamaulipan thorn scrub, agricultural area.

Specialty birds: *Resident*—Harris' Hawk, Groove-billed Ani, Common Pauraque, Buff-bellied Hummingbird, Green Jay, Long-billed Thrasher, Olive Sparrow. *Spring/Summer*—Brown-crested Flycatcher, Scissor-tailed Flycatcher. *Fall/Winter*—Vermilion Flycatcher. *Rarity*—Plain Chachalaca.

Other key birds: *Resident*—Crested Caracara, Roseate Spoonbill, Inca Dove, Ladder-backed Woodpecker, Curve-billed Thrasher, Pyrrhuloxia. *Spring/Summer*—Lesser Nighthawk, Painted Bunting.

Best times to bird: Fall, winter, spring.

Directions: U.S. Highway 77 intersects Farm-to-Market 624 in the 5 Points area of Corpus Christi. From the intersection, take FM 624 for 18.5 miles west to Orange Grove. In Orange Grove turn south on U.S. Highway 359. After 3 miles, look for a power substation on your right and Jim Wells County Road 308. Take a right on CR 308 and head west for 6 miles. CR 308 makes a very large S-turn; when it straightens out, you will see a sign for Tecolote Creek Ranch on the left. The ranch headquarters is 1 mile down a dirt road. You pass through two gates that should be left as found.

The birding

This ranch is about one third improved pasture with coastal Bermuda grass, where steers or heifers graze. The tall mesquites that remain in the pasture are ideal for Northern Harriers, Harris' Hawks, Crested Caracaras, and Great Horned Owls to use as hunting perches. Look here for Meadowlarks, Mourning Doves, Inca Doves, and White-winged Doves. The level fields are often used by Sandhill Cranes in the fall and winter. Cattle Egrets love the shaded concrete trough on the fence line near the second gate. Eastern Bluebirds, Vermilion Flycatchers, Scarlet Tanagers, and Loggerhead Shrikes have been seen here as well.

On the ranch road that goes to the headquarters, you will see Bobwhite Quail. At the headquarters, the owners have feeders to attract Northern Cardinals, Pyrrhuloxias, Green Jays, Ladderback Woodpeckers, and sometimes Plain Chachalacas. (These birds are highly unusual this far north. They live in the brush along the creek and come up to the feeders in the afternoon.) During the spring and summer, hummingbird feeders are also used with great success. Barn Owls and Great Horned Owls like to roost and hunt from the ranch headquarters. Often they are in the barns and silently glide to a perch on a mesquite tree when a car approaches. They also perch in the tall mesquites or the anaqua tree by the guesthouse.

The road continues south of the house across Tecolote Creek (*tecolote* is Spanish for "owl"). The creek is often dry, but this makes for an excellent trail through the habitat. Birders are able to walk the creek bed and look up into the trees for Car-

Wildlife-viewing blind on the Tecolote Creek Ranch.

olina Wrens, Crested Titmice, Blue-gray Gnatcatchers, and Ruby-crowned Kinglets. After about ¼ mile the road turns west and crosses the back third of the ranch. This is where you will find the Tamaulipan thorn scrub. There are many species to be seen here if one is patient: Greater Roadrunner, Eastern Phoebe, Curved-bill Thrasher, and Northern Mockingbird, among them. A Screech Owl has been heard in this area. Cenderas or cleared areas are plentiful on the ranch. These allow the birder to get off the road and explore the brush.

The road turns north and crosses a narrow dirt dam separating two small artificial lakes. Roseate Spoonbills, Great Blue Heron, and Belted Kingfishers are some of the birds seen at this location. The road then connects to the entry road and completes a 1.5-mile loop.

No hunting is allowed on the ranch. In the past, however, five deer blinds were used. These are now used for wildlife viewing. Barn Owls have nested in one or more of these blinds. The ranch has deer, feral pigs, raccoons, opossums, coyotes, bobcats, a lynx, a badger, and possibly a cougar.

General information: There is a fee, and you must call the owners to make an appointment. The 305-acre property was originally part of the Adams Ranch, which belonged to a longtime ranching family in the Orange Grove area. The current owners, Joe and Vickey Paschal, have worked to open part of the ranch for nature tourism. Clients are welcomed for day trips, or there is a three-bedroom, two-bath guesthouse available for overnight or weekend stays. Guests are allowed to explore the ranch on their own.

DeLorme: Texas Atlas & Gazetteer: Page 84 3D.

Elevation: 240 feet.

Hazards: Thorns, snakes, bees, fire ants.

Nearest food, gas, lodging: Orange Grove for food and gas; overnight lodging is available on the ranch.

For more information: Joe and Vickey Paschal, 9545 Paula Drive, Corpus Christi, TX 78410; (361) 946-1103; Tecolote Creek Ranch, 2558 County Road 308, Orange Grove, TX 78372; (361) 946-1103.

62 Wesley Seale Dam and the City of Corpus Christi Wildlife Sanctuary

Habitats: Tamaulipan thorn scrub, transitional riparian forest, freshwater lake.

Specialty birds: *Resident*—Least Grebe, Black-bellied Whistling-Duck, Harris' Hawk, White-tipped Dove, Common Pauraque, Green Kingfisher, Golden-fronted Woodpecker, Great Kiskadee, Couch's Kingbird, Long-billed Thrasher. *Spring/Summer*—Brown-crested Flycatcher, Scissor-tailed Flycatcher, Cave Swallow.

Other key birds: *Resident*—Neotropic Cormorant, Mottled Duck, Crested Caracara, Ringed Kingfisher. *Spring/Summer*—Anhinga. *Fall/Winter*—Greater White-fronted Goose, Ross's Goose. *Migrating*—Neotropic passerines.

Best times to bird: Winter, early spring.

Directions: Take Interstate 37 north from Corpus Christi. Take Exit 34, which is the first exit for Mathis. Go under the interstate to Spur 459, and go west for ½ mile. Turn left on Highway 359 and travel west for about 5 miles. You will notice signs for Corpus Christi State Recreational Area along the way. Turn right on to Park Road 25, which is just before the Nueces River bridge. The parking area for the City of Corpus Christi Wildlife Sanctuary is about 1 block on the left. There is a second entrance, and parking for this area is about 1 mile farther down PR 25.

To reach the Wesley Seale Dam area, return to Highway 359 and cross the Nueces River. On the other side you will notice Jim Wells County Road 365. Follow this road until it ends at the parking lot for the Wesley Seale Dam.

Ringed Kingfisher. PHOTO: TONY BAYLIS.

The birding

If you wish to cover the entire area of the City of Corpus Christi Wildlife Sanctuary, it is best to enter at one end and exit at the other. The first entrance will take you initially into an open area. Off to the left of this area is a trail that will eventually lead you back onto the path to the river. Or you can follow the river path by going straight until it meets with the trail paralleling the river. None of these trails are marked. Also, many thorny bushes are hiding under the tall grasses. Be sure to wear sturdy shoes at this site. These trails go through rocky overflow areas, which in rainy times can have enough water to make them impassable. The cedar elms, black willow, Arizona ash, and hackberry trees and dewberry vines make it fine habitat for birds. In the spring, the area is densely covered with bluebonnets and other wildflowers.

The entrance area has many resident Carolina Wrens. Listen for their "tea kettle, tea kettle" call. On the walk to the river and dam, look for Mockingbirds, Green Jays, Great Kiskadees, House Wrens, White-tipped Doves, Couch's Kingbirds, Ruby-crowned Kinglets, Golden-fronted Woodpeckers, Yellow-bellied Sapsuckers, American Robins, Long-billed Thrashers, Cedar Waxwings, and others. Crested Caracara and Red-shouldered Hawks are abundant here. In the early morning, watch for flyovers of Black-bellied Whistling-Ducks, American White Pelicans, herons, egrets, White Ibis, Neotropic and Double-crested Cormorants, Cave Swallows, Purple Martins, Red-winged Blackbirds, Sandhill Cranes, and Snow Geese. As you near the river, you will pass a small lake with great Anhinga habitat. Watch the trees for warblers, such as Black and White and Wilson's, and wrens, such as the Winter Wren. Once you reach the river, search for Belted and Green Kingfishers.

At the end of the trail you will see the spillway for the dam. Cormorants, pelicans, and ducks will be working this area. Ospreys fly over the water. The dam usually has a Black or Turkey Vulture on each possible roost. They are both thick in this park.

On the other side of the river, at the Wesley Seale Dam facility, the birder will spy most of the same birds. If you are looking for sparrows, this would be the better site to explore. The trail on this side is very straightforward, with large yellow signs announcing SHORTEST PATH TO THE RIVER and RIVER. This site has some large, beautiful specimens of live oak trees. A Barred Owl often takes to these trees. It is also said that this is a good habitat for the American Woodcock, though I have never seen one here.

In the spring, migrating passerines and Yellow-shafted and Red-shafted Flickers are noted at this site.

General information: This is a very primitive area with no facilities. Anglers walking to the Nueces River use this area heavily. Together, these sites are classified as CTC#79.

The dam was completed in 1958 and named in honor of Wesley E. Seale, chairman of the Lower Nueces River Water Supply District.

DeLorme: Texas Atlas & Gazetteer: Page 84 4C.

Elevation: 160 feet.

Hazards: Snakes, fire ants, thorns, poison ivy.

Nearest food, gas, lodging: Mathis.

Camping: Lake Corpus Christi State Park.

For more information: City of Corpus Christi, 1202 Leopard, Corpus Christi, TX 78401; (361) 880-3211.

63 Pernitas Point/Carmel Hills

Habitats: Transitional riparian forest, Tamaulipan thorn scrub, agricultural areas.

Specialty birds: *Resident*—Black-bellied Whistling-Duck, White-tailed Kite, Harris' Hawk, White-tipped Dove, Groove-billed Ani, Common Pauraque, Green Kingfisher, Golden-fronted Woodpecker, Greater Kiskadee, Couch's Kingbird, Green Jay, Long-billed Thrasher, Olive Sparrow, Cassin's Sparrow, Audubon's Oriole. *Spring/Summer*—Brown-crested Flycatcher, Scissor-tailed Flycatcher, Cave Swallow. *Fall/Winter*—Vermilion Flycatcher, Sprague's Pipit.

Other key birds: *Resident*—Mottled Duck, Crested Caracara, Scaled Quail, Inca Dove, Ladder-backed Woodpecker, Curve-billed Thrasher, Pyrrhuloxia. *Spring/Summer*—Anhinga, Lesser Nighthawk, Painted Bunting.

Best times to bird: Year-round, with summer least productive.

Directions: From Corpus Christi, take Interstate 37 north toward San Antonio. Get off at Exit 34, in the town of Mathis, about 30 miles north of Corpus Christi. Take Spur 459 west for ½ mile; merge onto Highway 359 West and continue for 9 miles. Turn right onto North Farm-to-Market 534 and go 4.6 miles to Farm-to-Market 369. Turn right and travel on FM 369 for 2.5 miles until you reach the unincorporated Village of Pernitas Point.

Return to FM 534. Turn right and continue for another 3.7 miles, then turn right on Carmel Hills Road. There will be a sign marked LAKESHORE. Travel 1.8 miles until you arrive at the entrance to the Lakeshore Subdivision.

Audubon's Oriole. PHOTO: TONY BAYLIS.

The birding

Except for Lake Corpus Christi State Park and the wildlife areas owned by the City of Corpus Christi, all of the land around this lake has been subdivided and developed. Both of these locations are rural residential areas, with all of the property privately owned. They are, however, well known for their diverse bird populations. Drive around either subdivision, or find a convenient place to park and walk on the paved streets to look for bird life. Just remember to be respectful of the residents.

In either subdivision it is possible to get close to the lake to look for ducks, cormorants, gulls, and so on. At Carmel Hills, a shallow inlet of the lake is especially nice and can easily be accessed. Here in some trees by the water, I saw Audubon's Orioles. In the brush along the roads, Green Jays and Curve-billed Thrashers are abundant. Watch the fields and utility lines for sparrows and raptors.

General information: About 270 people live in Pernitas Point which is in Live Oak County. (The community straddles Live Oak and Jim Wells Counties, but Live Oak has the greater share of the population.) Carmel Hills, which is somewhat smaller, is also in Live Oak County.

DeLorme: Texas Atlas & Gazetteer: Page 84 4C.
Elevation: 210 feet.

Nearest food, gas, lodging: Mathis.
Camping: Lake Corpus Christi State Park.

64 Lake Corpus Christi State Park and Recreation Area

Habitats: Transitional riparian, Tamaulipan thorn scrub, freshwater lake.

Specialty birds: *Resident*—Least Grebe, Black-bellied Whistling-Duck, White-tailed Kite, Harris' Hawk, White-tailed Hawk, White-tipped Dove, Groove-billed Ani, Common Pauraque, Buff-bellied Hummingbird, Green Kingfisher, Golden-fronted Woodpecker, Great Kiskadee, Couch's Kingbird, Green Jay, Long-billed Thrasher, Olive Sparrow, Cassin's Sparrow, Audubon's Oriole. *Spring/Summer*—Wood Stork, Brown-crested Flycatcher, Scissor-tailed Flycatcher, Cave Swallow. *Fall/Winter*—Vermilion Flycatcher, Sprague's Pipit. *Migrating*—Swallow-tailed Kite, Hudsonian Godwit.

Other key birds: *Resident*—Neotropic Cormorant, Mottled Duck, Fulvous Whistling-Duck, Crested Caracara, Inca Dove, Ladder-backed Woodpecker, Curved-bill Thrasher, Bronzed Cowbird, Pyrrhuloxia, Lesser Goldfinch. *Spring/Summer*—Anhinga, Lesser Nighthawk, Painted Bunting. *Fall/Winter*—Common Loon, Greater White-fronted Goose, Ross's Goose. *Migrating*—Raptors, shorebirds, Neotropic passerines.

Best times to bird: Fall, winter, spring

Directions: From Corpus Christi, take Interstate 37 north toward San Antonio. Get off at Exit 34, in the town of Mathis, about 30 miles north of Corpus Christi. Take Spur 459 west for ½ mile; merge onto Highway 359 West and continue for 4.8 miles. Turn right onto Park Road 25 and go 1.5 miles. The entrance for Lake Corpus Christi State Park will be on the left. There are plenty of brown state park signs along the way to mark every turn.

The birding

The focus of this state park is the 21,000-acre lake with boating and fishing. Consequently, there are no nature or hiking trails. Visitors are not encouraged to walk in the brush: It is thick and thorny, and the threat of snakes is ever present. This, however, should not discourage the bird-watcher in any way. The park is crisscrossed with many paved roads leading to campsites and shelters. An early morning or sunset walk along these roads could be very productive.

In many cases, the brush comes right up to the road, and birds such as Northern Cardinals, Northern Mockingbirds, White-winged and Inca Doves, and Green Jays are easy to spot. Other birds of this arid climate include Greater Roadrunners, Harris' Hawks, Groove-billed Anis, Brown-crested and Scissor-tailed Flycatchers, and Golden-fronted Woodpeckers. At wildflowers and flowering bushes, check for Black-chinned and Ruby-throated Hummingbirds, as well as many species of butterflies. At twilight, try to spot nightjars such as Lesser Nighthawks and Common Pauraques. Other dry land birds such as thrashers and sparrows should be observed. During spring migration, many Neotropic passerines use the mesquite brush and grasslands as a refueling stop.

Curve-billed Thrasher. PHOTO: TONY BAYLIS.

There is easy access to the lake at boat ramps and fishing piers. Waterbirds such as Purple Gallinules, Great Blue Herons, Great Egrets, and Black-bellied Whistling-Ducks can be spotted. In the fall and winter, geese and ducks such as Blue-winged Teal, Hooded Mergansers, and Ruddy Ducks will be abundant. Plovers and American Avocets stop here during their migrations, as will several species of sandpipers. Near both piers and fish-cleaning stations there are willow trees that may harbor Couch's Kingbirds, Greater Kiskadees, or other interesting passerines.

For a different look at the lake, go to the Old Pavilion, which was built by the Civilian Conservation Corp (CCC) in 1933–1934. There is an overlook of the lake behind the pavilion. Brick steps lead explorers down to a lower level for a closer look at the water. You will be able to tell from this vantage point that much of the lake shoreline has been developed. This makes the preservation of natural habitat within the park especially important.

There is a bird checklist available just for the asking. It includes several rarities for which the visiting bird-watcher could wish. I hope you are thrilled by spotting a Scaled Quail, Golden Eagle, White-tailed Kite, Northern Jacana, or White-tipped Dove.

General information: There is an entrance fee. Gates open at 7:00 A.M. and close at 10:00 P.M. Primitive camping, RV sites, and shelters are available. There are several restrooms and covered picnic tables. Swimming in the lake is permitted. This is CTC#80. It is wheelchair accessible.

The lake and the park have a long and interesting history. The original dam on the Nueces River near this point was called La Fruita Dam. It was constructed in 1929. Because of a washout, the Civilian Conservation Corps rebuilt the dam during the Great Depression. The CCC dam was replaced by the current dam in the 1940s. All of the large lakes, and most of the small lakes, within the borders of Texas are artificial. The Lake Corpus Christi Reservoir is one of these large artificial bodies of water.

By the way, the name *Corpus Christi* is Latin for "Body of Christ." It is said that the Spanish explorer Alonso de Piñeda, who sailed into the bay in 1519, named it Corpus Christi, honoring that feast day on the Catholic calendar. The city and later the lake took their name from the bay.

DeLorme: Texas Atlas & Gazetteer: Page 84 8C.

Elevation: 161 feet.

Hazards: Africanized bees, snakes, fire ants.

Nearest food, gas, lodging: Mathis.

Camping: Lake Corpus Christi State Park.

For more information: Lake Corpus Christi State Park, P.O. Box 1167, Mathis, TX 78368; (361) 547-2635.

65 Highway 624—McMullen County

Habitats: Tamaulipan scrubland, Tamaulipan thorn scrub.

Specialty birds: *Resident*—Harris' Hawk, White-tipped Dove, Common Pauraque, Golden-fronted Woodpecker, Long-billed Thrasher, Olive Sparrow, Cassin's Sparrow, Audubon's Oriole. *Spring/Summer*—Brown-crested Flycatcher, Scissor-tailed Flycatcher, Cave Swallow, Hooded Oriole. *Fall/Winter*—Vermilion Flycatcher.

Other key birds: *Resident*—Crested Caracara, Scaled Quail, Inca Dove, Curve-billed Thrasher, Bronzed Cowbird, Pyrrhuloxia, Lesser Gold-finch. *Spring/Summer*—Lesser Nighthawk,

Painted Bunting. *Rarity*—Black-tailed Gnat-catcher.

Best times to bird: Fall and spring.

Directions: Highway 77 intersects with Highway 624 in the 5 Points area of Corpus Christi. From the intersection, take Highway 624 for 21 miles west to the town of Orange Grove, in Jim Wells County. Continue through the town on Highway 624 to Live Oak County after another 15 miles and McMullen County, which is about 28 miles from Orange Grove. If you wish to continue to the Nueces River, stay on Highway 624 for another 45 miles.

The birding

This is one of those sites that will not appeal to everyone. First, it is a long way to McMullen County from Corpus Christi. Second, there is really no specific place to visit. When you arrive in the county, the only option is to pull off the road and walk a bit. But that isn't easy, as Highway 624 is two lanes with no shoulders. There are very few crossroads or even ranch gates by which to pull off.

Once you leave Orange Grove, you will immediately notice a change in the scenery. An official Texas highway sign at the outskirts of town warns the traveler that no gas will be available for 82 miles. Don't doubt that sign. There are no towns, or stores, or even many houses on this road. Bring enough gas and water. Right away you will think that you have somehow magically gotten to West Texas. The farmland of the Orange Grove area turns into rolling ranch terrain, with cactus, mesquite, sage, chaparral, and scrubby grasses. Limestone and caliche intertwine to form the "soil." It looks hot here even in the winter. Signs for Los Niños, Rancho Clegg, Los Dos Ranch, and Brazil Ranch will make you question if you're still in Texas.

Highway 624 intersects with two major state highways that go north and south—Highway 281 and Highway 59. Traffic that you meet will consist mostly of eighteen-wheelers hauling cattle or caliche. If solitude agrees with you, then this should be your pick of the sites in the book. I mean, McMullen County is over 1,000 square miles with only one real town, Tilden, and even that town has a population of around 500. After you cross Highway 59, don't expect to see any traffic at all.

Crested Caracara. PHOTO: TONY BAYLIS.

You can, however, expect to see lots of birds. On one trip, I saw more than one hundred Crested Caracaras. There were fourteen of these birds at one road kill, along with the ever-certain Turkey Vultures. At highway culverts, such as the one at Cow Creek, look for Cave/Cliff Swallows. Watch for Common Roadrunners crossing in front of you or giving you a short chase. You should have no trouble spotting White-wing Doves, Common Ground Doves, and, if you're lucky, Scaled Quail. If you are looking for that bird, this might just be your best bet.

Check the fence lines for Scissor-tailed Flycatchers, Loggerhead Shrikes, and Northern Mockingbirds. In the winter, look at the same fences for Vermilion Fly-catchers. Watch the utility poles for Harris and Red-tailed Hawks. If you arrive before sunrise, listen for Common Pauraque and Common Poorwill. There are three spectacular orioles that like this habitat. While walking along the road, it would be lovely to spot a Bullock's, Audubon, or Hooded Oriole. In the grasses, you may see sparrows such as Black-throated or Cassin's. Check the brush for Verdins and Cactus Wrens. Black-tailed Gnatcatchers have been listed in this county in the past.

General information: Jim Wells County was named for James B. Wells Jr. who was a figure in the early 1900s in the Lower Rio Grande Valley. Live Oak County is named for the trees. McMullen County is named for John McMullen, an Irish empresario.

DeLorme: Texas Atlas & Gazetteer: All of page 84.
Elevation: 150 feet to 400 feet.

Hazards: Snakes, lack of roadside assistance.
Nearest food, gas, lodging: Orange Grove or Tilden.

66 La Ramireña Ranch

Habitats: Transitional riparian forest, Tamaulipan scrubland, Tamaulipan thorn scrub, oak savanna, freshwater ponds.

Specialty birds: *Resident*—Black-bellied Whistling-Ducks, White-tailed Kite, Harris' Hawk, White-tipped Dove, Groove-billed Ani, Common Pauraque, Green Kingfisher, Golden-fronted Woodpecker, Couch's Kingbird, Green Jay, Long-billed Thrasher, Olive Sparrow, Cassin's Sparrow, Audubon's Oriole. *Spring/Summer*—Wood Stork, Brown-crested Flycatcher, Scissor-tailed Flycatcher, Cave Swallow. *Fall/Winter*—Vermilion Flycatcher.

Other key birds: *Resident*—Mottled Duck, Crested Caracara, Inca Dove, Ladder-backed Woodpecker, Curved-billed Thrasher, Bronzed Cowbird, Lesser Goldfinch. *Spring/Summer*—Anhinga, Lesser Nighthawk, Painted Bunting. *Fall/Winter*—Greater White-fronted Goose, Ross's Goose.

Best times to bird: Fall, winter, spring.

Directions: From Corpus Christi, take Interstate 37 north toward San Antonio. Travel 40 miles to Exit 47, at Sweeny Switch. Turn left onto South Farm Road 534 toward Dinero. Go west 3.6 miles. At Dinero, make a hard left to stay on Farm-to-Market 534. Travel 6.5 miles to the ranch. The gate is on the right at the top of a rise. The sign on the gate announces LA RAMIREÑA RANCH, GATE #3. There is a push-button gate control. The caliche ranch road curves around to the main house and available rentals.

The birding

To me it seems that good bird-watchers eventually become habitat lovers. At this ranch, you will feel that way sooner rather than later. This is a beautiful 1,026-acre ranch that is lovingly cared for.

The ranch is used for many outdoor activities. Some cattle range on the property. During the appropriate seasons, turkey, quail, dove, ducks, deer, and wild hogs are hunted here. Also, on a portion of the ranch called Rich's Pond, there is catch-and-release bass fishing. The ranch participates in the annual Coastal Bend Wildlife Photo Contest sponsored by the Coastal Bend Wildlife Habitat Education Program.

Two bungalows are available for rent. The first cottage has one bedroom, with two double beds, and one bathroom. It includes a living room with additional sleeping available and a kitchen. The other rental is a bunkhouse that sleeps four and has one bath. Both are comfortable and nicely decorated. Between the two is a gorgeous outdoor living area that contains a complete *cocina* (kitchen), barbecue, fire ring, outdoor seating, hammock, and swimming pool. Seed and nectar feeders are kept well stocked. Black-chinned and Ruby-throated Hummingbirds buzz by for a drink. Part of Lake Corpus Christi can be seen from this lovely vista. The owner lives on the property, but bird-watchers, with a little orientation and instruction, are free to wander on foot or vehicle around the property. The ranch roads are passable even in the worst weather.

La Ramireña Ranch.

These roads traverse most of the property, including the Tamaulipan thorn scrub characterized by mesquite, cactus, Spanish yucca, lantana, and purple sage. While walking here, look and listen for Cactus Wren, Lark and Black-throated Sparrows, and Curve-billed Thrashers. Scaled Quail have never been seen on the ranch, but Bobwhite Quail certainly have.

The thorn scrub quickly turns to Tamaulipan scrubland, with more grasses visible, as well as huisache and agarita. Keep your eyes and ears open for Long-billed Thrashers, Green Jays, Pyrrhuloxia, White-eyed Vireos, and Bewick's Wrens. The Painted Bunting is a brilliant bird of this habitat.

A savanna with old, large stands of live oaks dominates another section of the ranch. The ranch has an abundance of Wild Turkey. Look for them in this area. You should see a Greater Roadrunner, Northern Mockingbirds, Blue-gray Gnatcatchers, and Ladder-backed and Golden-fronted Woodpeckers. The ranch has several deer blinds that can be used by birders. A small part of the ranch is usually planted in a feed crop for birds and other wildlife. In the winter, Sandhill Crane, ducks, and geese frequent the ranch.

There are several water elements on the ranch. Sandpipers, herons, and egrets visit these areas. Wood Storks have been spotted in June and July. Where the road crosses the Ramireña Creek, willows line the area, making it a desirable spot for many birds, including passerines. There is also a deep creek section known as Gator Hole. In spring, this area and most of the ranch are covered with beautiful wildflowers that draw in more hummingbirds and many butterfly species.

There is an artificial tank used by ducks such as mallards, shovelers, and teal. Yet another water feature is the artesian well that was dug in 1984. Since that time, it has produced 1 gallon of water per minute, which is now funneled into a cattail pond. Black-bellied Whistling-Ducks nested there recently.

This area of Texas is famous for hawks. La Ramireña Ranch is no different. Look up every so often to watch for Red-tailed, Harris, Red-shouldered, and Cooper's Hawks. A special treat would be a Crested Caracara or a White-tailed Kite.

Many visitors to the ranch have commented on the abundance of horny toads, which were once common throughout Texas but are seldom seen anymore. They are usually a good indicator of the environmental health of an area.

General information: This ranch was originally part of the Mexican land grant given in the early 1800s to two Irish settlers, John McMullen and James McGloin. About 3 miles upstream, Ramireña Creek runs through the ranch on which J. Frank Dobie, the famous Texas historian, was raised. Ramireña Creek is mentioned in his books on South Texas. Perhaps the creek was named for the Ramirez brothers, who had built a fort on the creek for protection from natives. Or maybe the name comes from two Spanish words: *rami* for "brush" and *reña* for "queen." Queen of the Brush absolutely fits as a name for this ranch.

DeLorme: Texas Atlas & Gazetteer: Page 84 3B.

Elevation: 85 feet to 210 feet.

Hazards: Snakes, alligators, mosquitoes.

Nearest food, gas, lodging: Lodging on the ranch; gas and food in Mathis, south on I-37.

For more information: La Ramireña Ranch, c/o Richard Phillips, P.O. Box 87, Dinero, TX 78350; (361) 547-2249.

⑥⑦ Veteran's Memorial Park

Habitats: Transitional riparian forest, Tamaulipan scrubland, prairie, oak woodland.

Specialty birds: *Resident*—Black-bellied Whistling-Duck, Groove-billed Ani, Common Pauraque, Golden-fronted Woodpecker, Great Kiskadee, Couch's Kingbird, Green Jay, Long-billed Thrasher, Cassin's Sparrow, Audubon's Oriole. *Spring/Summer*—Brown-crested Flycatcher, Scissor-tailed Flycatcher. *Fall/Winter*—Vermilion Flycatcher.

Other key birds: *Resident*—Inca Dove, Ladder-backed Woodpecker, Curve-billed Thrasher, Bronzed Cowbird, Pyrrhuloxia, Lesser Goldfinch. *Spring/Summer*—Painted Bunting. *Migrating*—Neotropic passerines.

Best times to bird: Year-round.

Directions: From Corpus Christi, take Interstate 37 north toward San Antonio. Take exit 56 (U.S. Highway 59); this is about 50 miles out of Corpus Christi. Turn right onto US 59 and travel east for 18 miles to Beeville. Turn left on Farm Road North 673. The entrance to Veteran's Memorial Park is 0.3 mile on the left.

The birding

This 200-acre park has the feel of a large county park. As you enter, notice baseball and football fields, but continue by staying to the right. Cross the road over the slow-moving Poesta Creek into the back section of the park. There are a few tables back here, and a Frisbee golf course cuts through the large open field. Many lovely live oak trees and some mesquites highlight this section of the park. This is a fine place for Meadowlarks, White-winged Doves, Northern Mockingbirds, Cliff Swallows, Scissor-tailed Flycatchers, Couch's Kingbirds, Western Kingbirds, and even Eurasian Collared Doves. The road circles around and will return you to the park's main road.

The creek, which runs through most of the park, is lined with willows and cedar elms. It is situated so that the bird-watcher can walk the banks on either side to look for water-loving birds, including the Belted Kingfisher. There is also a dirt road that follows the creek behind the sports fields.

Following the main road to its end, you arrive at the clubhouse of the eighteen-hole public golf course, which borders the upper edge of the park. This area of the park is manicured and has numerous tables and a restroom. In the winter, look for a Vermilion Flycatcher perched on a low wire or an American Kestrel peering down from a utility line.

Take the road to the right to access another secluded section of the park with a birding trailhead. A sign explains that it is a bird-viewing area. It marks the entrance to the trail. There is parking here as well. A wooden bridge begins the trail. A wire pulled through posts marks the rest of the trail. You are led in two directions, but this is actually a loop. Feel comfortable going either way. Expect

Northern Cardinals, Loggerhead Shrikes, Great Kiskadees, Bronze-headed Cowbirds, Red-winged Blackbirds, and Black-bellied Whistling-Ducks. Beeville brags that it is the one Coastal Bend city where you can see Green Jays and Blue Jays at the same feeder. In May, I saw Eastern Bluebirds. Could they have been a remnant of the Rio Grande subspecies? The spring wildflowers along this short trail are awesome. Many of these flowers draw in Ruby-throated Hummingbirds.

General information: Veteran's Memorial Park, which was dedicated on March 22, 1981, is a joint project of the City of Beeville, Texas Parks and Wildlife, and the National Park Service. It is open daily from 7:00 A.M. to 10:00 P.M.

Texas has 254 counties, each with a unique courthouse. The Bee County Courthouse in Beeville is special. Drive by it at the corner of Highway 59 and U.S. Business Highway 181. There is also a small but wonderful art museum in Beeville that is open every day except Sunday.

DeLorme: Texas Atlas & Gazetteer: Page 78 4K.

Elevation: 214 feet.

Hazards: Mosquitoes, snakes.

Nearest food, gas, lodging: Beeville.

For more information: City of Beeville, 400 North St. Mary's, Beeville, TX 78102; (361) 358-4641; Beeville Art Museum, 401 East Fannin, P.O. Box 1236, Beeville, TX 78104; (361) 358-8615.

68 Berclair Loop

Habitats: Transitional riparian forest, Tamaulipan scrubland, prairie, agricultural areas.

Specialty birds: *Resident*—Black-bellied Whistling-Duck, White-tailed Kite, Harris' Hawk, White-tipped Dove, Groove-billed Ani, Common Pauraque, Golden-fronted Woodpecker, Great Kiskadee, Couch's Kingbird, Green Jay, Long-billed Thrasher, Olive Sparrow, Cassin's Sparrow, Audubon's Oriole. *Spring/Summer*—Brown-crested Flycatcher, Scissor-tailed Flycatcher, Cave Swallow. *Fall/Winter*—Vermilion Flycatcher.

Other key birds: *Resident*—Crested Caracara, Inca Dove, Ladder-backed Woodpecker, Curve-billed Thrasher, Bronzed Cowbird, Pyrrhuloxia, Lesser Goldfinch. *Spring/Summer*—Lesser Nighhawk, Painted Bunting. *Migrating*—Raptors.

Best times to bird: Year-round.

Directions: From the junction of U.S. Highway 181 and U.S. Highway 59 at Beeville, go 13 miles east on US 59 until you reach Farm-to-Market 883 in Berclair. Turn left and go north on FM 883 for 13.5 miles to Farm-to-Market 2442. Turn right and travel for 7.8 miles to Newton-Powell Road. This road is plainly marked by a sign, but be sure to watch for it, as highway maps do not include this one-lane road. After 8.3 miles, this ranch road dead-ends into Farm-to-Market 1351; however, the road is not marked at that point. Turn left, but from there on stay to your right, and another 8.4 miles will return you to US 59. Left will take you on to Goliad, or turn right and travel 10 miles back to Berclair.

The birding

This tour loop is not for everyone; it is definitely the road less traveled.

Newton-Powell Road is only one lane, and in some patches it is not even paved. Very few people live out this way, and when I took the 47-mile tour, I saw only four vehicles. I had read about this loop in Mark Elwonger's out-of-print book, *Finding Birds on the Central Texas Coast,* and was encouraged to try it. Believe me, the birds are there. The trick is figuring out where to stop to look for them. Obviously, the best places are near water. The roads cross Miller's Creek in several places, and I would certainly suggest that you get out and look around at those spots. In most cases the trees come right out to the roadway, and in other places there is no fence. Therefore, the birder will want to consider stopping at those places that look most promising. Don't forget that all of this is private property.

If you are trying to see the Common Pauraque or the Lesser or Common Nighthawk, you must be on location before the sun comes up or perhaps as it is going down. The Harris' Hawks and other raptors will be easy to spot overhead or in the tops of trees or on utility lines. Cave Swallows swarm around the roadside culverts and should be easily seen. Orioles, Lesser Goldfinches, and any warblers should be near areas with water. Look for Bronzed Cowbirds and flycatchers, including the Vermilion, perched on lines or fences. Thrashers, Painted Buntings, and Olive Sparrows like the dry brush and may be hard to see from the road or at

Golden-fronted Woodpecker. PHOTO: TONY BAYLIS.

least while seated in your car. Green Jays will most likely cross the road in front of your car. They are usually hard to miss. Look in the grassy edges for sparrows like the Cassin's and Grasshopper.

General information: Berclair is just a spot in the road. However, the twenty-two-room Berclair Mansion is open for touring the last Sunday of each month. It is furnished with fabulous antiques, some dating to the 1600s.

DeLorme: Texas Atlas & Gazetteer: Page 78 5J.

Elevation: 210 feet.

Hazards: Lack of roadside assistance.

Nearest food, gas, lodging: Beeville and Goliad.

For more information: Bee County Chamber of Commerce/Convention and Visitors Bureau, 705 North St. Mary's, Beeville, TX 78102; (361) 358-3267; Berclair Mansion, (361) 358-4480.

69 Barnhart Q5 Ranch

Habitats: Transitional riparian forest, Tamaulipan scrubland, prairie, agricultural areas.

Specialty birds: *Resident*—Black-bellied Whistling-Duck, White-tailed Kite, Harris' Hawk, White-tipped Dove, Groove-billed Ani, Common Pauraque, Buff-bellied Hummingbird, Golden-fronted Woodpecker, Green Jay, Long-billed Thrasher, Olive Sparrow. *Spring/Summer*—Brown-crested Flycatcher, Scissor-tailed Flycatcher. *Fall/Winter*—Vermilion Flycatcher.

Other key birds: *Resident*—Crested Caracara, Inca Dove, Ladder-backed Woodpecker, Curve-billed Thrasher, Bronzed Cowbird, Pyrrhuloxia. *Spring/Summer*—Lesser Nighthawk, Painted Bunting. *Migrating*—Raptors.

Best times to bird: Year-round.

Directions: From the junction of U.S. Highway 181 and U.S. Highway 59 at Beeville, go 13 miles east on US 59 until you reach Farm-to-Market 883 in Berclair. Turn left and go north on FM 883 for 8.2 miles to the entrance for Barnhart Q5 Ranch on the right. Inside the gate, which you will close after going through, take the left road to the ranch house. It is 0.8 mile down the dirt road to the headquarters. You must cross two cattle guards. Drive slowly across the iron cattle guards in the roadway.

The birding

How would you like to meet Jim Bowie, Rosa Parks, and Pablo Picasso all on the same day at the same place? You can at the Barnhart Q5 Ranch. Surprised? They are members of the herd of Mediterranean miniature donkeys bred at the ranch. What does this have to do with bird watching? The ranch is also a premier wildlife and bird-watching destination.

The 706 acres of the Q5 Ranch have been divided into quadrants with something to attract wildlife to each. There are several miles of flagged hike and bike trails. Each quadrant has at least one water feature, including a total of eight ponds and Indian Creek and Turkey Creek. Eight photography blinds with feeders also dot the ranch. Small groups are welcome for day use, but the ranch's focus is on overnight guests, who are free to roam on their own after they are given an initial overview tour by the owners. A golf cart is available for guests, but most choose to hike the many trails and cenderos on the ranch.

Rest in one of the blinds and watch Green Jays, Northern Cardinals, Pyrrhuloxias, or Common Ground Doves at the feeder. In the winter, Sandhill Crane and Canada Geese have been listed. Hike through the native grasses and look for sparrows such as Vesper, White-crowned, White-throated, Song, and Savannah. If you want to see Black-chinned, Ruby-throated, or Buff-bellied Hummingbirds, study the nectar feeders near the house or the numerous wildflowers that blanket the ranch in the spring. Of course, the flowers draw in many species of butterflies as well.

Many beautiful stands of live oaks grace the Q5 Ranch. Near these trees would be a good place to look for Wild Turkeys and Northern Bobwhite Quail. Raptors are represented on the property by Great Horned Owls, Red-tailed Hawks, Harris' Hawks, Northern Harriers, and even a Ferruginous Hawk.

Even though none of the water features on the ranch are large, many water-loving birds use them, including ducks, egrets, ibis, herons, and grebes. The two creeks are lined by a nice stand of trees. These would be prime stopovers for migrating passerines in the spring. Woodpeckers love these trees. Golden-fronted and Downy Woodpeckers are known to visit the ranch, and there is a suggested sighting of a Pileated Woodpecker.

Other wildlife noted on the ranch are deer, bobcat, coyote, red and gray fox, javelina, feral hog, cottontail and jackrabbits, and snakes. Horny toads are numerous, and a jaguarundi with cubs was seen in the southeast pasture in December 2004.

The adorable donkeys and the Texas hospitality are worth the trip to this ranch. The variety and accessibility to the bird life will not disappoint the avid bird-watcher.

General information: There is a fee, and reservations are necessary for day use or overnight stays. The historic guesthouse, the Maetze–von Dohlen Home, was originally located in Goliad and was built about 1875. It was moved to the ranch in August 2005. It features three bedrooms, two baths, two living rooms, a new kitchen, and a wraparound porch. It can sleep eight to ten people.

In addition to the donkeys, the ranch raises a small herd of cattle. The livestock is maintained in a limited area of the ranch. This location is far removed from any night lights and would be a fine spot for stargazing. The ranch is sometimes leased to hunters during deer season. In 2004 the Barnhart Q5 Ranch won the Texas Lone Star Land Steward Award. The ranch owners live on the property.

DeLorme: Texas Atlas & Gazetteer: Page 78 5J.

Elevation: 210 feet.

Hazards: Fire ants, snakes, poor road conditions in rainy weather.

Nearest food, gas, lodging: Beeville and Goliad.

For more information: Barnhart Q5 Ranch, 8212 FM 883, P.O. Box 626, Berclair, TX 78107; (361) 375-2824.

70 Choke Canyon State Park

Habitats: Transitional riparian forest, Tamaulipan thorn scrub, freshwater lake, agricultural areas.

Specialty birds: *Resident*—Least Grebe, Brown Pelican, Black-bellied Whistling-Duck, White-tailed Kite, Harris' Hawk, White-faced Ibis, Groove-billed Ani, Common Pauraque, Green Kingfisher, Golden-fronted Woodpecker, Great Kiskadee, Couch's Kingbird, Green Jay, Long-billed Thrasher, Olive Sparrow, Cassin's Sparrow, Audubon's Oriole. *Spring/Summer*—Brown-crested Flycatcher, Scissor-tailed Flycatcher, Cave Swallow, Hooded Oriole. *Fall/Winter*—Ringed Kingfisher, Vermilion Flycatcher, Sprague's Pipit. *Migrating*—Hudsonian Godwit.

Other key birds: *Resident*—Neotropic Cormorant, Mottled Duck, Crested Caracara, Scaled Quail, Little Blue Heron, Roseate Spoonbill, Gull-billed Tern, Inca Dove, Ladder-backed Woodpecker, Curve-billed Thrasher, Bronzed Cowbird, Pyrrhuloxia, Lesser Goldfinch. *Spring/Summer*—Anhinga, Lesser Nighthawk, Painted Bunting. *Fall/Winter*—Greater White-fronted Goose, Ross's Goose, Rufous Hummingbird. *Migrating*—Raptors, shorebirds, Neotropic passerines.

Best times to bird: Winter, spring.

Directions: Choke Canyon is about halfway between Corpus Christi and San Antonio off Interstate 37. Take Exit 69, which is about 70 miles north of Corpus Christi. Travel on Highway 72 West. You will go through the town of Three Rivers. The Frio, Nueces, and Atascosa Rivers meet near here. Highway 72 makes a jog in the town, but the signs are easily seen and followed. As you leave Three Rivers and cross the Frio River, note a sign for Tips Park. This thirty-one-acre city park is known for its Lesser Goldfinches. After 6 miles, you arrive at the entrance to the first unit of Choke Canyon State Park, South Shore Unit. The South Shore Unit is in Live Oak County. The second unit, Calliham Unit, is another 8½ miles on Highway 72. Turn right on Recreation Road 8 and travel for 1 mile to the park entrance. Again, everything is plainly marked. The Calliham Unit is in McMullen County.

The birding

It is hard to beat Choke Canyon State Park for enjoyable birding. The Choke Canyon Reservoir brings in waterfowl and wading birds, while the riparian and mesquite habitats attract owls, raptors, woodpeckers, and passerines. The park is so large that you must pick your area to start and then enjoy.

The first unit on Highway 72 is the South Shore Unit. This is the smaller of the two units. Stop at the park headquarters for a map of the park and a bird checklist of the 220+ birds seen here. The best birding is below the dam. Take the first road to the right after the park entrance. This will lead you up to the dam, where there is an overlook at the top. Continue on the road by veering to the right down from the overlook. Watch the telephone poles for Harris or Red-tailed Hawks. The road ends at the outlet channel for the Frio River. Park here. You can look over the channel toward the spillway to spot Great Blue Herons, Little Blue Herons, Green

Herons, Great Egrets, Snowy Egrets, and White and White-faced Ibis. Black-bellied Whistling-Ducks, Gadwalls, Northern Shovelers, and Cinnamon, Green-winged, and Blue-winged Teal can be seen in the spillway when water pools. The outlet channel attracts Yellow-rumped Warblers in the fall and winter. In the spring, look for neotropical migrating warblers and vireos.

From here, you can walk for a short distance to the right along the Frio River. This is a reliable place to look for Green Kingfishers. Check for them on the river bluff in the tangled growth. This is a secretive bird and difficult to find. It makes a sound like two small pebbles bumping together; so listen carefully. Say's Phoebes are known in this area as well. A Blue Grosbeak or a Painted Bunting could thrill you along the river.

As you leave the parking lot, there is a nice picnic area on the left that offers covered tables. Cliff, Cave, and Barn Swallows nest under the roofs. Behind table 33 is an entrance to a bird trail. This is a "mowed" ¼-mile path through cedar elms. Look for Black-crested Titmouse, House Wrens, White-eyed Vireos, Ruby-crowned and Golden-crowned Kinglets, and Orange-crowned Warblers. Both Ladder-backed and Golden-fronted Woodpeckers should be here. The trail continues across the paved road and eventually leads to a camping area. The outer edges of the park are fenced, but look across the fence for Savannah, White-crowned, and Black-throated Sparrows. The trees are loaded with ball moss, which attracts several species. You may spot a Winter Wren here, too. On a recent trip, I saw American Goldfinches, Pine Siskins, Titmice, and Brown-headed Cowbirds in the campground. Inca Doves and a Loggerhead Shrike were also in the region.

Farther down Highway 72 is the Calliham Unit. After the entrance, follow the road to the right and down to a closed boat ramp on 75 Acre Lake. Boating is no longer allowed on 75 Acre Lake. Look for ducks, coots, gulls, cormorants, herons, and egrets. There is also a boat ramp on the road leading off to the left. Here is another good place to look for waterfowl and wading birds. At both ramps, Turkey Vultures and Black Vultures hang out. Near the recreational facilities watch for Meadowlarks and American Pipits. The trees along the shore have produced Great Kiskadees, Scissor-tailed and Vermilion Flycatchers, and rarely a Black Phoebe.

Across from the recreation hall, a bird trail begins. The first part of the trail is paved and can be used by birders with disabilities. However, be sure to follow the arrows and continue down the mowed portion of the path after the pavement ends. Expect to find Golden-fronted and Ladder-backed Woodpeckers, White-eyed Vireos, Yellow-rumped Warblers, Olive Sparrow, Common Pauraque, and even Green Jays and Audubon's Orioles here. All along the trail you will note various birdhouses placed to attract nesters. I've seen Eastern Screech owls nesting in the bluebird boxes.

There are some benches along the trail where you can rest and listen for wrens and thrashers. A small pond is located near the end of the trail. This is a great location to spot Least Grebes and Anhingas. Don't be surprised if you see a Harris'

Bird-watchers at Choke Canyon State Park.

Hawk or Crested Caracara, too. The trail ends at a paved road, where a flock of Wild Turkey roams in the park. A Greater Roadrunner may dart on and off the road and into the thorny brush.

At the trailer camping area at the end of the park road, you will find the Bird Sanctuary. One of the frequent guests, Gregg Shivers, with financial help from Mr. and Mrs. Victor Roberts and Friends of Choke Canyon, built a water feature and feeding stations to attract passerines. Appropriate signs labeled DOVER'S LANE, QUAIL TRAIL, and WREN INN suggest which birds you may see here: Bobwhite

Quail, Spotted Towhee, Audubon and Bullock's Oriole, American Goldfinch, Green Jay, and many others. The sanctuary is fenced with tables nearby.

About halfway between the two units (not on park property), there is an opportunity to view Scaled Quail, Olive Sparrow, Verdin, Spotted Towhee, Pyrrhuloxia, Cactus Wren, Lark Bunting, and Black-throated Sparrow. Go south on paved County Road 1545 for about 1 mile and then west again on dirt County Road 426. This dirt road dead-ends after several miles. All of this is fenced private property, so stay out. But there is great birding up and down both roads.

General information: This is CTC#82. There is an entrance fee to the state park. The park is open daily for day use from 8:00 A.M. to 10:00 P.M. Many areas of the park are wheelchair accessible. The land for Choke Canyon State Park was acquired from the Bureau of Reclamation, the City of Corpus Christi, and the Nueces River Authority in 1981 in a fifty-year cooperative agreement. The 26,000-acre Choke Canyon Reservoir, which provides drinking water for Corpus Christi, was created when the Frio River was dammed. The South Shore Unit covers 385 acres, the Calliham Unit contains 1,100 acres. This beautiful state park was named for the steep banks near the dam site that "choked" the Frio River during floods.

Both units provide for camping with or without hook-ups, picnicking, boating (including boat ramps), hiking, fishing, and wildlife viewing. There are many restrooms. A sports complex with facilities for tennis, volleyball, basketball, swimming, softball, and shuffleboard is available. There are group facilities and a recreation hall. Several fishing tournaments are held there throughout the year. Sections of the park are closed at scheduled times for public hunting.

There is a primitive camping area, which includes equestrian trails, across the dam on the north shore. This area has been closed to the general public since September 11, 2001. Special permits and reservations are required to use this area.

DeLorme: Texas Atlas & Gazetteer: Page 78 1J, 2J, 1K, 2K.

Elevation: 220 feet.

Hazards: Snakes, fire ants, alligators.

Nearest food, gas, lodging: Three Rivers.

Camping: Choke Canyon State Park.

For more information: Choke Canyon State Park, Calliham Unit, P.O. Box 2, Calliham, TX 78007; (361) 786-3868; Choke Canyon State Park, South Shore Unit, P.O. Box 1548, Three Rivers, TX 78007; (361) 786-3538.

71 James E. Daughtrey Wildlife Management Area

Habitats: Transitional riparian forest, Tamaulipan thorn scrub, freshwater lake.

Specialty birds: *Resident*—Least Grebe, Brown Pelican, Black-bellied Whistling-Duck, White-tailed Kite, Harris' Hawk, White-faced Ibis, Groove-billed Ani, Common Pauraque, Golden-fronted Woodpecker, Great Kiskadee, Couch's Kingbird, Green Jay, Long-billed Thrasher, Olive Sparrow, Cassin's Sparrow, Audubon's Oriole. *Spring/Summer*—Brown-crested Flycatcher, Scissor-tailed Flycatcher, Cave Swallow. *Fall/ Winter*—Vermilion Flycatcher.

Other key birds: *Resident*—Neotropic Cormorant, Mottled Duck, Crested Caracara, Scaled Quail, Little Blue Heron, Roseate Spoonbill, Gull-billed Tern, Inca Dove, Ladder-backed Woodpecker, Curve-billed Thrasher, Bronzed Cowbird, Pyrrhuloxia, Lesser Goldfinch. *Spring/Summer*—Anhinga, Lesser Nighthawk, Painted Bunting. *Fall/Winter*—

Greater White-fronted Goose, Ross's Goose, Rufous Hummingbird. *Migrating*—Raptors, shorebirds, Neotropic passerines.

Best times to bird: Winter, spring.

Directions: From Corpus Christi, take Interstate 37 north to Exit 69, which is about 70 miles north of Corpus Christi. Travel west on Highway 72. You will go through the town of Three Rivers. Highway 72 makes a jog in the town, but the signs for it are easily spotted and followed. Stay on Highway 72 for 24.5 miles. You will pass the entrance to Choke Canyon State Park. Highway 72 runs into Highway 16 at Tilden. Turn right on Highway 16 and travel another 2.8 miles to Farm-to-Market 3445. Turn right from FM 3445 and go 5.7 miles to the entrance and another 0.9 mile to the headquarters of the James E. Daughtrey Wildlife Management Area.

The birding

The James E. Daughtrey Wildlife Management Area is a 4,400-acre expanse near Choke Canyon Reservoir. The actual size of this preserve shrinks and expands with the level of the lake. Mostly anglers and hunters use the area. By special permit and in season, hunters may take turkey, quail, javelina, doves, deer, and ducks. Some of the scheduled hunts are for archers.

Bird-watchers would not find this area appealing during any of these hunting seasons. Otherwise, the small part of the preserve that is open to nature lovers is secluded and can be very active with bird life. To the left of the headquarters is a check-in and camping area. Hunters use these primitive campsites, and there is a paved road with paved pullouts. At the front of this area is the trailhead for a short nature trail. The ¼-mile trail includes labeled plant life and a mowed path. The birder should find woodpeckers, Common Ground Doves, thrashers, and other scrubland birds. The trail makes a loop that returns you to the parking lot. A sign at the beginning of the trail warns of snakes.

The bird-watching possibilities are even better about ½ mile farther down FM 3445 toward the public boat ramp. Here you will find a slough created by water from the Choke Canyon Reservoir. Many dead trees spot the slough. In one quick stop, I saw Great Egrets, Great Blue Herons, Cattle Egrets, a Little Blue Heron, two Green Herons, a Purple Gallinule, Common Moorhens, Pied-bill Grebes, a Black-necked Stilt, a White-faced Ibis, and Black-bellied Whistling-Ducks. On the road to this spot, I flushed a Harris' Hawk from a utility pole.

Continue another 0.3 mile to the boat ramp for a view of the lake. Here I saw Anhingas and a flycatcher.

General information: The original purpose of the James E. Daughtrey Wildlife Management Area was to provide an ecological buffer around the water source for cities downstream. Since 1981 the Texas Parks and Wildlife Department has managed it for wildlife, and some limited public access is allowed. There is a portable toilet but no drinking water. During hunting seasons, the bird-watcher should avoid this area. At those times a limited public use permit or Texas Conservation Passport is required.

James E. Daughtrey WMA is named in honor of the McMullen County state game warden who was fatally injured while pursuing game law violators.

DeLorme: Texas Atlas & Gazetteer: Page 78 1K.

Elevation: 220 feet.

Hazards: Snakes, fire ants.

Nearest food, gas, lodging: Tilden.

Camping: Choke Canyon State Park.

For more information: Texas Parks and Wildlife Department, 4200 Smith School Road, Austin, TX 78744; (800) 792-1112.

Vermilion Flycatcher. PHOTO: TONY BAYLIS.

South of
Corpus Christi

The area south of Corpus Christi, either along U.S. Highway 77 or U.S. Highway 281, is the quintessential South Texas ranch land. The history and lifestyle of the King Ranch exemplifies the area. This is the Wild Horse Desert, with caliche underfoot, very few trees, and a thorn on every plant. The birds in this region, except for the coastal birds near Riviera, thrive in the dry, sparse habitat. Expect to spot Greater Roadrunners, Cactus Wrens, Bobwhite Quail, and Curve-billed Thrashers.

72. La Copita at Ben Bolt

73. Bishop City Park and Lawrence Guess Nature Trail

74. King Ranch (IBA)

75. Dick Kleberg Park

76. Santa Gertrudis Creek Bird Sanctuary

77. Drum Point/Kaufer-Hubert Memorial County Park/Riviera Beach Fishing Pier

78. Sarita/Hawk Alley

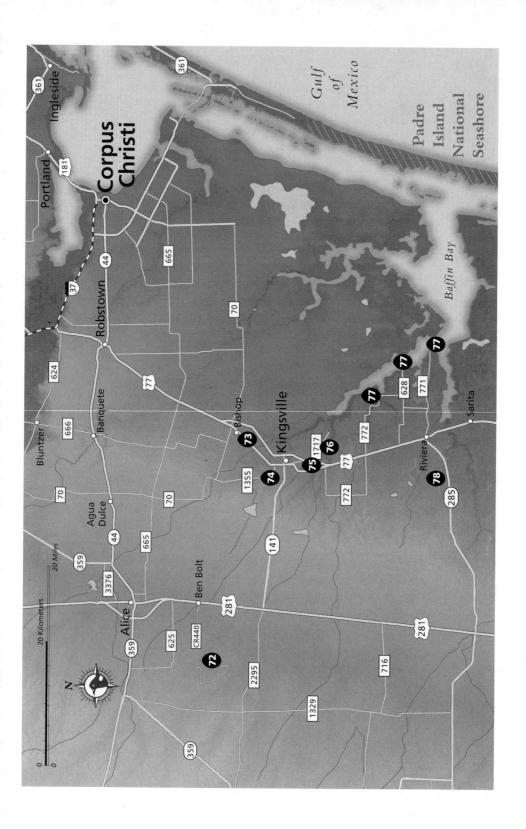

72 La Copita at Ben Bolt

Habitats: Tamaulipan thorn scrub, Tamaulipan scrubland.

Specialty birds: *Resident*—Harris' Hawk, White-tipped Dove, Groove-billed Ani, Common Pauraque, Golden-fronted Woodpecker, Green Jay, Long-billed Thrasher, Olive Sparrow, Cassin's Sparrow, Audubon's Oriole. *Spring/Summer*—Brown-crested Flycatcher, Scissor-tailed Flycatcher, Cave Swallow, Hooded Oriole. *Fall/Winter*—Vermilion Flycatcher.

Other key birds: *Resident*—Crested Caracara, Inca Dove, Ladder-backed Woodpecker, Curve-billed Thrasher, Pyrrhuloxia. *Spring/Summer*—Lesser Nighthawk, Painted Bunting.

Best times to bird: October and November, January through April.

Directions: La Copita is about 13 miles southwest of Alice. From Corpus Christi, take Highway 44 to Alice. From there, head south on U.S. Highway 281 toward Ben Bolt. At Ben Bolt, turn right on County Road 465 at the blinking yellow light. Follow CR 465 for 0.9 mile and turn left onto County Road 440. Be careful here, as you do not see the road sign until after you have turned. Stay on CR 440 for 7 miles. The road makes some curves and turns before you come to the ranch gate on the right side of the road. The ranch office is another ½ mile in on a dirt road.

The birding

This ranch is open to the public by reservation only.

There are two short interpretive trails near the headquarters. Both are great for birding and observing native plants and cacti. A nice observation blind with picnic tables is nearby. Feeders and water are used to entice birds for the bird-watcher or photographer. Professionally designed photography blinds for morning and for evening can be reserved. A 1-mile loop trail leads to another large picnic table and wildlife observation blind with feeders and water. Birders may walk or travel on a trailer/wagon.

The ranch has extensive native plant diversity and is home to birds typical for this habitat. It also gets birds often considered western species. You will see thrashers—Northern Mockingbirds, Long-billed Thrashers, Curve-billed Thrashers, and even Sage Thrashers. You will certainly find Northern Cardinal and Pyrrhuloxia. Bobwhite Quail are common, as are sparrows. Look for Black-throated Sparrow, White-crowned Sparrow, Lark Bunting, and Cassin's Sparrow. This is excellent habitat for Verdin. If you don't see Barn Owls, Great Horned Owls, and Screech Owls, you will surely hear them if you spend the night. There will be no trouble finding Crested Caracaras, Harris' Hawks, Northern Harriers, American Kestrel, and Red-tailed Hawks. Audubon Orioles are usually found at the feeders near the blinds. Cactus and Bewick's Wrens are numerous. The birder can see Lark Buntings in the winter and Painted Buntings in the spring/summer. Daytime finds of Common Pauraque and Lesser Nighthawks are possibilities.

General information: There is a fee, and you must have a reservation. This 3,000-acre ranch in the "Wild Horse Desert" was donated to Texas A&M University in 1982 by Robert Muil to be used for research and demonstrations that benefit ranchers and the general public. In addition to nature tourism, the ranch operations include cattle, goat, and wildlife management. *Copita* means "little cup" in Spanish. Tours with a focus on ranching and heritage are also provided.

DeLorme: Texas Atlas & Gazetteer: Page 84, 2F.

Elevation: 300 feet.

Hazards: Snakes, fire ants, thorns.

Nearest food, gas, lodging: Ben Bolt for food and gas; Alice for lodging. The ranch operates a guesthouse with four bedrooms, two baths, and a kitchen.

For more information: La Copita, 3091 County Road 440, Alice, TX 78332; (361) 664-1093.

73 Bishop City Park and Lawrence Guess Nature Trail

Habitats: Urban park, freshwater lake, Tamaulipan thorn scrub, prairie.

Specialty birds: *Resident*—White-tailed Hawk, Harris' Hawk, Groove-billed Ani, Buff-bellied Hummingbird, Golden-fronted Woodpecker, Great Kiskadee, Green Jay, Long-billed Thrasher, Olive Sparrow. *Spring/Summer*—Brown-crested Flycatcher, Scissor-tailed Flycatcher, Cave Swallow, Hooded Oriole. *Fall/Winter*—Peregrine Falcon, Vermilion Flycatcher.

Other key birds: *Resident*—Crested Caracara, Roseate Spoonbill, Inca Dove, Bronzed Cowbird, Pyrrhuloxia, Lesser Goldfinch. *Spring/Summer*—Anhinga.

Best times to bird: Year-round.

Directions: Bishop is 35 miles south of Corpus Christi on U.S. Highway 77. From the US 77 Bypass, take the Sixth Street Exit. Travel ½ mile on Sixth Street, and turn left onto Birch Lane for a short distance to the Bishop City Park entrance. Or take the Meadowbrook Street Exit and stay on that street until it dead-ends at the back trailhead for the nature trail.

The birding

Bishop City Park features a freshwater lake with a trail encircling it. There is a gazebo and another observation deck jutting out over the lake. Waterfowl are regular visitors here; however, some domesticated ducks and geese are permanent residents. Other birds associated with water, such as Belted Kingfishers, White Ibis, Roseate Spoonbill, Anhingas, and cormorants, may be seen. In spring and summer, a colony of Cave Swallows lives under the highway bridge at the lower end of the lake.

From Birch Street or Meadowbrook Street, you can enter the Lawrence Guess Nature Trail. This is a cement sidewalk that runs along Carreta Creek and through native scrubland. The creek is crossed in one place by a wooden footbridge and in another by a metal footbridge. Therefore, the birder can make a circle around the creek. There are two observation decks along the way. The trail is less than 1 mile long and completely wheelchair accessible, including the decks. Beyond the creek and trail are farm fields. The trail is a nice sliver of habitat for many local species. Expect to see Great Kiskadees, Long-billed Thrashers, Vermilion Flycatcher, Northern Cardinals, Northern Mockingbirds, Olive Sparrow, Golden-fronted Woodpeckers, and Green Jays. Warblers, tanagers, and orioles could be present at certain times of the year.

General information: The park has many facilities, including restrooms, picnic tables, a swimming pool, and sports fields. The nature trail was named for Judge

Lawrence Guess who was an avid nature lover and photographer. The City of Bishop has dubbed itself "A Birder's Paradise." This is CTC#85. It is wheelchair accessible.

DeLorme: Texas Atlas & Gazetteer: Page 84 4G.

Elevation: 59 feet.

Hazards: Snakes, fire ants.

Nearest food, gas, lodging: Bishop.

For more information: City of Bishop, 500 East Texas Avenue, P.O. Box 356, Bishop, TX 78343; (361) 584-2567.

74 King Ranch (IBA)

Habitats: Tamaulipan scrubland, primary and secondary bays, freshwater lakes, agricultural areas.

Specialty birds: *Resident*—Least Grebe, Black-bellied Whistling-Duck, Harris' Hawk, White-tailed Hawk, Reddish Egret, White-faced Ibis, White-tipped Dove, Common Pauraque, Golden-fronted Woodpecker, Great Kiskadee, Couch's Kingbird, Green Jay, Long-billed Thrasher, Olive Sparrow, Cassin's Sparrow, Audubon's Oriole. *Spring/Summer*—Wood Stork, Brown-crested Flycatcher, Scissor-tailed Flycatcher, Cave Swallow, Botteri's Sparrow, Hooded Oriole. *Fall/Winter*—Piping Plover, Vermilion Flycatcher, Sprague's Pipit. *Migrating*—Buff-breasted Sandpiper, Hudsonian Godwit.

Other key birds: *Resident*—Neotropic Cormorant, Mottled Duck, Fulvous Whistling-Duck, White-tailed Kite, Crested Caracara, Little Blue Heron, Roseate Spoonbill, Clapper Rail, American Oystercatcher, Gull-billed Tern, Inca Dove, Ladder-backed Woodpecker, Curve-billed Thrasher, Bronzed Cowbird, Pyrrhuloxia, Lesser Goldfinch. *Spring/Summer*—Anhinga, Wilson's Plover, Lesser Nighthawk, Painted Bunting. *Fall/Winter*—Greater White-fronted Goose, Ross's Goose, Rufous Hummingbird. *Migrating*—Raptors, shorebirds, Neotropic passerines.

Best times to bird: Fall, winter, spring.

Directions: There are several ways to get from Corpus Christi to Kingsville. I recommend taking Interstate 37 and exiting onto U.S. Highway 77. Kingsville is about 30 miles south on US 77. Stay on US 77 Bypass rather than U.S. Business Highway 77. In Kingsville take the Highway 141 exit or the Santa Gertrudis Avenue exit. In either case, you will go 3.5 miles to the entrance of the King Ranch. After you enter the gate, signs direct you to the visitor center.

The birding

If the adage "You get what you pay for" is true, then the King Ranch is undercharging for its bird tours. These are excellent, well-guided tours. Several types are available, including half-day, full-day, and private. Be sure to check the King Ranch Web site (www.kingranch.com) to determine which outing would suit your needs. The ranch has had holdings around the world, but today in South Texas, the ranch consists of 825,000 acres in four divisions. Birding tours explore three of the divisions: the Santa Gertrudis Division, the Norias Division, and the Laureles Division. The ranch comprises many of the habitats found in this book. However, I have listed only those generally seen on the tours. All tours are taken in a fifteen-passenger van with an expert guide. They begin at the visitor center, which also has a gift shop and restrooms.

At the visitor center several birdseed and hummingbird feeders dot a nearby picnic area. This is a pleasant place to pass the time while others arrive. You can watch Northern Cardinals, Pyrrhuloxias, White-winged Doves, Great Kiskadees,

Northern Bobwhite, Golden-fronted Woodpeckers, and Northern Mockingbirds. At the right time of year, look for Ruby-throated and Buff-bellied Hummingbirds while you wait for the start of the excursion.

Do not think in any way that the tour will be "sanitized." This is a real off-road birding trip. The guide will drive down some paved roads, but most of the trip is on dirt roads through the ranch, on levees near reservoirs, around cattle pens, or past agricultural fields used in the ranch's vast farming operations. Occasionally, the van stops for the group to take a short walk in order to get a better look at a particular site. Guides bring along a tripod-mounted scope and are very willing to set it up if any member of the group needs a better look. They are also eager to help

Sprague's Pipit. PHOTO: TONY BAYLIS.

birders list new birds. At a few places, seeds and fruits are regularly put out in the brush to attract birds.

Name an order of bird, and there is generally a species found on the ranch to represent it. In the brushy areas of the ranch, White-tipped and Common Ground Doves, Green Jays, Long-billed and Curve-billed Thrashers, Pyrrhuloxias, Cactus and Bewick's Wrens, and Olive Sparrows will be seen. At the large reservoirs, the birder will find Lesser Scaups, Northern Shovelers, Black-bellied Whistling-Ducks, Roseate Spoonbills, Great Blue Herons, Anhingas, Great White Egrets, Green Herons, Tricolored Herons, Cliff and Cave Swallows, and so on. The water's edges support sandpipers such as Solitary, Western, and Least. Name a North American plover—it's been seen on the ranch. So have all three kingfishers.

At or near the cow pens, expect Brewer's Blackbirds, Bronzed Cowbirds, Great Tailed Grackles, and Eastern and Western Meadowlarks. Snow Geese, White-fronted Geese, Ross's Geese, and Sandhill Cranes concentrate in the open fields in the winter. Burrowing Owls, American and Sprague's Pipits, Mountain Plovers, and Killdeer will be in the agricultural areas. Twenty-one species of flycatchers have been spotted.

You will be mesmerized by the quantity and variety of raptors: Barn Owls, Short-eared Owls, Great Horned Owls, White-tailed Hawks, Harris' Hawks in groups of four or more, Red-tailed Hawks, Red-shouldered Hawks, Merlin, Northern Harrier, Swainson's Hawk, Ferruginous Hawk, Osprey, and Crested Caracara, to name a few.

Let me just sum it up by saying that the ranch bird list covers 340 species.

The ranch also offers wildlife tours. The birding tours usually end up being a two-for-one deal, as you will more than likely see deer, javelina, coyote, and even a bobcat.

There are tours to the southernmost division of the ranch, the large Norias Division. That area would be south of the realm of this book, but those tours might well be worth your while. Rarities such as the Ferruginous Pygmy Owl, Tropical Parula, Northern Beardless Tyrannulet, and Botteri's Sparrow are often spotted on those tours in the spring and summer.

General information: Captain Richard King, a former river boat captain, founded the ranch in 1853. It is best known for the development of the Santa Gertrudis breed of cattle and the first registered American quarter horse. Historic tours of the ranch are also available. The King Ranch Museum and the King Ranch Saddle Shop are located in the town of Kingsville. This is CTC#87.

DeLorme: Texas Atlas & Gazetteer: Page 84 3H.

Elevation: 66 feet.

Hazards: Many on the ranch, but you will be in a van.

Nearest food, gas, lodging: Kingsville.

For more information: King Ranch Visitor Center, P.O. Box 1090, Kingsville, TX 78364; (361) 592-8055.

⑦⑤ Dick Kleberg Park

Habitats: Urban park, freshwater creek with dam and pond.

Specialty birds: *Resident*—Least Grebe, White-tailed Kite, Golden-fronted Woodpecker, Great Kiskadee, Couch's Kingbird, Green Jay, Long-billed Thrasher, Olive Sparrow. *Spring/ Summer*—Brown-crested Flycatcher, Scissor-tailed Flycatcher, Cave Swallow, Hooded Oriole. *Fall/Winter*—Vermilion Flycatcher, Sprague's Pipit.

Other key birds: *Resident*—Neotropic Cormorant, Inca Dove, Ladder-backed Wood-pecker, Curve-billed Thrasher. *Spring/ Summer*—Anhinga, Painted Bunting.

Best times to bird: Fall, winter, spring.

Directions: Take U.S. Highway 77 to Kingsville. Stay on Bypass US 77 rather than Business Highway 77. At the southern city limits, take a right onto Farm-to-Market 1717, and travel for 1 block to Escondido Road; turn left. Escondido curves around until you reach the Dick Kleberg Park at about 0.4 mile.

The birding

This 211-acre park has been cleared of most understory brush. However, it still sports a beautiful stand of mesquite and live oak trees. Some areas of the park habitat are not so bare, and you should have better birding in those areas. A paved road circles the park, so drive around and get a feel for the area. In the trees and on the edges look for Green Jays, Golden-fronted and Ladder-backed Woodpeckers, Vermilion Flycatchers, Long-billed and Curve-billed Thrashers, Olive Sparrows, Orchard and Hooded Orioles, Black-crested Titmice, and Loggerhead Shrikes. Migrating warblers and vireos also use this as a stopover. In the undeveloped section of the park are extensive areas of short grass. In the winter, these grasses host American Pipits and occasionally Sprague's Pipits.

At the rear of the park is Escondido Creek and a freshwater reservoir lined with picnic tables and a sidewalk. Here you will find ducks and cormorants and perhaps Least Grebes or Anhingas. A Belted Kingfisher defends his territory here. Also present will be Forster's Terns, Great Kiskadees, Cave Swallows, and Couch's Kingbirds.

General information: The park is open daily from 7:30 A.M. to 9:00 P.M. There are restrooms, playgrounds, picnic tables, a swimming pool, and several sports fields. The J. K. Northway Exposition Center and Rodeo Grounds are also located within the park. The park was named for Dick Kleberg Sr., who was a U.S. Congressman from 1934 to 1936. He also served as chairman for the King Ranch Board from 1950 to 1955. Kingsville is located in Kleberg County. This is CTC#88.

Kingsville is the home of Texas A&M, Kingsville. The John E. Conner Museum and the Kleberg Hall of Natural History are both located on the campus.

DeLorme: Texas Atlas & Gazetteer: Page 84 4H.

Elevation: 65 feet.

Nearest food, gas, lodging: Kingsville.

For more information: City of Kingsville, 200 East Kleberg, Kingsville, TX 78363; (361) 595-8002.

76 Santa Gertrudis Creek Bird Sanctuary

Habitats: Freshwater marsh, transitional riparian forest.

Specialty birds: *Resident*—Black-bellied Whistling-Duck, Great Kiskadee, Couch's Kingbird, Green Jay, Long-billed Thrashers. *Spring/Summer*—Cave Swallows.

Other key birds: *Resident*—Mottled Duck, Curve-billed Thrasher.

Best times to bird: Year-round.

Directions: At the southern city limits of Kingsville, Farm-to-Market 1717 crosses the U.S. Highway 77 Bypass. Turn east on FM 1717 and travel for 1.8 miles. The Santa Gertrudis Creek Bird Sanctuary will be on the left just as you pass Santa Gertrudis Creek. There is a large parking lot.

The birding

There is a short walk on a gravel path to an observation platform.

Along the walk are some benches and trash cans. Unfortunately, the marsh at the site is very overgrown, and birding is not the easiest. A cattail marsh is close to the walk. A scope would be needed to see any birds farther out on the pond. Cliff, Cave, and Barn Swallows use the culverts that channel the creek under FM 1717. Check the utility lines to and from the site for hawks.

General information: This is CTC#89. The Great Texas Coastal Trail maps list another site on Santa Gertrudis Creek near the King Ranch. The sign is gone from the CTC#86 site, and I would not recommend a stop there. There is no place to park off the road, and there is a lot of fast-moving traffic.

DeLorme: Texas Atlas & Gazetteer: Page 84 4H.

Elevation: 65 feet.

Hazards: Snakes, mosquitoes.

Nearest food, gas, lodging: Kingsville.

For more information: Kingsville Convention and Visitors Bureau, 1501 Highway 77, Kingsville, TX 78363; (361) 592-8516, (800) 333-5032.

77 Drum Point/Kaufer-Hubert Memorial County Park/Riviera Beach Fishing Pier

Habitats: Tamaulipan thorn scrub, secondary bay, freshwater pond, agricultural areas.

Specialty birds: *Resident*—Black-bellied Whistling-Duck, Harris' Hawk, Reddish Egret, White-faced Ibis, Groove-billed Ani, Common Pauraque, Buff-bellied Hummingbird, Golden-fronted Woodpecker, Great Kiskadee, Couch's Kingbird, Green Jays, Long-billed Thrasher, Olive Sparrow. *Spring/Summer*—Wood Stork, Scissor-tailed Flycatcher, Hooded Oriole. *Fall/Winter*—Piping Plover, Vermilion Flycatcher, Sprague's Pipit. *Migrating*—Buff-breasted Sandpiper, Hudsonian Godwit.

Other key birds: *Resident*—Neotropic Cormorant, Mottled Duck, Crested Caracara, Roseate Spoonbill, Clapper Rail, American Oystercatcher, Gull-billed Tern, Ladder-backed Woodpecker, Inca Dove, Curve-billed Thrasher, Bronzed Cowbird, Pyrrhuloxia. *Spring/Summer*—Wilson's Plover, Sandwich Tern, Painted Bunting. *Fall/Winter*—Greater White-fronted Goose, Ross Goose, Marble Godwit. *Migrating*—Raptors, shorebirds.

Best times to bird: Fall and winter.

Directions: If you decide to try these three sites, I know that you will be glad to have these directions. They are difficult enough to find with directions and a map, impossible without. Also, they are rather remote and yet close to each other. When you choose to go to one of these sites, it makes sense to bird all three at the same time.

To reach Drum Point, leave Corpus Christi on U.S. Highway 77 heading south toward Kingsville and the Rio Grande Valley. Stay on the U.S. Highway 77 Bypass around Kingsville. Continue through the small community of Ricardo. Begin looking for Farm-to-Market 772. It is approximately 8 miles from

Kingsville to FM 772. Turn left (east) on FM 772 and travel for 4 miles. At the stop sign, FM 772 bends to the right. Make that turn and keep going. You will travel another 4.7 miles to Kleberg County Road 2250E. Turn left (east) onto this very narrow paved road. After 1 mile, the road crosses another paved road. Keep going, but start to look for large tanks on the left. After traveling down County Road 2250E for a total of 2.3 miles, turn left (north) onto County Road 1132. This one-lane paved road is not marked. You will go 1.2 miles down this road. At one point it curves to the right, and a sign reads CR 2230E, but it looks like the same road to me, and there is no other way to go. When you reach the water, congratulate yourself, because you are almost at Drum Point. Along the shore, a caliche road of sorts continues. Depending on the beach conditions and your vehicle, you can drive north along the shore to reach Drum Point. I must confess that I did not complete the trip, but I am told that it is another 3 miles or more to the actual point.

To travel to Kaufer-Hubert Memorial County Park, return to CR 2250E and turn left toward Baffin Bay. When the road ends, go right on CR 1144S; I did not see a sign for this road. You will know that you are in the right place as the bay and several houses will be on your left. Soon you come to a stop sign and a convenience store. Turn left onto Farm-to-Market 628. The road curves to the right, but just keep going for 1.2 miles to the entrance for the county park. (If you want to skip Drum Point: FM 628 meets US 77 before the town of Riviera. Take FM 628 11 miles to the park.)

Next, to bird *Riviera Beach Fishing Pier* from Kaufer-Hubert Memorial County Park, return to

FM 628 and go south (left). Continue for 3 miles to a stop sign; turn left (south) on Farm-to-Market 1546/County Road 1140S. Go 1.1 miles to another stop sign. You have reached Farm-to-Market 771. Turn left (east) and travel for 2.7 miles until the state maintenance ends. County Road 2327 continues here for

0.3 mile. Turn right on County Road 2360 for another 0.1 mile to the pier. (If you want to skip Drum Point and Kaufer-Hubert Memorial County Park: FM 771 intersects US 77 in the town of Riviera. Take FM 771 for 9.3 miles to CR 2327, and follow directions above.)

The birding

One reason to bird at Drum Point is to look out over Cayo Del Grullo (*grullo* means "crane") for ducks. Get out your field guide and turn to the section on ducks. Pick one; it's probably been seen at Drum Point. Most common are Red-heads, Buffleheads, and Lesser Scaups. Rarities such as Long-tailed Duck and White-winged Scoter have been seen there. White Pelicans and both cormorants

Black-bellied Whistling-Ducks. PHOTO: TONY BAYLIS.

favor this area. Shorebirds and wading birds should be numerous. Look for the Reddish Egret, Wilson's Plover, Black Skimmers, Least Terns, and many others.

While traveling to these sites, you pass many agricultural fields. In or near the roads, you find Mourning, White-winged, Common Ground, and Inca Doves. I flushed some Bobwhite Quail at one farm. Watch the high lines and fence posts for raptors in the fall and for Scissor-tailed and Vermilion Flycatchers in the summer. Crested Caracara will always be around. I saw many Common Nighthawks early one summer morning. In the winter, Greater White-fronted, Snow, and Ross's Geese will move in and out of these fields. Sandhill Cranes feed here, too. In the late fall and winter, a careful birder should be able to locate both the American Pipit and the Sprague's Pipit.

At the entrance to Kaufer-Hubert Memorial County Park, there is a large mudflat. Every egret and heron is likely to be there, as are spoonbills and ibis. Near the boat ramp parking lot, the Bird Trail begins. This is an old dirt road that leads for about ⅓ mile through some scrubby brush. You might see a thrasher, Green

Jay, or oriole here, but the main reason for the trail is to reach a bench at the end of the trail. Here you can watch the bay and the mouth of Vattmann Creek for herons, egrets, plovers, Long-billed Curlews, Black-necked Stilts, and American Avocets. The list of sandpipers includes White-rumped, Western, Least, Solitary, Spotted, Stilt, Pectoral, and Semipalmated.

Several rare-for-here ducks have been listed in this park: Black Scoter, Surf Scoter, and Greater Scaup. Speaking of ducks, look in the freshwater pond in the SeaWind RV park for Black-bellied Whistling-Ducks. A sign notes that only campers are allowed in this part of the county facility, but if you stop at the office and sign in, birders are welcome. An artificial pond is at the center of the camp-sites. Perhaps a more productive area is at the far end of the trailer sites. There, water from the treatment plant has created a large cattail marshy area. Benches are provided there, and campers verify that the birding is surprisingly good.

The fishing pier at Riviera Beach is rather straightforward. Look here for peli-cans and other waterfowl. Watch in the nearby brush for Groove-billed Anis.

General information: Drum Point is CTC#91. Cayo del Grullo is part of Baffin Bay.

Kaufer-Hubert Memorial County Park is CTC#92. Leo Kaufer was a beloved county commissioner. Vernie Hubert donated forty acres of land to establish the SeaWind RV campsite. The county park has restrooms, many picnic tables and pits, playground equipment, boat ramp, lighted fishing pier, and an excellent observation tower. The RV park offers 134 camping sites, recreation hall, restrooms, and laundry facilities. The RV park has planned activities from November 1 through March 31.

Riviera Beach Fishing Pier is CTC#93. Theodore Koch donated the land for this site, and the pier was completed in 1973. Recently, renovations were com-pleted on the pier. There are restrooms.

There are two other sites associated with this area. B Bar B Ranch Inn, CTC#90, is now closed. The two-plus-acre Louise Trant Bird Sanctuary, CTC#94, is located in the town of Riviera. The CTC sign is still on the highway, but there is no place to park, and the site is in serious decline. The sanctuary belongs to the Audubon Outdoor Club of Corpus Christi, and members hope to restore the site in the future.

DeLorme: Texas Atlas & Gazetteer: Page 84 5I and 5J.

Elevation: 50 feet.

Hazards: Fog, narrow roads, possibility of get-ting stuck, snakes, mosquitoes.

Nearest food, gas, lodging: Kingsville and Riviera. A well-known seafood restaurant, King's Inn, is on FM 628.

Camping: SeaWind.

For more information: SeaWind, 1066 East FM 628, Riviera, TX 78379; (361) 297-5738; Kleberg County Parks and Recreation Depart-ment, P.O. Drawer 512, Kingsville, TX 78364; (361) 595-8591; Audubon Outdoor Club of Corpus Christi, Inc., P.O. Box 3352, Corpus Christi, TX 78463.

78 Sarita/Hawk Alley

Habitats: Tamaulipan thorn scrub, prairie, agricultural areas.

Specialty birds: *Resident*—White-tailed Kite, Harris' Hawk, White-tailed Hawk, White-tipped Dove, Golden-fronted Woodpecker, Long-billed Thrasher. *Spring/Summer*—Scissor-tailed Flycatcher, Cave Swallow, Hooded Oriole. *Fall/Winter*—Vermilion Flycatcher. *Migrating*—Swallow-tailed Kite, Zone-tailed Kite.

Other key birds: *Resident*—Crested Caracara, Inca Dove, Curve-billed Thrasher, Bronzed Cowbird, Pyrrhuloxia, Lesser Goldfinch. *Migrating*—Raptors.

Best times to bird: All year, but summer is the least productive.

Directions: If you are leaving the Corpus Christi area to continue your bird watching in the Lower Rio Grande Valley, there are two ways to go. U.S. Highway 77 will take you south to Raymondville, Harlingen, and Brownsville. If you go that way, you will pass through the small town of Sarita, which is about 20 miles south of Kingsville.

Alternatively, you can turn at Riviera onto Highway 285 and go over to U.S. Highway 281 at Falfurrias. US 281 will take you to Edinburg, Pharr, and McAllen. The 30-mile stretch of Highway 285 is known as Hawk Alley.

Harris' Hawk. PHOTO: TONY BAYLIS.

The birding

Sarita is the county seat of Kenedy County. About 200 people live there. A visiting judge services the county courthouse every other month, but there is no public gasoline station. Quaint, right? The town of Sarita is on the west side of US 77. The birder should just drive around the town, which acts as an oasis for birds. The Rufous-backed Robin, Hooded Oriole, and Altamira Oriole are three of the rarities that have been seen there. There is also an unmarked road that goes east from Sarita for about 3 miles before it comes to a ranch gate. There is good birding along the road. Again, stay off private property. North and south of Sarita, ponds develop in wet years. If present, these wetlands are visible from US 77.

South of Sarita is a rest stop. This once was another good birding stop. A couple of years ago, the rest stop was upgraded, and it seemed to "scare off" the birds. It is a long way before another place to stop, so you might try having a look around there. Also, I think some of the habitat has begun to rebound. On US 77 south of this rest stop, I have almost always spotted white-tailed deer to the east of the road. Coyotes and wild turkey are a possibility as well.

Twenty-six species of hawks have been reported along Highway 285. My personal bird list includes first-time sightings of Harris' Hawk, Swainson's Hawk, and Ferruginous Hawk on this road. There is nothing hard about finding raptors here. They will be on telephone poles, at the tops of trees, and occasionally on fence posts. The hard part will be deciding how many times you want to stop the car to use your binoculars. Ranches along this road sometimes use controlled burns to reduce brush that can hamper their cattle operations. These fires bring in White-tailed and Harris' Hawks who are looking for small rodents and other animals fleeing the area.

Once you turn south at Falfurrias, you still see many hawks. My daughter and I once counted over fifty between Corpus Christi and McAllen.

General information: Hawk Alley is CTC#95. The land for the town of Sarita was originally part of the Kenedy Ranch. John G. Kenedy named the town for his daughter Sarita. The town, established in 1904, flourished as a ranching center and a stop on the St. Louis, Brownsville, and Mexico Railway. Consider stopping at the Kenedy Ranch Museum of South Texas in Sarita. It is open Tuesday to Saturday from 10:00 A.M. to 4:00 P.M., Sunday from noon to 4:00 P.M.

DeLorme: Texas Atlas & Gazetteer: Page 84 2J, 3J, 4J.

Elevation: 65 feet.

Nearest food, gas, lodging: Riviera and Falfurrias.

For more information: Kenedy District and County Clerk, P.O. Box 227, Sarita, TX 78385; (361) 294-5220; Kenedy Ranch Museum of South Texas, 200 East La Parra Avenue, P.O. Box 70, Sarita, TX 78385; (361) 294-5751.

Appendix A: Addresses and Phone Numbers

Alice Chamber of Commerce, 612 East Main, P.O. Box 1609, Alice, TX 78332; (361) 664–3454

American Bird Conservancy, P.O. Box 249, The Plains, VA 20198; (540) 253–5780

Aransas Bird and Nature Club, P.O. Box 308, Fulton, TX 78358; (361) 729–0521

Aransas First, P.O. Box 266, Rockport, TX 78381; (361) 790–8384

Aransas National Wildlife Refuge, P.O. Box 100, Austwell, TX 77950; (361) 286–3559

Aransas Pass Chamber of Commerce, 130 West Goodnight, P.O. Box 1949, Aransas Pass, TX 78336; (361) 758–2750, (800) 633–3028

Asian Cultures Museum and Educational Center, 1809 North Chaparral, Corpus Christi, TX 78401; (361) 882–2641

Audubon Outdoor Club of Corpus Christi, Inc., P.O. Box 3352, Corpus Christi, TX 78463

Audubon Texas, 2525 Wallingwood, Suite 301, Austin, TX 78746; (512) 306–0225

Barnhart Q5 Ranch, 8212 FM 883, P.O. Box 626, Berclair, TX 78107; (361) 375–2824

Bee County Chamber of Commerce/Convention and Visitors Bureau, 1705 North Saint Mary's, Beeville, TX 78102; (361) 358–3267

Beeville Art Museum, 401 East Fannin, P.O. Box 1236, Beeville, TX 78104; (361) 358–8615

Berclair Mansion, (361) 358–4480

Bishop Chamber of Commerce, 213 East Main Street, P.O. Box 426, Bishop, TX 78343; (361) 584–2214

Choke Canyon State Park, Calliham Unit, P.O. Box 2, Calliham, TX 78007; (361) 786–3868

Choke Canyon State Park, South Shore Unit, P.O. Box 1548, Three Rivers, TX 78071; (361) 786–3538

City of Alice, 500 East Main Street, P.O. Box 3229, Alice, TX 78332; (361) 668–7210

City of Aransas Pass, 600 West Cleveland Boulevard, Aransas Pass, TX 78336; (361) 758–5301

City of Austwell, 108 South Gisler, P.O. Box 147, Austwell, TX 77950; (361) 286–3523

City of Bayside, P.O. Box 194, Bayside, TX 78340; (361) 529–6520

City of Beeville, 400 North St. Mary's, Beeville, TX 78102; (361) 358–4641

City of Bishop, 500 East Texas Avenue, P.O. Box 356, Bishop, TX 78343; (361) 584–2567

City of Corpus Christi, 1202 Leopard Street, Corpus Christi, TX 78401; (361) 880–3211

City of George West, 406 Nueces Street, George West, TX 78022; (361) 449–1556

City of Goliad, 152 West End Street, Goliad, TX 77963; (361) 645–3454

City of Ingleside, P.O. Box 400, 2671 San Angelo, Ingleside, TX 78362; (361) 776–2517

City of Kingsville, 200 East Kleberg, Kingsville, TX 78363; (361) 595–8002

City of Mathis, 411 East San Patricio, Mathis, TX 78368; (361) 547–3343

City of Orange Grove, P.O. Box 1350, Orange Grove, TX 78372; (361) 384–2322

City of Port Aransas, 710 West Avenue A, Port Aransas, TX 78373; (361) 749–4111

City of Port Aransas Parks and Recreation Department, 710 West Avenue A, Port Aransas, TX 78373; (361) 749–4158

City of Portland, 900 Moore Avenue, Portland, TX 78374; (361) 643–6501

City of Refugio, 609 Commerce Street, P.O. Box 1020, Refugio, TX 78377; (361) 526–5361

City of Rockport, 622 East Market, P.O. Box 1059, Rockport, TX 78381; (361) 729–2213

City of Sinton, 301 East Market, Sinton, TX 78387; (361) 364–2381

City of Three Rivers, P.O. Box 398, Three Rivers, TX 78071; (361) 786–2528

Coastal Bend Audubon Society, P.O. Box 3604, Corpus Christi, TX 78463; (361) 442–9437

Coastal Bend Bays and Estuaries Program, 1305 North Shoreline Boulevard, Suite 205, Corpus Christi, TX 78401; (361) 885–6202

Coastal Conservation Association (CCA) Texas, 6919 Portwest, Suite 100, Houston, TX 77024; (800) 201–FISH, (713) 626–4234

Coastal Coordination Council, P.O. Box 12873, Austin, TX 78711; (800) 998–4GLO, (512) 475–0773

Coleto Creek Reservoir and Park, P.O. Box 68, Fannin, TX 77960; (361) 575–6366

Copano Bay State Fishing Pier Concession Operation, P.O. Box 39, Fulton, TX 78358; (361) 729–7762

Corpus Christi Area Heritage Society, 411 Upper Broadway, Corpus Christi, TX 78403; (361) 882–8691

Corpus Christi Botanical Gardens and Nature Center, 8545 South Staples, Corpus Christi, TX 78413; (361) 852–7875

Corpus Christi Convention and Visitors Bureau, 1823 North Chaparral, Corpus Christi, TX 78401; (361) 766–2322

Corpus Christi Museum of Science and History, 1900 North Chaparral, Corpus Christi, TX 78401; (361) 883–2862

Crane House St. Charles Bay Retreat, 1401 North Terry Street, Rockport, TX 78382; (361) 729–7239

Fennessey Ranch, P.O. Box 99, Bayside, TX 78340; (361) 529–6600

Friends of Connie Hagar, P.O. Box 586, Rockport, TX 78381; (361) 729–6887

Fulton Mansion State Historic Site, 317 Fulton Beach Road, Rockport, TX 78358; (361) 729–0386

George Blucher House Bed and Breakfast Inn, 211 North Carrizo Street, Corpus Christi, TX 78401; (361) 884–4884, (866) 884–4884

George West Chamber of Commerce, 400 North Nueces, P.O. Box 359, George West, TX 78022; (888) 909–3154, (361) 449–2033

Goliad County Chamber of Commerce, 231 South Market Street, Goliad, TX 77963; (800) 848–8674, (361) 645–3563

Goliad State Park, 108 Park Road 6, Goliad, TX 77963; (361) 645–3405

Goose Island State Park, 202 South Palmetto Street, Rockport, TX 78382; (361) 729–2858

Guadalupe Delta WMA, Texas Parks and Wildlife Department, 2601 North Azalea, Suite 31, Victoria, TX 77901; (361) 576–0022, (361) 790–0308

HawkWatch International, 1800 South West Temple, #226, Salt Lake City, UT 84115; (800) 726–4295

Hazel Bazemore County Park, P.O. Box 4343, County Road 69, Corpus Christi, TX 78410; (361) 387–4231

Heritage Park, 1600 block of North Chaparral Street, Corpus Christi, TX 78410; (361) 883–0639

Hilltop Community Center, 11425 Leopard Street, Corpus Christi, TX 78410; (361) 241–3754

I. B. Magee Beach Park, 321 North on the Beach, Port Aransas, TX 78373; (361) 749–6117

Indian Point Pier, (361) 643–1600

Ingleside Chamber of Commerce Information and Tourist Center, 2665 San Angelo Street, Ingleside, TX 78362; (361) 776–2906

Kenedy District and County Clerk, P.O. Box 227, Sarita, TX 78385; (361) 294–5220

Kenedy Ranch Museum of South Texas, 200 East La Parra Avenue, P.O. Box 70, Sarita, TX 78385; (361) 294–5751

King Ranch Visitor Center, P.O. Box 1090, Kingsville, TX 78364; (361) 592–8055

Kingsville Bird and Wildlife Club, c/o Milton Kimball, (361) 592–6002

Kingsville Convention and Visitors Bureau, 1501 Highway 77, Kingsville, Texas 78363; (361) 592–8516, (800) 333–5032

Kleberg County Parks and Recreation Department, P.O. Drawer 512, Kingsville, TX 78364; (361) 595–8591

Knolle Farm and Ranch Bed, Barn, and Breakfast, FM Road 70, Route 1, P.O. Box 81, Sandia, TX 78383; (361) 547–2546

Labonte Park Visitor Center, 1433 Interstate 37, Corpus Christi, TX 78410; (361) 241–1464

La Copita, 3091 County Road 440, Alice, TX 78332; (361) 664–1093

Lake Corpus Christi State Park, P.O. Box 1167, Mathis, TX 78368; (361) 547–2635

La Ramireña Ranch, c/o Richard Phillips, P.O. Box 87, Dinero, TX 78350; (361) 547–2249

McFaddin Cafe, 1859 FM 445, McFaddin, TX 77973; (361) 573–0301

Mustang Island State Park, P.O. Box 326, Port Aransas, TX 78373; (361) 749-5246

Mustang Riding Stables, 8159 Highway 361 on The Island, Corpus Christi, TX 78418; (361) 991–7433

National Wildlife Refuge System, (800) 344–WILD

Nueces County Parks and Recreation Department,15802 South Padre Island Drive, Corpus Christi, TX 78408; (361) 949–8122

Nueces River Authority, Coastal Bend Division, Natural Resources Center, 6300 Ocean Drive, Suite 3100, Corpus Christi, TX 78412; (361) 825–3193

Padre Island National Seashore, P.O. Box 18130, Corpus Christi, TX 78480-1300; (361) 949–8068

Padre Island Visitors Center, 14252 South Padre Island Drive, Corpus Christi, TX 78418; (361) 949–8743

Paschal, Joe and Vickey, 9545 Paula Drive, Corpus Christi, TX 78410; (361) 946–1103

Port Aransas Convention and Visitor's Bureau, 421 West Cotter, Port Aransas, TX 78373; (800) 452–6278

Port of Corpus Christi Authority, 222 Power Street, Corpus Christi, TX 78401; (361) 882–5633

Portland Chamber of Commerce, 2000 Billy G. Webb Drive, Portland TX 78374; (361) 643–2475

Presidio La Bahia, Friends of the Fort, P.O. Box 57, Goliad, Texas 77963; (361) 645–3752

Refugio County Chamber of Commerce, 301 North Alamo, Refugio, TX 78377; (361) 526–2835

Rockport-Fulton Area Chamber of Commerce, 404 Broadway, Rockport, TX 78382; (800) 242–0071, (361) 729–6445

Rose Hill Memorial Park, 2731 Comanche, Corpus Christi, TX 78408; (361) 882–5497

San Patricio County Judge, 400 West Sinton, Sinton, TX 78387; (361) 364–6120

SeaWind, 1066 East FM 628, Riviera, TX 78379; (361) 297–5738

Sinton Chamber of Commerce, 218 West Sinton, Sinton, TX 78387; (361) 364–2307

South Texas Institute for the Arts, 1902 North Shoreline, Corpus Christi, TX 78401; (361) 825–3500

Tecolote Creek Ranch, 2558 County Road 308, Orange Grove, TX 78372; (361) 946–1103

Tejano R.O.O.T.S. Hall of Fame and Museum, 213 North Wright Street, Alice, TX 78332; (361) 664–8000

Texas A&M University, Corpus Christi, 6300 Ocean Drive, Corpus Christi, TX 78412; (361) 825–3100

Texas A&M University, Kingsville, 700 University Boulevard, Kingsville, TX 78363; (361) 593–2111

Texas Coastal Management Program, 1700 North Congress Street, Austin Building, Austin, TX 78701; (512) 463–5054

Texas Department of Transportation Travel and Information Division, P.O. Box 5064, Austin, TX 78763; (800) 452–9292

Texas Maritime Museum, 1202 Navigation Circle, Rockport, TX 78382; (361) 729–1271

Texas Ornithological Society, PMB #189, 6338 North New Braunfels Avenue, San Antonio, TX 78209

Texas Parks and Wildlife Department, 4200 Smith School Road, Austin, TX 78744; (800) 792–1112

Texas Parks and Wildlife Rates and Reservations, (512) 389–8900

Texas Partners in Flight, 4200 Smith School Road, Austin, TX 78744; (512) 389–4470

Texas State Aquarium, 2710 North Shoreline, Corpus Christi, TX 78402; (361) 881–1200, (800) 477–4853

Three Rivers Chamber of Commerce, P.O. Box 1648, Three Rivers, TX 78071; (361) 786–4330

United States Environmental Protection Agency, Region 6 Office, 1445 Ross Avenue, Suite 1200, Dallas, TX 75202; (214) 665–6444

United States Fish and Wildlife Service, Department of the Interior, 1849 C Street NW, Washington, DC 20240; (202) 208–5634

University of Texas at Austin, Marine Science Institute, Cotter Street, Port Aransas, TX 78387; (361) 749–6805

U.S.S. *Lexington* Museum, 2914 North Shoreline Boulevard, P.O. Box 23076, Corpus Christi, TX 78403; (361) 888–4873

Welder Wildlife Foundation, P.O. Box 1400, Sinton, TX 78387; (361) 364–2643

Womack Family Ranch, c/o Jesse Womack, 711 Navarro, Suite 404, San Antonio, TX 78205; (361) 570–4796

Appendix B: Web sites

Alice Chamber of Commerce, www.alicetx.org

American Bird Conservancy, www.abcbirds.org

American Birding Association, http://americanbirding.org

America's National Wildlife Refuge System, www.fws.gov/refuges

Aransas Bird and Nature Club, www.birdRockport.com

Aransas Pass Chamber of Commerce, www.aransaspass.org

Asian Cultures Museum and Educational Center, www.asianculturesmuseum.org

Audubon Outdoor Club of Corpus Christi, www.ccbirding.com/aoc

Audubon Texas, http://tx.audubon.org

Barnhart Q5 Ranch, www.barnhartdonkeys.com

Bee County Chamber of Commerce, www.beeville.net/chamber

Bishop Chamber of Commerce, www.bishoptx.org

Blucher Audubon Nature Center, www.tx.audubon.org/centers/blucher.htm

Central Texas Coast Birding Patches, www.ccbirding.com/aoc/patches

City of Alice, www.ci.alice.tx.us

City of Aransas Pass, www.aransas-pass-texas.com/Home

City of Bayside, www.geocities.com/baysidecityhall

City of Beeville, www.beeville.net/CityofBeeville

City of Corpus Christi, www.cctexas.com

City of George West, www.georgewest.org/cityofgw.htm

City of Goliad, www.goliad.org/goliad.html

City of Ingleside, www.inglesidetx.org

City of Kingsville, www.kingsvilletexas.com, www.kingsville.org

City of Mathis, http://cityofmathis.com

City of Port Aransas, www.portaransas.org

City of Portland, www.portlandtx.com

City of Rockport, www.rockportnet.com

Coastal Bend Audubon Society, www.ccbirding.com/cbas

Coastal Bend Bays and Estuaries, www.cbbep.org

Coastal Bend Wildlife Photo Contest, www.wildlifephotocontest.com

Coastal Conservation Association (CCA) Texas, www.ccatexas.org/ccatexas/Default.asp

Coastal Coordination Council, www.glo.state.tx.us/coastal/cmp.html

Coleto Creek Reservoir and Park, www.coletocreekpark.com

Corpus Christi Botanical Gardens and Nature Center, www.ccbotanicalgardens.org

Corpus Christi Museum of Science and History, www.ci.corpuschristi.tx.us/services/museum

Corpus Christi Padre Island Convention and Visitors Bureau, www.corpuschristi cvb.com/index.htm

Crane House St. Charles Bay Retreat, www.cranehouseretreat.com

Endangered Birds in Texas, www.tpwd.state.tx.us/nature/endang/animals/birds

Fennessy Ranch, www.fennessyranch.com

George West Chamber of Commerce, www.georgewest.org

Goliad County Chamber of Commerce, www.goliadcc.org

Hawk Watch International, www.hawkwatch.org

Heritage Park, www.ci.corpuschristi.tx.us

Ingleside Chamber of Commerce, www.inglesidetxchamber.org

Kenedy Ranch Museum of South Texas, www.kenedymuseum.org

King Ranch, www.kingranch.com

Kingsville Chamber of Commerce, www.kingsville.org

Kleberg County Parks and Recreation Department, www.klebergpark.org

Knolle Farm and Ranch Bed, Barn, and Breakfast, www.knolle.com

La Copita, http://lacopita.com

Port Aransas Chamber of Commerce, www.portaransas.org

Portland Chamber of Commerce, www.portlandtx.org

Presidio La Bahia, www.presidiolabahia.org

Refugio County Chamber of Commerce, www.refugiocountytx.com

Rockport–Fulton Area Chamber of Commerce, www.rockport-fulton.org

Sinton Chamber of Commerce, www.sintonchamber.com

South Texas Institute of the Arts, www.stia.org

Tecolote Creek Ranch, www.tcrgenetics.com/contact.html

Tejano R.O.O.T.S. Hall of Fame, www.tejanorootshalloffame.org

Texas A&M University, Corpus Christi, www.tamucc.edu

Texas A&M University, Kingsville, www.tamuk.edu

Texas Coastal Management Program, www.glo.state.tx.us/coastal/cmp.html

Texas Department of Public Safety, www.txdps.state.tx.us

Texas Department of Transportation, www.dot.state.tx.us

Texas Hawk Watchers, www.ccbirding.com/thw/hb.html

Texas Highways Magazine online, www.texashighways.com

Texas Maritime Museum, www.texasmaritimemuseum.org

Texas Ornithological Society, www.texasbirds.org

Texas Parks and Wildlife Department, www.tpwd.state.tx.us

Texas State Aquarium, www.texasstateaquarium.com

Three Rivers Chamber of Commerce, www.threeriverstx.org

Welder Wildlife Foundation, www.welderwildlife.org

Womack Family Ranch, www.womackranch.com.

Appendix C: Boat Operators

Whooping Crane Trips
MV *Molly Anna* or *Pisces,* Rockport Harbor; (800) 245–9324, (361) 729–7525

Rockport Birding and Kayak Adventures on the *Skimmer,* Fulton Harbor; (877) TXBIRDS, (877) 892–4737; www.RockportAdventures.com

Whooping Crane Boat Tours on the *Wharf Cat,* Fisherman's Wharf, Port Aransas and Rockport Harbor, (800) 605–5448, (361) 749–5448; Rockport; (800) 782–2473, (361) 729–4855; www.texaswhoopers.com

Whooping Crane Nature Tours on the *Mustang,* 920 Fulton Beach Road, Rockport; (866) 729–2997, (361) 729–2997

Nature/Birdwatching Tours (not Whooping Crane)
Woody's Sports Center, 136 West Cotter, Port Aransas; (361) 749–5271, (361) 749–5252; www.woodysonline.com

Jetty Boat (passenger ferry), Fisherman's Wharf, Port Aransas; (800) 605–5448, (361) 749–5448; www.wharfcat.com

Private Charters
Aransas Bay Birding Charters on the *Jack Flash,* Sea Gun Marina at Copano Causeway, Rockport; (361) 790–3746; www.texasbirdingcentral.com

Capt. Sally's Reel Run Charters, (361) 729–9095; www.captainsally.com

Crystal Blue Charters, P.O. Box 1875, Port Aransas; (800) 920–0931, (361) 815–7747, (361) 749–5904; www.crystalbluecharters.com

El Gato Charters, Port Aransas, (361) 749–5488, (361) 749–5554; www.texas coastalfishing.com

Friebele's Guide Service, (361) 729–5676

Gold Spoon Charters, Inc., (361) 727–9178; www.goldspooncharters.com

Handsome Sailor Yacht Charters, Hampton's Landing in Aransas Pass, (361) 758–1377; www.handsomesailor.com

Nauti Charters, Port Aransas, (361) 441–4077, (361) 758–4604; www.nauticharters .com

Out to Sea Adventures, P.O. Box 3344, Port Aransas; (361) 749–0093

Padres Island Sarais, 84l Flour Bluff Drive, Corpus Christi; (361) 937–8446; www .billysandifer.com

Shallow Water Guide Service, (361) 729–9265; www.shallow-water.com

Tecolote Charter Service, (361) 729–1529; www.gcaa.com/tecolotecharters.htm

Texas Excursions, (361) 937–2375; www.texasexcursionsonline.com

Web Foot Guide Service, (361) 790–8354

Kayak Rentals

Aransas Bay Birding Charters and Kayak Express, (361) 790–3746; www.texasbirdingcentral.com

Coastal Bend Kayak, 1808 West Wheeler, Aransas Pass; (361) 537–8668, (361) 758–7520

Corpus Christi Kayak Tours and Rentals, c/o Ken Johnson, (361) 855–3926; home.earthlink.net/~johnsonkw/kayak-corpus

Jubilee Boat and Kayak Rentals, Macport Marina Cove Harbor, (361) 727–9835; www.jubileeguideservice.com

Rockport Kayak Outfitters, Fulton Harbor, (800) 729–1505, (361) 729–1505; www.kayakrockport.com

South Bay Bait and Charters, Port Aransas Causeway, (361) 758–2632, (361) 779–8389; www.fishportaransas.com

Appendix D: Birding Organizations in the Coastal Bend

Aransas Bird and Nature Club, P.O. Box 308, Fulton, TX 78358; www.bird Rockport.com

Audubon Outdoor Club of Corpus Christi, P.O. Box 3352, Corpus Christi, TX 78463; www.ccbirding.com/aoc
Meets at 7:00 P.M. at the Corpus Christi Museum of Science and History on the second Tuesday of every month except July and August

Audubon Texas, 2525 Wallingwood, Suite 301, Austin, TX 78746; (512) 306–0225; http://tx.audubon.org

Coastal Bend Audubon Society, P.O. Box 3604, Corpus Christi, TX 78463; (361) 442–9437; www.ccbirding.com/cbas
Meets at 7:00 P.M. at the Corpus Christi Museum of Science and History on the first Tuesday of every month except July and August

Kingsville Bird and Wildlife Club, c/o Milton Kimball; (361) 592–6002
Meets at 7:30 P.M. on the fourth Tuesday of every month at the First Presbyterian Church of Kingsville except June, July, and August

Texas Ornithological Society, PMB #189, 6338 North New Braunfels Avenue, San Antonio, TX 78209; www.texasbirds.org

Appendix E: Birding Festivals in the Area

January/February

Three Rivers: Choke Canyon Birding Festival

Port Aransas: A Celebration of Whooping Cranes and Other Birds

April

Corpus Christi: Earth Day/Bay Day

The Central Texas Coast: Great Texas Birding Classic

The Central Texas Coast: International Migratory Bird Day

Corpus Christi: America's Birdiest City Contest

May

American Wetlands Month

August

Corpus Christi: A Celebration of Flight (Hawk Watch). Runs August through November, with special events in September.

September

Rockport: Hummer/Bird Celebration

October

Your Favorite National Wildlife Refuge: Refuge Week

Goliad State Park: Lone Star Legacy

November

Kingsville: South Texas Wildlife and Birding Festival

December

The Central Texas Coast: Christmas Bird Count. Many local towns hold this in late December or early January.

Appendix F: Campground Reservations

National Parks

Padre Island National Seashore, P.O. Box 18130, Corpus Christi, TX 78480-1300; (361) 949–8068

Texas State Parks

Choke Canyon State Park, Calliham Unit, P.O. Box 2, Calliham, TX 78007; (361) 786–3868

Choke Canyon State Park, South Shore Unit, P.O. Box 1548, Three Rivers, TX 78071; (361) 786–3538

Goliad State Park, 108 Park Road 6, Goliad, TX 77963; (361) 645–3405

Goose Island State Park, 202 South Palmetto Street, Rockport, TX 78382; (361) 729–2858

Lake Corpus Christi State Park, P.O. Box 1167, Mathis, TX 78368; (361) 547–2635

Mustang Island State Park, P.O. Box 326, Port Aransas, TX 78373; (361) 749–5246

County Campgrounds

Bee County Coliseum, 214 South FM 251, Beeville, TX 78102; (361) 362–3290

I. B. Magee Beach Park, 321 North on the Beach, Port Aransas, TX 78373; (361) 749–6117

Padre Balli Park, 15820 Park Road 22, Corpus Christi, TX 78418; (361) 949–8121

San Patricio de Hibernia Perserve (this county park is still under development)

SeaWind, 1066 East FM 628, Riviera, TX 78379; (361) 297–5738

City Campgrounds

Austwell City RV Park, (361) 286–3523

Labonte Park, 1433 Interstate 37, Corpus Christi, TX 78410; (361) 241–1464

Lions/Shelly Park and Jeter RV Park, City of Refugio, 609 Commerce Street, Refugio, TX 78377; (361) 526–5361

Live Oak City Park, City of Ingleside, P.O. Box 400, Ingleside, TX 78362; (361) 776–2517

Rob and Bessie Welder Park, City of Sinton, 301 East Market, Sinton, TX 78387; (361) 364–2381

Tips Park, Highway 72 West at Frio River, Three Rivers, TX 78071; (361) 786–4324

Private Campgrounds by Town

Alice

Paisano Mobile Home Park, Highway 359, Alice, TX 78332; (361) 664–3909

Aransas Pass

Country Villa RV/Mobile Home Park, 3780 FM 1069, Aransas Pass, TX 78336; (361) 776–7534

Fin and Feather Marina and RV Park, 100 Stedman Island, Aransas Pass, TX 78336; (361) 758–7414

Hampton's Landing, 430 Ransom Road, Aransas Pass, TX 78336; (361) 758–1562

Harbor Village, 128 East Mrytle Avenue, Aransas Pass, TX 78336; (361) 758–5218

Hummer Haven RV Park, 1708 South Commercial Street, Aransas Pass, TX 78336; (361) 758–5602

ICW RV Park, 427 Ransom Road, Aransas Pass, TX 78336; (361) 758–1044

Mobile Village RV Park, 164 Stone, Aransas Pass, TX 78336; (361) 758–8367

Portobelo Village, 2009 West Wheeler, Aransas Pass, TX 78336; (361) 758–3378, (888) 412–2671

Ransom Road RV Park, 240 Ransom Road, Aransas Pass, TX 78336; (361) 758–2715

Bayside

Evans Bait Stand and RV Park, 103 Salt Flat Road, Bayside, TX 78340; (361) 529–6656

Beeville

Country Villa Park, 214 Private Oxford Lane, #41, Beeville, TX 78102; (361) 358–0341

Hill Top Mobile Ranch, 1300 Hill Top Ranch Road, Beeville, TX 78102; (361) 358–9595

Mabray's, 115 Private Kelsey Lane, Beeville, TX 78102; (361) 358–0524

Corpus Christi

Anchor Harbor RV Community, 8100 South Padre Island Drive, Corpus Christi, TX 78412; (361) 991–3292

Colonial Del Rey, 1717 Waldron Road, Corpus Christi, TX 78418; (800) 580–2435, (361) 937–2435

Gateway Mobile, 1545 North Lexington Boulevard, Corpus Christi, TX 78409; (361) 289–1191

Greyhound RV Park, 5402 Leopard Street, Corpus Christi, TX 78408; (361) 289–2076

Gulfway RV Park, 7436 South Padre Island Drive, Corpus Christi, TX 78412; (361) 991–0106

Gulley's RV Park, 8225 Leopard Street, Corpus Christi, TX 78409; (361) 241–4122

Hatch RV, 3101 Valero Way (formerly Up River Road), Corpus Christi, TX 78408; (800) 332–4509, (361) 883–9781

Laguna Shore Village, 3828 Laguna Shores Road, Corpus Christi, TX 78418; (361) 937–4259

Lakeside RV Park, 515 Lakeside Drive, Corpus Christi, TX 78418; (361) 937–5296

Marina Village, 229 NAS Drive, Corpus Christi, TX 78418; (361) 937–2560

Padre Palms RV, 131 Skipper Lane, Corpus Christi, TX 78418; (361) 937–2125

Puerto Del Sol Park, 5100 Timon, Corpus Christi, TX 78402; (361) 882–5373

Shady Grove RV, 2919 Waldron Road, Corpus Christi, TX 78418; (361) 937–1314

George West
Smith Trailer and RV Park, P.O. Drawer 1520, George West, TX 78022; (361) 449–1498

Goliad
Aranama RV Park, 2205 Alcalde de La Bahia, Goliad, TX 77963; (361) 645–8003

Coleto Creek Park, P.O. Box 68, Fannin, TX 77960; (361) 575–6366

Dos Vecinos Dry Camping, 700 Block Highway 59, Goliad, TX 77963; (361) 645–8288

Encino Grande RV Park, 914 FM 1351, Goliad, TX 77963; (361) 645–8133

Salones' RV Park, 302 North Fort, Goliad, TX 77963; (361) 645–2647

Ingleside
County Villa Motor Home and RV Park, 378 FM 1069, Ingleside, TX 78362; (361) 776–7534

Indian Trail RV and Motor Home Park, 1618 Highway 361, Ingleside, TX 78362; (361) 776–1961

Ingleside Trailer Park, Avenue F, Ingleside, TX 78362; (361) 960–6064

Kingsville
Kings Manor Estates Mobile Home Park, 1700 North First Street, Kingsville, TX 78363; (361) 592–0711

Oasis RV and Mobile Home Park, 2415 East Santa Gertrudis, Kingsville, TX 78363; (361) 592–0764

Wright's Mobile Home and RV Park, 1639 Carlos Truan Boulevard, Kingsville, TX 78363; (361) 592–7243

Mathis

Camp Bell RV and Marina, FM 3162 and Boat Ramp Road, Sandia, TX 78383; (361) 547–0606

County Estates Mobil Ranch, 2336 FM 1717 South, Mathis, TX 78363; (361) 592–4659

Fiesta Marina Resort, 250 Boat Ramp Road, Sandia, TX 78383; (361) 547–3462

Lake Corpus Christi KOA Campgrounds, Route 1, P.O. Box 158B, Mathis, TX 78368; (361) 547–5201

Mathis Motor Inn and RV, 1223 North Front, Mathis, TX 78363; (361) 547–0177

Riverlake Drive Inn and RV Park, South Highway 359, Mathis, TX 78368; (361) 547–9853

Sunrise Beach, Park Road 25, P.O. Box 189, Mathis, TX 78368; (877) 547–9796, (361) 547–7722

Wilderness Lakes RV Resort, Park Road 25, Mathis, TX 78368; (361) 547–9995

Port Aransas

Beachway RV Park, 223 North Station Street, Port Aransas, TX 78373; (361) 749–6351

Funtime RV Park, 400 West Avenue C, Port Aransas, TX 78373; (361) 749–5811

Gulf Waters RV, 5601 State Highway 361, Port Aransas, TX 78373; (361) 749–8888

Island RV Resort, P.O. Box 1377, 700 Sixth Street, Port Aransas, TX 78373; (361) 749–5600

Kazen RV Parks, 1129 South Eleventh Street, Port Aransas, TX 78373; (361) 749–4844

Mustang RV and Trailer, 300 East Cotter Avenue, Port Aransas, TX 78373; (361) 749–5343

On the Beach RV Park, 907 Beach Access Road 1A, Port Aransas, TX 78373; (361) 749–4909

Pioneer Beach Resort, 120 Gulfwind Drive, Port Aransas, TX 78373 (888) 480–3246, (361) 749–6248

Surf Side RV and Resort, P.O. Box 179, 1820 South Eleventh Street, Port Aransas, TX 78373; (888) 565–5929, (361) 749–2208

Tropic Island RV Resort, P.O. Box 748, 315 Cutoff Road, Port Aransas, TX 78373; (888) 221–7179, (361) 749–6128

Portland

Sea Breeze RV Park, 1026 Seabreeze Lane, Portland, TX 78374; (361) 643–0744

Riviera

Bayview RV Park and Campground, 662 South County Road 1150, Riviera, TX 78379; (361) 297–5726

Riviera Beach RV Park, 991 East FM 771, Riviera, TX 78379; (361) 297–5254

Robstown

Evelyn's RV Park, 1645 East CR 48, Robstown, TX 78380; (361) 387–3777

Rockport/Fulton

Ancient Oaks RV Park, 1222 Highway 35 South, Rockport, TX 78382; (361) 729–5051, (800) 962–6134

At Watersedge RV Park, 717 N Fulton Beach Road, Rockport, TX 78382; (361) 729–1100

Bahia Vista Waterfront RV Park and Cottages, 5801 FM 1781, Rockport, TX 78382; (800) 953–1226, (361) 729–1226

Bay View RV Resort, 5451 Highway 35 North, Rockport, TX 78382; (866) 275–5172, (361) 729–1334

Beacon RV Park and Marina, P.O. Box 238, Fulton, TX 78358; (361) 729–3906

Big D RV Resort, 3101 FM 1781, Rockport, TX 78382; (361) 790–9373

Blue Heron RV Park, 1136 Heron Lane, Rockport, TX 78382; (361) 727–1136

Circle W RV Ranch, 1401 Smokehouse Road, Rockport, TX 78382; (361) 729–1542

Copano Hideaway RV, 3966 FM 1781, Rockport, TX 78382; (361) 729–9292

Country Oaks Mobile Home and RV, 2431 FM 1781, Rockport, TX 78382; (361) 729–9651

Driftwood RV Haven, 701 Mesquite, Fulton, TX 78358; (361) 729–2452

E-Z Liv'n RV Park, 2121 FM 3036, Fulton, TX 78358; (361) 727–0688

Fulton Oaks Park, P.O. Box 1908, Fulton, TX 78358; (361) 729–4606

J&V Travel Trailer Park, 606 West Market Street, Rockport, TX 78382; (361) 729–9558

Lagoons RV Resort, 600 Enterprise Boulevard, Rockport, TX 78382; (361) 729–7834

The Last Resort, 4321 Highway 35 South, Rockport, TX 78382; (361) 727–1958

Palm Harbor Marina, 151 Port Avenue, Rockport, TX 78382; (361) 729–8540

Palm Harbor RV Park, 170 Port Avenue, Rockport, TX 78382; (361) 729–0113

Paradise Trailer Park 212 North Hood Street, Rockport, TX 78382; (361) 729–8554

Quiet One Travel Trailer Park, 600 West James Street, Rockport, TX 78382; (361) 729–2668

RV Resort of Rockport, 2455 FM 1781, Rockport, TX 78382; (361) 729–3013

Raintree RV Park, 1924 West Terrace Boulevard, Rockport, TX 78382; (361) 729–7005

Rockport 35 RV Park Inc., 4851 Highway 35 North, Rockport, TX 78382; (800) 392–2930, (361) 729–2307

Sandollar Resort and RV Park, 919 North Fulton Beach Road, Fulton, TX 78358; (361) 729–2381

Seahorse RV and Mobile Home Park, 3802 Highway 35 North, Rockport, TX 78382; (361) 729–2760

Shady Oaks RV Park, 1301 Smokehouse Road, Rockport, TX 78382; (800) 781–1962, (361) 729–6511

Sunny Acres Travel Trailer Park, 602 West Sixth Street, Rockport, TX 78382; (361) 729–1248

Taylor Oaks RV Park, 707 South Pearl, Rockport, TX 78382; (800) 551–4996, (361) 729–5187

Watersedge RV Park, 717 North Fulton Beach Road, Fulton, TX 78358; (361) 729–1100

Woody Acres RV Resort, 1202 West Mesquite Street, Fulton, TX 78358; (800) 526–9264, (361) 729–5636

Sinton

Hitching Post RV Park, 900 West Sinton, Sinton, TX 78387; (361) 364–3615

Three Rivers

Choke Canyon RV Park, 2625 Highway 72 West, Three Rivers, TX 78071; (361) 449–7620

Appendix G: Plans for Future Sites

The hobby of bird watching grows every year, and future birding sites are exciting prospects. At the time of publication, five new sites are being considered in the Corpus Christi area.

1. **The Coastal Bend Regional Park** will be a 1,600-acre multiuse park near Corpus Christi. The proposed location is the property bounded by Highway 286, Farm-to-Market 43, Farm-to-Market 763, and Oso Creek. If this park is developed, it could include a number of facilities such as a golf course, an equestrian venue, a zoological park, and a green space with hike and bike trails. The planners are sincere about incorporating accommodations for bird-watchers.

    Coastal Bend Regional Park Foundation, Inc.
    600 Leopard Street, Suite 2700
    Corpus Christi, TX 78473
    (361) 698–3726

2. The Texas Department of Transportation (DOT) had long planned an overpass on Highway 181 near **Sinton.** Land was acquired, and then plans changed. The DOT and the City of Sinton have agreed to convert this right-of-way into a birding habitat park. Right now it is referred to as the Unnamed Bird Site, Sinton, Texas. This eight-acre site, set for construction in spring/summer of 2006, is found at the junction of U.S. Highway 181 and County Road 962 (or CR 28A). It is located south of the Rob and Bessie Welder Park on US 181 approximately 3 miles north of Sinton in San Patricio County. This site includes dense brush dominated by retama, mesquite, huisache, and hackberry, which attracts Northern Cardinals, Red-eyed Vireos, Cattle Egrets, Turkey Vultures, and butterflies. Initial plans are to complete a parking lot, an educational and tourism kiosk, and a beginning trail.

    Texas Department of Transportation
    Attention: Suzanne Contreras, Environmental Specialist
    P.O. Box 9907
    Corpus Christi, TX 78469
    (361) 808–2250

3. The Coastal Bend Bays and Estuaries Program and The Nature Conservancy of Texas purchased the **Nueces Delta Preserve** of 1,600 acres in 2003. A plan was developed to move freshwater into the area to revitalize the wetlands, crucial to the environmental health of this dynamic ecosystem. The property is home to raptors, passerines, and wetland birds. At present, the preserve is not open to the public, but future plans include construction of a

parking lot, restrooms, and trails marked by signs, with the hope of using the facilities for educational purposes. The Nueces Delta Preserve is located on Highway 77 south of the City of Odem. It is about 3 miles north of the Interstate 37, Exit 17.

Coastal Bend Bays and Estuaries Program
1305 North Shoreline, Suite 205
Corpus Christi, TX 78401
(361) 885–6202

4. Port Aransas acquired 1,100 acres through the Texas General Land Office and is purchasing another 1,800 acres from private owners in order to complete the **Port Aransas Nature Preserve.** The property, known to the locals as Charlie's Pasture, is adjacent to the Leonabelle Turnbull Birding Center. The preserve will include wetlands and grasslands that are home to many Coastal Bend birds.

City of Port Aransas
710 West Avenue A
Port Aransas, TX 78373
(361) 749–4111

5. The Corpus Christi port commissioners are considering a plan for a long-term lease of fifty-four acres at the north end of the **Rincon Industrial Park** on the north side of the port. If approved, the project would include a hotel resort and a bird sanctuary.

Port of Corpus Christi Authority
222 Power Street
Corpus Christi, TX 78401
(361) 882–5633

Appendix H: Bibliography

Alsop, Fred J. III. *Birds of Texas.* New York: Dorling Kindersley, Inc., 2002.

American Bird Conservancy: Globally Important Bird Areas of the United States. Available at www.abcbirds.org.

Aransas National Wildlife Refuge. Washington, D.C.: U.S. Fish and Wildlife Service, 2002.

Aransas National Wildlife Refuge: Birds. Washington, D.C.: U.S. Fish and Wildlife Service, 2004.

Audubon Club of Corpus Christi. Available at www.ccbirding.com.

Baird, Mike. "Channel's History Steeped in Longhorns, Their Bones." *Corpus Christi Caller Times,* 16 February 2005, p. 3B.

Baird, Mike. "Padre Island Nation Seashore: Visitors Voicing Concerns." *Corpus Christi Caller Times,* 14 February 2005, p. 1B.

Beshur, Alison. "An Oil-and-Waterfront Mix." *Corpus Christi Caller Times,* 11 September 2005, p. 1D.

Birding the Corpus Christi Area. Compiled by members of Audubon Outdoor Club of Corpus Christi, 1996.

Birds of Choke Canyon State Park. Austin: Texas Parks and Wildlife, 2003.

"Birdwatching on Padre Island." National Park Service. Available at park entrance.

Blacklock, Gene W. *Birds of the Lake Corpus Christi State Recreation Area: A Field Checklist.* Austin: Texas Parks and Wildlife, 1988.

A Checklist of Birds of Padre Island National Seashore. Tucson, AZ: Southwest Parks and Monuments Association, 2000.

Chipley, Robert M., et. al. *The American Bird Conservancy Guide to the 500 Most Important Bird Areas in the United States.* New York: Random House, 2003.

Coastal Bend Bays and Estuaries Web site. Available at www.cbbep.org.

Connie Hagar. Available at www.birdRockport.com.

Cooksey, M. *Birds of Mustang Island State Park and Vicinity.* Austin: Texas Parks and Wildlife Department, 2002.

Corpus Christi Padre Island Convention and Visitors Bureau. Available at www .corpuschristicvb.com.

Dollar, Brent, ed. *Texas State Travel Guide, 2004.* Austin: Texas Department of Transportation, 2004.

Endangered Birds in Texas. Available at www.tpwd.state.tx.us.

Elwonger, Mark. *Birds and Butterflies of the Angel of Goliad Trail.* 2003. Available at trailhead.

Elwonger, Mark. *Finding Birds on the Central Texas Coast*. Victoria, Texas: Mark Elwonger, 1995.

Garza, Adriana. "Port A Nature Preserve Plans Viewed." *Corpus Christi Caller Times,* 31 August 2005, p. 3B.

Garza, Alicia A. "Jim Wells County." *Handbook of Texas.* Austin: Texas Historical Association, 2005.

Goodloe, Carolyn. *Winter Birding Corpus Christi Botanical Gardens and Nature Center. 2005.* Unpublished.

Graczyk, Michael. "Bird Lover Monitors Cranes on Their Own Turf." *Corpus Christi Caller Times,* 17 April 2005, p. 6B.

Graham, Frank, Jr. *Audubon's Introduction to Important Bird Areas.* New York: National Audubon Society, 2002.

The Great Texas Coastal Birding Trail: Central Texas Coast. Austin: Texas Parks and Wildlife and Texas Department of Transportation.

Guthrie, Keith. *History of San Patricio County.* Austin: Nortex, 1986.

Hanna, Bill. "Goose Island Campers to Get Web Access." *Corpus Christi Caller Times,* 30 December 2004, p. 4B.

Hike and Bike (map). Available at www.tamucc.edu/hike_bike/#dist.

Hodge, Larry D. "Of Cows and Crawdads." *Texas Parks and Wildlife Magazine,* September 2002.

Holgersen, Norman. *Birds at Coleto Creek Park.* Coleto Creek Park Newsletter, 2002.

Holt, Harold R. *A Birder's Guide to the Texas Coast.* Colorado Springs: American Birding Association, 1993.

Huson, Hobart. *Refugio: A Comprehensive History of Refugio County from Aboriginal Times to 1953.* Woodsboro, Texas: Rooke Foundation, 1953.

Jasinski, Laurie E. "Sarita, Texas." *Handbook of Texas Online.* Available at www.tsha .utexas.edu/handbook/online.

Johnson, John G. "Copano Bay State Fishing Pier." *Handbook of Texas Online.* Available at www.tsha.utexas.edu/handbook/online.

Jones, Barry. *A Birder's Guide to Aransas National Wildlife Refuge.* Albuquerque, NM: Southwest Natural and Cultural Heritage Association, 1992.

Kemper, John. *Birding Northern California.* Guilford, Connecticut: The Globe Pequot Press, 2001.

Konrad, Paul M. "WildBird's Top 50 Birding Hotspots." *WildBird,* September 1996, pp. 31–45.

Kutac, Edward A. *Birder's Guide to Texas.* Houston: Gulf Publishing Co., 1998.

Leatherwood, Art. "Aransas Pass." *Handbook of Texas.* Austin: Texas State Historical Association, 2002.

LeBaron, Geoffrey S. "The 104th Christmas Bird Count." *American Birds,* Vol. 58, pp. 2–7.

Leffler, John. "McMullen County." *Handbook of Texas.* Austin: Texas State Historical Commission, 2005.

Littleton, Johnnie Sue. "Sinton to Be Home for New Birding Sanctuary." *San Pat County News, 20,* p. 9, 2006.

Lockwood, Mark, and Brush Freeman. *The Texas Ornithological Society Handbook of Texas Birds.* College Station: Texas A&M University Press, 2004.

Nipper, M., J. A. Sanchez Chavez, & J. W. Tunnell, Jr., ed. *2004 GulfBase.* Available at www.gulfbase.org.

"Padre Island." National Park Service, 2002.

Palmer, Paul C. *Birder's Guide to Kingsville–Kleberg County.* Kingsville, Texas: Kingsville Visitor Center, 1990.

Parks in Portland. Available at www.portlandtx.com/parks.cfm.

Rappole, John H., and Gene Blacklock. *Birds of Texas.* College Station, Texas: A&M University Press, 1994.

Rappole, John H., and Gene Blacklock. *Birds of the Texas Coastal Bend Abundance and Distribution.* College Station, Texas: A&M University Press, 1985.

"Record Number of Whooping Cranes Expected to Winter Here This Year." *Winter/Spring Visitor's Guide, 30* October 2004, p. 6.

Riskind, David, and Mark Lockwood. *Birding Texas.* Austin: Texas Parks and Wildlife, 1997.

"Rockport–Fulton Visitor's Guide." *Rockport Pilot Newspaper, 30* April 2005.

Schwennesen, Tricia. "Dedication Is Today for 2 Wetlands Overlooks." *Corpus Christi Caller Times, 31* October 2002.

Shackelford, Clifford E., and Mark W. Lockwood. *Rare and Declining Birds of Texas: Conservation Needed.* Austin: Texas Parks and Wildlife.

Species Information: Threatened and Endangered Animals and Plants. Available at http://endangered.fws.gov/wildlife.html.

Texas Hawk Watchers. Available at www.ccbirding.com.

Texas Ornithological Society: Corpus Christi Meeting Bird Report, April 26–28, 2001. Available at www.texasbirds.org/cc_meeting_birds.html.

Texas Poisonous Snakes. Available at www.tpwd.state.tx.us/kids.

Tucci, Tony. *On the Waterfowl of Texas: Ducks, Geese and Swans.* Austin: Texas Parks and Wildlife, 2001.

"Victoria County Land Owner Is Top 2002 Lone Star Land Steward." *TPW News,* 3 June 2002.

Wauer, Roland H., and Mark A. Elwonder. *Birding Texas.* Guilford, Connecticut: The Globe Pequot Press, 1998.

Welder, Mrs. Patrick. "Rob and Bessie Welder Wildlife Foundation and Refuge." *Handbook of Texas Online.* Available at www.tsha.utexas.edu/handbook/online.

Welder Wildlife Foundation. Available at www.welderwildlife.org.

White, Mel. *Exploring the Great Texas Coastal Birding Trail.* Guilford, Connecticut: The Globe Pequot Press, 2004.

The Whooping Crane—An Endangered Species. Washington, D.C.: U.S. Fish and Wildlife Service.

Yochem, Phyllis. "Bird Guides Lead Productive Trip to Guadalupe Delta." *Corpus Christi Caller Times,* 27 February 2001.

Yochem, Phyllis. "Catching Up on This Season's Sightings." *Corpus Christi Caller Times,* 28 May 2005.

Appendix I: Status and Distribution Chart

Chart Key:

C = common: present in significant numbers in the proper habitat

F = fairly common: a few are present in the proper habitat

U = uncommon: sometimes present in the proper habitat

R = rare: occur regularly but in small numbers

I = irregular: a few occur occasionally

V = vagrant: well out of the species' normal range

BIRD SPECIES	JAN.	FEB.	MAR.	APR.	MAY	JUNE	JULY	AUG.	SEPT.	OCT.	NOV.	DEC.
Common Loon	F	F	F	U	U						U	U
Least Grebe	U	U	U	U	U	U	U	U	U	U	U	U
Pied-billed Grebe	C	C	C	C	C	C	C	C	C	C	C	C
Horned Grebe	R	R	R							R	R	R
Eared Grebe	F	F	F	F	U					U	F	F
Western Grebe	V	V								V	V	V
Northern Gannet	U	U	U	U						U	U	U
American White Pelican	C	C	C	C/U	U	U	U	U	U	U/C	C	C
Brown Pelican	F	F	F	F	F	F	F	F	F	F	F	F
Double-crested Cormorant	C	C	C	C	R	R	R	R	R	R/C	C	C
Neotropic Cormorant	U	U	U	F	F	F	F	F	F	U	U	U
Anhinga	R	R	R	F	F			F	F	R	R	R
Magnificent Frigatebird	R	R	R	R	R	U	U	R	R	R	R	R
American Bittern	U	U	U							U	U	U
Least Bittern	R	R	U	U	U	U	U	R	R	R	R	R
Great Blue Heron	C	C	C	C	C	C	C	C	C	C	C	C
Great Egret	C	C	C	C	C	C	C	C	C	C	C	C
Snowy Egret	C	C	C	C	C	C	C	C	C	C	C	C
Little Blue Heron	F	F	F	U	U	U	U	F	F	F	F	F
Tricolored Heron	C	C	C	C	C	C	C	C	C	C	C	C
Reddish Egret	F	F	F	F	F	F	F	F	F	F	F	F
Cattle Egret	C	C	C	C	C	C	C	C	C	C	C	C
Green Heron	R	R	R	F	F	F	F	F	F	R	R	R
Black-crowned Night-Heron	F	F	F	F	F	F	F	F	F	F	F	F
Yellow-crowned Night-Heron	R	R	R	R	F	F	F	F	R	R	R	R
White Ibis	U	U	U	F	F	F	F	F	F	U	U	U
Glossy Ibis			I	I	I	I						
White-faced Ibis	U	U	F	F	F	F	F	F	U	U	U	U
Roseate Spoonbill	U	U	U	F	F	F	F	F	F	F	U	U
Wook Stork					U	U	U	U	U			
Fulvous Whistling-Duck	U	U	U	U	U	U	U	U	U	U	U	U
Black-bellied Whistling-Duck	U	U	U	F	F	F	F	F	F	F	U	U
Greater White-fronted Goose	F	F	F	I	I						F	F
Snow Goose	C	C	I	I							C	C
Ross's Goose	R	R	R								R	R
Canada Goose	F	F	F								F	F
Wood Duck	U	U	U	U	U	U	U	U	U	U	U	U
Green-winged Teal	C	C	C	U	U					C	C	C
Mottled Duck	C	C	C	C	C	C	C	C	C	C	C	C
Mallard	U	U	U	R							U	U
Northern Pintail	C	C	C	C	R					R	C	C
Blue-winged Teal	F	F	C	C	C	U	U	U	C	C	F	F
Cinnamon Teal	U	U	U	U	R					U	U	U
Northern Shoveler	C	C	C	C	U					U	C	C
Gadwall	F	F	F	F	R	R				R	F	F

BIRD SPECIES	JAN.	FEB.	MAR.	APR.	MAY	JUNE	JULY	AUG.	SEPT.	OCT.	NOV.	DEC.
American Wigeon	C	C	C	C	V	V				C	C	C
Canvasback	U	U	U	R	R					U	U	U
Redhead	F	F	F	U	U	U					F	F
Ring-necked Duck	U	U									U	U
Greater Scaup	R	R	R								R	R
Lesser Scaup	C	C	C	U	U	U				C	C	C
Long-tailed Duck	R	R									R	R
Surf Scoter	R	R									R	R
White-winged Scoter	R	R									R	R
Common Goldeneye	U	U	U								U	U
Bufflehead	F	F	U	U	U						F	F
Hooded Merganser	U	U	U	R						R	R	U
Common Merganser	R	R									R	R
Red-breasted Merganser	F	F	F	U							F	F
Ruddy Duck	F	F	F	F	R	R	R	R	R	R	F	F
Masked Duck	R	R	R	R	R	R	R	R	R	R	R	R
Black Vulture	C	C	C	C	C	C	C	C	C	C	C	C
Turkey Vulture	C	C	C	C	C	C	C	C	C	C	C	C
Osprey	U	U	U	U					U	U	U	U
Swallow-tailed Kite				R	R	R	R	R				
White-tailed Kite	U	U	U	U	U	U	U	U	U	U	U	U
Mississippi Kite				F				F				
Bald Eagle	I	I	I	I	I	I	I	I	I	I	I	I
Northern Harrier	C	C	C	U	U	U	U	U	U	C	C	C
Sharp-shinned Hawk	U	U	U	U						U	U	U
Cooper's Hawk	U	U	U	U	V	V	V	V	U	U	U	U
Harris's Hawk	C	C	C	C	C	C	C	C	C	C	C	C
Red-shouldered Hawk	F	F	F	F	F	F	F	F	F	F	F	F
Broad-winged Hawk				F	F				F	F		
Swainson's Hawk					F				F			
White-tailed Hawk	U	U	U	U	U	U	U	U	U	U	U	U
Red-tailed Hawk	C	C	C	U	U	U	U	U	U	U	C	C
Ferruginous Hawk	I	I	I	I						I	I	I
Rough-legged Hawk	R	R									R	R
Golden Eagle	V	V	V								V	V
Crested Caracara	C	C	C	C	C	C	C	C	C	C	C	C
American Kestrel	C	C	C	I					I	C	C	C
Merlin	R	R	R	R						R	R	R
Peregrine Falcon	R	R	R	F					F	R	R	R
Prairie Falcon	I	I	I							I	I	I
Wild Turkey	F	F	F	F	F	F	F	F	F	F	F	F
Northern Bobwhite	F	F	F	F	F	F	F	F	F	F	F	F
Scaled Quail	R	R	R	R	R	R	R	R	R	R	R	R
Yellow Rail	I	I	I	I						I	I	I
Black Rail	R	R	R	R	R	R	R	R	R	R	R	R
Clapper Rail	F	F	F	F	F	F	F	F	F	F	F	F
King Rail	U	U	U	U	U	U	U	U	U	U	U	U
Virginia Rail	U	U	R	R					R	U	U	U
Sora	R	R	R	U					U	U	R	R
Purple Gallinule				U	U	U	U	U	R	R	R	R
Common Moorhen	F	F	F	F	F	F	F	F	F	F	F	F
American Coot	C	C	C	C	C	C	C	C	C	C	C	C
Sandhill Crane	F	F	U							U	F	F
Whooping Crane	F	F	F								F	F
Black-bellied Plover	C	C	C	C	R	R	R	R	R	C	C	C
American Golden-Plover				R					R			
Snowy Plover	R	R	R	U	U	U	U	U	R	R	R	R
Wilson's Plover	R	R	R	F	F	F	F	F	F	R	R	R
Semipalmated Plover	F	F	F	F	U			U	F	F	F	F
Piping Plover	U	U	F	F	R	R	R	R	F	F	U	U
Killdeer	C	C	C	C	C	C	C	C	C	C	C	C

BIRD SPECIES	JAN.	FEB.	MAR.	APR.	MAY	JUNE	JULY	AUG.	SEPT.	OCT.	NOV.	DEC.
Mountain Plover	I	I	R	R					R	I	I	I
American Oystercatcher	F	F	F	F	F	F	F	F	F	F	F	F
Black-necked Stilt	R	U	U	C	C	C	C	C	U	R	R	R
American Avocet	F	F	F	F	F	F	F	F	F	F	F	F
Northern Jacana	I	I	I	I	I	I	I	I	I	I	I	I
Greater Yellowlegs	F	F	F	F	U	U	U	U	F	F	F	F
Lesser Yellowlegs	U	U	F	F	R	R	R	F	F	U	U	U
Solitary Sandpiper	R	U	U	U	R	R	R	U	U	R	R	R
Willet	C	C	C	C	C	C	C	C	C	C	C	C
Spotted Sandpiper	F	F	F	F	F			F	F	F	F	F
Upland Sandpiper			F	F				U	U			
Whimbrel	R	R	R	F	R	R	R	R	R	R	R	R
Long-billed Curlew	F	F	F	F	F	R	U	U	F	F	F	F
Hudsonian Godwit				U	U			U				
Marbled Godwit	U	U	U	U	U	R	R	U	U	U	U	U
Ruddy Turnstone	F	F	F	F	F	R	R	R	F	F	F	F
Red Knot	R	R	R	R	R	R	R	R	R	R	R	R
Sanderling	C	C	C	C	C	C	C	C	C	C	C	C
Semipalmated Sandpiper			R	F	F	R	R	R	R	R	R	
Western Sandpiper	F	F	F	F	R	R	R	R	F	F	F	F
Least Sandpiper	C	C	C	C	R	R	R	R	C	C	C	C
White-rumped Sandpiper					F		R	R				
Baird's Sandpiper				F			R					
Pectoral Sandpiper			F	F	F			F	F			
Dunlin	F	F	F	F			U	U	F	F	F	F
Stilt Sandpiper	R	R	R	U				U	U	F	F	F
Buff-breasted Sandpiper			U	U				U	U			
Ruff				V					V	V	V	
Short-billed Dowitcher	F	F	F	F	R	R	R	R	F	F	F	F
Long-billed Dowitcher	C	C	C	C			U	U	C	C	C	C
Common Snipe	F	F	F	F					F	F	F	F
American Woodcock	R	R									R	R
Wilson's Phalarope			U	U	U			U	U	U		
Pomarine Jaeger	U	U	U									U
Parasitic Jaeger	I	I	I							I	I	I
Laughing Gull	C	C	C	C	C	C	C	C	C	C	C	C
Franklin's Gull				U	F					F	U	
Bonaparte's Gull	F	F	U	U							U	F
Ring-billed Gull	C	C	C	C	U	U	U	U	U	C	C	C
California Gull	I	I	I							I		I
Herring Gull	C	C	C	C	U	U	U	U	U	U	C	C
Lesser Black-backed Gull	I	I	I								I	I
Glaucous Gull	I	I	I									I
Gull-billed Tern	U	U	U	F	F	F	F	F	F	F	U	U
Caspian Tern	F	F	F	F	F	F	F	F	F	F	F	F
Royal Tern	F	F	F	C	C	C	C	C	C	F	F	F
Sandwich Tern	R	R	U	F	F	F	F	F	F	U	R	R
Common Tern	U	U	U	F						F	U	U
Forster's Tern	C	C	C	C	C	C	C	C	C	C	C	C
Least Tern				C	C	C	C	C	C			
Sooty Tern				R	R	R	R	R	R			
Black Tern				U	F	F	F	F	U			
Black Skimmer	U	U	C	C	C	C	C	C	C	C	U	U
Rock Pigeon	C	C	C	C	C	C	C	C	C	C	C	C
White-winged Dove	U	U	C	C	C	C	C	C	C	U	U	U
Mourning Dove	F	F	F	F	F	F	F	F	F	F	F	F
Inca Dove	F	F	F	F	F	F	F	F	F	F	F	F
Common Ground-Dove	F	F	F	F	F	F	F	F	F	F	F	F
White-tipped Dove	U	U	U	U	U	U	U	U	U	U	U	U
Eurasian Collared-Dove	R	R	R	R	R	R	R	R	R	R	R	R
Black-billed Cuckoo				R	R			R	R			

BIRD SPECIES	JAN.	FEB.	MAR.	APR.	MAY	JUNE	JULY	AUG.	SEPT.	OCT.	NOV.	DEC.
Yellow-billed Cuckoo				U	F	U	U	U	U			
Greater Roadrunner	U	U	U	U	U	U	U	U	U	U	U	U
Groove-billed Ani	R	R	U	U	U	U	U	U	R	R	R	R
Barn Owl	F	F	F	F	F	F	F	F	F	F	F	F
Eastern Screech-Owl	U	U	U	U	U	U	U	U	U	U	U	U
Great Horned Owl	F	F	F	F	F	F	F	F	F	F	F	F
Burrowing Owl	R	R	R							R	R	R
Barred Owl	F	F	F	F	F	F	F	F	F	F	F	F
Short-eared Owl	R	R	R							R	R	R
Lesser Nighthawk				F	F	F	F	F	F			
Common Nighthawk				F	C	C	C	C	C	F		
Common Pauraque	U	U	U	U	U	U	U	U	U	U	U	U
Chuck-will's-widow				R	R	R	R	R	R	R	R	
Whip-poor-will	R		R	R						R	R	R
Chimney Swift				U	F	F	F	F	F	U		
Buff-bellied Hummingbird	R	R	R	R	R	R	R	R	R	R	R	R
Ruby-throated Hummingbird	U	U	U	F	F	U	U	F	F	U	U	U
Black-chinned Hummingbird			R	R	R	R	R	R	R			
Rufous Hummingbird	I	I	I				I	I	I	I	I	I
Ringed Kingfisher	I	I	I	I	I	I	I	I	I	I	I	I
Belted Kingfisher	F	F	F	U					U	F	F	F
Green Kingfisher	R	R	R	R	R	R	R	R	R	R	R	R
Red-headed Woodpecker	R	R	R	R	R	R	R	R	R	R	R	R
Golden-fronted Woodpecker	C	C	C	C	C	C	C	C	C	C	C	C
Red-bellied Woodpecker	F	F	F	F	F	F	F	F	F	F	F	F
Yellow-bellied Sapsucker	F	F	F	U					U	F	F	F
Ladder-backed Woodpecker	F	F	F	F	F	F	F	F	F	F	F	F
Downy Woodpecker	F	F	F	F	F	F	F	F	F	F	F	F
Northern Flicker	F	F	F	U						F	F	F
Northern Beardless-Tyrannulet	I	I	I	I	I	I	I	I	I	I	I	I
Olive-sided Flycatcher				R			R	R				
Eastern Wood-Pewee				F	F			F	F	U		
Yellow-bellied Flycatcher				U	U			U	U	U		
Acadian Flycatcher				U	U			U	U			
Alder Flycatcher				R	R			R	R			
Willow Flycatcher				R	R			R	R			
Least Flycatcher	R	R	R	R	R			R	R	R	R	R
Eastern Phoebe	F	F	F	U					U	F	F	F
Say's Phoebe	R	R	R								R	R
Vermilion Flycatcher	U	U	I	I	I	I	I	I	I	I	U	U
Ash-throated Flycatcher				R	U	U	U	U	R			
Great Crested Flycatcher				F	U			F	U			
Brown-crested Flycatcher				U	U	U	U	U	U			
Great Kiskadee	U	U	U	U	U	U	U	U	U	U	U	U
Couch's Kingbird	R	R	R	U	U	U	U	U	U	U	R	R
Western Kingbird			R	R	R	R	R	R	R	R	R	
Eastern Kingbird			U	C	C			C	C	U		
Scissor-tailed Flycatcher	R	R	R	R	C	C	C	C	C	C	R	R
Horned Lark	F	F	F	F	F	F	F	F	F	F	F	F
Purple Martin			R	R	C	C	C	C	C	R		
Tree Swallow	U	U	U	C	C		U	C	C	U	U	U
Northern Rough-winged Swallow	R	R	R	F			R	C	C	R	R	R
Bank Swallow			R	F	R			R	F	R	R	
Cliff Swallow				U	U	U	U	U	U			
Cave Swallow	R	R	R	F	F	F	F	F	R	R	R	R
Barn Swallow				F	F	U	U	U	F	U		
Green Jay	F	F	F	F	F	F	F	F	F	F	F	F
Carolina Chickadee	U	U	U	U	U	U	U	U	U	U	U	U
Tufted Titmouse	F	F	F	F	F	F	F	F	F	F	F	F
Verdin	F	F	F	F	F	F	F	F	F	F	F	

BIRD SPECIES	JAN.	FEB.	MAR.	APR.	MAY	JUNE	JULY	AUG.	SEPT.	OCT.	NOV.	DEC.
Red-breasted Nuthatch	I	I	I	I							I	I
Brown Creeper	U	U	U								U	U
Cactus Wren	U	U	U	U	U	U	U	U	U	U	U	U
Carolina Wren	C	C	C	C	C	C	C	C	C	C	C	C
Bewick's Wren	F	F	F	F	F	F	F	F	F	F	F	F
House Wren	F	F	F	U	U						F	F
Winter Wren	R	R	R								R	R
Sedge Wren	F	F	F	U							F	F
Marsh Wren	F	F	F	F	F					F	F	F
Golden-crowned Kinglet	U	U	U							U	U	U
Ruby-crowned Kinglet	F	F	F	F							F	F
Blue-gray Gnatcatcher	C	C	C	C	R	R	R	R	C	C	C	C
Eastern Bluebird	U	U	U	R	R	R	R	R	R	U	U	U
Veery				U	U			R	R	R		
Gray-cheeked Thrush				U	U			R	R	R		
Swainson's Thrush				F	F				R	R		
Hermit Thrush	F	F	F	U							F	F
Wood Thrush						F	U			U	U	
American Robin	C	C	C	C	V	V	V	V	V	C	C	C
Gray Catbird	R	R	R	F	F				F	F	R	R
Northern Mockingbird	C	C	C	C	C	C	C	C	C	C	C	C
Sage Thrasher	R	R	R	R						R	R	R
Brown Thrasher	F	F	F	F	R	R	R	R	F	F	F	F
Long-billed Thrasher	F	F	F	F	F	F	F	F	F	F	F	F
Curve-billed Thrasher	F	F	F	F	F	F	F	F	F	F	F	F
American Pipit	F	F	F							F	F	F
Sprague's Pipit	R	R	R							R	R	R
Cedar Waxwing	F	F	F	F								F
Loggerhead Shrike	F	F	F	F	U	U	U	U	F	F	F	F
European Starling	C	C	C	F	F	F	F	F	F	F	C	C
White-eyed Vireo	U	U	F	F	F	U	U	F	F	U	U	U
Bell's Vireo				R	R	R	R	R	R			
Blue-headed Vireo	U	U	U	F	F					F	U	U
Yellow-throated Vireo				U	U				U			
Warbling Vireo				U	U					R		
Philadelphia Vireo					U				R			
Red-eyed Vireo				F	U			R	R	R		
Blue-winged Warbler				U	U			R	R	R		
Golden-winged Warbler					U				R	R		
Tennessee Warbler					U				U	U		
Orange-crowned Warbler	F	F	F	F							F	F
Nashville Warbler				U					F	F		
Northern Parula			U	U					U	U		
Tropical Parula	I	I	I	I	I	I	I	I	I	I	I	I
Yellow Warbler				F	F			F	F			
Chestnut-sided Warbler					F			U	U	U		
Magnolia Warbler					F			U	U	U		
Cape May Warbler				V	V							
Black-throated Blue Warbler			R	R					R			
Yellow-rumped Warbler	C	C	C	R							C	C
Black-throated Gray Warbler	R	R	R	R							R	R
Hermit Warbler				R								
Black-throated Green Warbler					F			U	U			
Blackburnian Warbler					F			U				
Yellow-throated Warbler	I	I	I	I						I	I	I
Pine Warbler	I	I	I								I	I
Prairie Warbler				I					I			
Palm Warbler	I	I	I								I	I
Bay-breasted Warbler				F	F					I	I	
Blackpoll Warbler				U	U				I	I		
Cerulean Warbler				U	U				I			
Black-and-white Warbler	I	I	F	F				U	F	I	I	

BIRD SPECIES	JAN.	FEB.	MAR.	APR.	MAY	JUNE	JULY	AUG.	SEPT.	OCT.	NOV.	DEC.
American Redstart			I	F					F	F	I	I
Prothonotary Warbler				F			U	U				
Worm-eating Warbler				U				R				
Swainson's Warbler				U				R				
Ovenbird					F					U		
Northern Waterthrush					U			U	U			
Louisiana Waterthrush			U	U						R	R	
Kentucky Warbler			U	U				U	U			
Connecticut Warbler						R			R			
Mourning Warbler			R	R					U	U		
MacGillivray's Warbler			R	R					R	R		
Common Yellowthroat	F	F	F	F	U	U	U	U	F	F	F	F
Hooded Warbler				F				U	U			
Wilson's Warbler	R	R	R	R	U				U	F	R	R
Canada Warbler					R				R			
Yellow-breasted Chat				F					F	F		
Summer Tanager				F	U	U	U	U	F			
Scarlet Tanager					U					R		
Western Tanager	I	I	I								I	I
Northern Cardinal	C	C	C	C	C	C	C	C	C	C	C	C
Pyrrhuloxia	F	F	F	F	F	F	F	F	F	F	F	F
Rose-breasted Grosbeak				F	F				U	U		
Black-headed Grosbeak	R	R	R							R	R	R
Blue Grosbeak				F	U	U	U	U	F	F		
Indigo Bunting	I	I	I	F	F	I	I	I	F	F	I	I
Varied Bunting				I	I	I	I	I				
Painted Bunting	I	I	I	I	F	F	F	F	F	I	I	I
Dickcissel	I	I	I	F	F	U	U	U	F	I	I	I
Olive Sparrow	F	F	F	F	F	F	F	F	F	F	F	F
Green-tailed Towhee	R	R	R									R
Spotted Towhee	U	U	U	U							U	U
Botteri's Sparrow	I	I	I	I	I	I	I	I	I	I	I	I
Cassin's Sparrow	U	U	U	F	F	F	F	F	F	U	U	U
Chipping Sparrow	F	F	F	U						U	F	F
Clay-colored Sparrow	I	I	I	F							I	I
Field Sparrow	U	U	U	I	I	I	I	I	I	I	U	U
Vesper Sparrow	F	F	F	I	I						F	F
Lark Sparrow	F	F	F	F	F	F	F	F	F	F	F	F
Black-throated Sparrow	U	U	U	U	U	U	U	U	U	U	U	U
Lark Bunting	U	U	U								U	U
Savannah Sparrow	C	C	C	C	U						C	C
Grasshopper Sparrow	U	U	U	I	I	I	I	I	I	I	U	U
Henslow's Sparrow	I	I	I	I	I	I	I	I	I	I	I	I
Le Conte's Sparrow	U	U	U								U	U
Nelson's Sharp-tailed Sparrow	U	U	U	U							U	U
Seaside Sparrow	F	F	F	F	F	F	F	F	F	F	F	F
Fox Sparrow	I	I	I									I
Song Sparrow	F	F	U								U	U
Lincoln's Sparrow	F	F	F	F							F	F
Swamp Sparrow	F	F	F	U							F	F
White-throated Sparrow	C	C	C								C	C
White-crowned Sparrow	U	U	U	U							U	U
Harris's Sparrow	I	I	I									I
Dark-eyed Junco	U	U	U								U	U
Bobolink				R	R				R			
Red-winged Blackbird	C	C	C	C	C	C	C	C	C	C	C	C
Eastern Meadowlark	C	C	C	C	C	C	C	C	C	C	C	C
Western Meadowlark	U	U	U	U	R	R	R	R	R	R	U	U
Yellow-headed Blackbird			I	U						I	I	I
Rusty Blackbird	R	R	R									R
Brewer's Blackbird	C	C	C								C	C

BIRD SPECIES	JAN.	FEB.	MAR.	APR.	MAY	JUNE	JULY	AUG.	SEPT.	OCT.	NOV.	DEC.
Great-tailed Grackle	C	C	C	C	C	C	C	C	C	C	C	C
Boat-tailed Grackle	F	F	F	F	F	F	F	F	F	F	F	F
Common Grackle	C	C	C	F	F	F	F	F	F	C	C	C
Bronzed Cowbird	F	F	F	C	C	C	C	C	C	F	F	F
Brown-headed Cowbird	C	C	C	C	C	C	C	C	C	C	C	C
Orchard Oriole				F	F	U	U	U	F	F		
Hooded Oriole				R	R	R	R	R	R			
Audubon's Oriole	R	R	R	R	R	R	R	R	R	R	R	R
Baltimore Oriole	R	R	R	F	R	R	R	R	F	R	R	R
House Finch	I	I	I	I	I	I	I	I	I	I	I	I
Pine Siskin	U	U	U									U
Lesser Goldfinch	I	I	I	U	U	U	U	I	I	I	I	I
American Goldfinch	F	F	F								F	F
House Sparrow	C	C	C	C	C	C	C	C	C	C	C	C

Index

About the Author

Jamie Ritter has lived in Corpus Christi, Texas, for the past twenty-five years. She was raised in McAllen, Texas, in the Lower Rio Grande Valley. Her parents valued wildlife and the out-doors. She was a casual bird-watcher all of her life but has treated it as a serious hobby for five years. She is a member of the Audubon Outdoor Club of Corpus Christi, a member of the Corpus Christi Botanical Gardens, and the recording secretary of the Coastal Bend Audubon Society. She has participated in Birdiest City Contests and Christmas Counts.

Jamie is the mother of two daughters, Annette and Carrie, and the grand-mother of Chloe. She teaches Texas and United States History at Smith Junior High in Sinton, Texas. In addition to bird watching, she enjoys painting, sewing, scrapbooking, and reading. She loves to travel.

PHOTO: K. KASTNER PHOTOGRAPHY